A CANOEING AND KAYAKING GUIDE TO THE CAROLINAS

BOB BENNER *and* DAVID BENNER

MENASHA RIDGE PRESS
Birmingham, Alabama

Once there was a legend that told of a river that went to hear a fountain sing. The song was so beautiful that the river decided to sing it to the ocean. All the way to the shores of the ocean the river sang. Soon, the mountains heard of the song that the river was singing and came from all over the land to listen. And because the song was so beautiful the mountains settled down and stayed to listen forever.

—*Algonquin Indian Legend*

A CANOEING AND KAYAKING GUIDE TO THE CAROLINAS

Benner, Bob.
  A canoeing and kayaking guide to the carolinas/Bob Benner
  and David Benner.
    p.cm.
  ISBN 0-89732-520-6
        1. Canoes and canoeing—North Carolina—
  Guidebooks. 2. Canoes and canoeing—South Carolina—
  Guidebooks. 3. Kayaking—North Carolina—Guidebooks. 4.
  Kayaking—South Carolina—Guidebooks. 5. North
  Carolina—Guidebooks. 6. South Carolina—Guidebooks.
  I. Benner, Dave, 1955– II. Title.

  GV776.N74 B45 2002
  917.56—dc21
                                                    2002016573

Cover photo: Copyright © Comstock Images
Cover design: Bud Zehmer
Text design: Ann Marie Healy

Table *of* Contents

part**One**

HIAWASSEE & LITTLE TENNESSEE WATERSHED

part**Two**

BROAD & FRENCH BROAD RIVER SYSTEM/WATERSHED

part**Three**

WATAUGA, NEW RIVER, & CATAWBA WATERSHED

partFour

YADKIN RIVER BASIN

partFive

NEARBY RIVERS

partSIX

INDEX

Maps

Acknowledgments

The authors would like to acknowledge the many people whose assistance made such an undertaking possible. There are so many, too numerous to mention, who have lent a helping hand in some way or another. A few whose efforts require a special note of thanks are:

Members of the Blue Ridge Outing Club and the Carolina Canoe Club for providing invaluable feedback for the new edition. Vann and Laura Evans for their notes on the Haw River. Leonard Baker and R.B. Binegar for their willingness to go well beyond the call of duty. Donna Benner for her patience in typing the work in progress—little pay but many thanks.

And last, but certainly not least, all of the many friends for joining in "interesting" exploratory trips, undoubtedly questioning the advisability of the friendship at times when such trips turned into hikes down dry stream beds, ice breakers, and major engineering feats—but always turned into memorable outings.

We have all followed the wild goose and hopefully are the better for having done so.

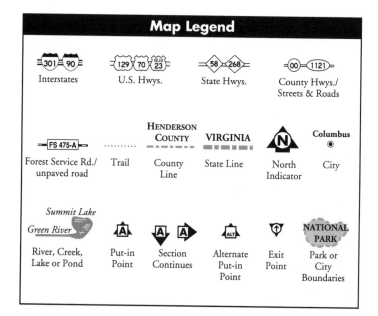

Introduction

This guide, originally written for the use of the recreational open boater, has been expanded to include stretches of water that will challenge the most advanced decked canoe and kayak paddler. Much of the water, however, is suitable for the novice paddler. The more difficult runs are not recommended for those thrill-seekers who wish to try their wings. One's wings need to be fully grown before attempting these highly technical, and quite often danger-ous, stretches. In classifying rapids it is difficult to remain totally objective because judgment is generally relative to experience.

As the sport of paddling grows, more and more clubs are being organized with paddling as their main interest. Some long-time paddlers question the need for such growth or organization and rightly so, but this is one of the few safe proving grounds available for aspiring paddlers. It is primarily through clubs that paddlers can obtain competent instruction toward improving skills and learning safe paddling practices. Also, it is only by organization that our free-flowing rivers are going to be saved for future generations.

Information on safety has been included because of certain haz-ards involved in the sport. Hopefully the suggestions made will lessen the possibilities of accidents other than normal swampings and dunkings that are likely to occur.

Along with these suggestions are rules that will be helpful for the paddler who decides that Labor Day shouldn't necessarily mean the end of his season. More and more paddlers are ventur-ing forth in the middle of winter to experience a completely dif-ferent world. The risks increase as the air and water temperatures decrease. A familiarity with certain facts relating to exposure can cut down considerably on these inherent risks.

The average paddler in North Carolina seems to harbor the idea that he has an inalienable right to paddle on any stream that has enough water to float his canoe. This most certainly is a miscon-ception under present interpretation of state law and an attempt to clarify what the rights of the paddler may be is discussed.

An explanation of the book's overall format has been included so that the reader can fully understand the organization of the materials on the streams and the various sections that it may be divided into. In *Canoeing White Water,* Randy Carter established such an understandable outline in describing rivers that it has been followed very closely.

This book is organized into six chapters. The first four consist of groups of rivers in neighboring counties in the foothills and mountains of the state: these are further grouped by watershed. The fifth chapter contains the Chattooga, the Chauga, the Doe

and the Tyger, located in neighboring states. The Haw River, a stream of the Piedmont, has also been included due to its extreme popularity. The last section has very little whitewater, but has been included to offer the paddler a selection of some 200 miles suitable for camping trips.

This eighth edition of Carolina Whitewater presents new maps for the paddler. Though these maps are as accurate as any can be (they are based primarily on county road maps), some amount of error is to be expected. Using these maps in conjunction with county maps will help you set shuttles quickly and accurately.

The original reason for undertaking such a work as this was to provide a source of information for those who would like to take their pleasure in paddling the many beautiful rivers of Western Carolina. The effort will have been worthwhile if any small portion of the great pleasure the authors have experienced on the several hundred miles contained herein is imparted to the reader.

Carolina Overview

Physiographically, North and South Carolina are very similar. Both are bordered on the west by the Blue Ridge Mountains and on the east by the Atlantic Ocean. Moving west to east in either state, three major physiographic regions are encountered: The Blue Ridge Mountains, the Piedmont, and the Coastal Plain. In both states the Coastal Plain is locally referred to as the "lowlands," while the Piedmont and Mountain regions are collectively known as "uplands" or "highlands."

The Blue Ridge Mountains are the eastern part of the Appalachian Mountain System, extending from Southeastern Pennsylvania across Maryland, Virginia, North Carolina, South Carolina, and Northern Georgia. In North Carolina, the Blue Ridge forms the eastern section of a mountain chain more than 75 miles wide, where cross-ridges connect the more westerly Black Mountains and Great Smokies. In this area, known as the "Land of the Sky," are 43 peaks of over 6,000 feet, and 125 others of more than 5,000 feet. Mountain valleys here are characteristically narrow, deep, and densely forested with elevations consistently above 2,000 feet.

By contrast, Western South Carolina extends only slightly into the Blue Ridge Mountains, where a small number of peaks not exceeding 3,600 feet rise rather abruptly from the foothills. Where mountains occupy approximately 6,000 square miles in North Carolina, there are only about 500 square miles of mountain terrain in South Carolina. The highest point in South Carolina is Sassafras Mountain (3,560 feet), situated on the North Carolina/South Carolina state line.

The coolest and wettest portion of both states, the Blue Ridge Mountain region is not farmed extensively nor densely populated, with the steepness of the terrain making the land more suitable for forest than for farms.

Geologically, the region is underlain by "crystalline" rocks such as granite, slate, and gneiss, which are dense and hard. The mountains are usually steep with V-shaped valleys. Slopes are covered with thick soil and luxurious forests which retard run-off.

Many rivers are born high in the mountains of the Carolinas, flowing down in all directions. Typically running along steep, rocky channels, the streams roll swiftly down the mountains over an abundance of rapids and falls, broadening when they reach the valley floors. West of the Blue Ridge the streams flow north and west, forming a major part of the Tennessee River drainage area. To the north are the headwaters of the New, which eventually empties into the Ohio. On the southeastern slopes of the Blue Ridge, the Broad, Catawba, and Yadkin are born. These merge with other drainages after crossing into South Carolina and finally find their way to the Atlantic Ocean. To the south are the headwaters of the Savannah River, which follows the South Carolina/Georgia border to the sea.

Beyond the Blue Ridge to the east, the Carolinas drop out of the mountains onto the rolling plateau of the Piedmont. Extending from the Blue Ridge Escarpment to the Fall Line where the topography suddenly drops off onto the flat expanse of the Coastal Plain, the Piedmont descends at roughly 3.5 feet per mile with the terrain changing gradually from rolling hills to flat upland. Deeply cut by rivers and creeks, the hills of the Piedmont rise from 400 to 1,500 feet above sea level. Though the Piedmont is underlain by the same crystalline rock as the Blue Ridge region, it lacks the mountains' high relief. Only occasionally are the rolling plains punctuated by a prominent hill. Comprising about 40 percent of the area of both Carolinas, the Piedmont is generally well developed and populated. Rivers flowing through the Piedmont, while lacking the high gradient and pristine setting of the mountains, are attractive, some endowed with a variety of rapids and falls.

The Coastal Plain region of the Carolinas begins at the Fall Line, where the underlying geology abruptly changes from hard crystalline rock to sandy loam over marl. Known locally as the "low country," the plain was at the bottom of the Atlantic Ocean in past geologic ages. The Fall Line, where a dramatic drop in elevation occurs as one moves east from the Piedmont into the Coastal Plain, runs very roughly on the line of Falls-of-the-Roanoke to Durham to Columbia to Augusta (GA). Near the Fall Line the Coastal Plain consists of small hills. Moving toward the

ocean, the terrain flattens. Swamp and marsh characterize the coastline corridor to the far east with many natural lakes occurring. Below the mouth of the Cape Fear River, the coastal environs assume a more tropical look with black water (caused by tannic acid from decaying vegetation), thick groves of palmettos, magnolias, tall cypress draped with Spanish Moss, and live oak.

The Carolinas are alive with beautiful and diverse flora and fauna. Because of their great variety of climate and soil, they have the greatest variety of plant life of any area in the Eastern U.S. Longleaf pine dominates the upper coastal plain along with water oaks and hickories. In the Piedmont, pine remains plentiful but hardwood forests are the order of the day with deciduous oak being most prevalent, followed by beech, birch, ash, maple, black walnut, sycamore, and yellow poplar. On the mountains the forest is generally comprised of oak, chestnut, laurel, white pine, and hemlock. Wildlife is abundant and varied, especially birds, many of which winter and breed in the coastal marshes.

Climate in the Carolinas is equable and pleasant, being cool in the mountains and almost subtropical on the Coastal Plain with the Piedmont representing the middle of the spectrum. Temperatures average approximately 10 degrees cooler in the mountains than in the low country. The mean annual temperature for North Carolina is about 59 degrees and for South Carolina 63 degrees, with January being the coldest month and July the warmest. North Carolina receives more rain than South Carolina owing to its larger mountain region. Averages for both states approximate 54 in. on the mountains, 47 in. on the Piedmont, and 48 in. on the Coastal Plain. On the east slope of some of the mountains the precipitation is exceptionally heavy. Heavy snow is unusual except in the mountains. Winds are variable and seldom violent except during the storms of fall along the coast.

Clubs and Organizations

There are a number of local and national organizations that the paddler should be aware of. We have listed those groups that we are acquainted with that are active in the surrounding area.

Most local clubs have as their main objectives the training of members toward safer canoeing and the preservation of the streams on which they paddle. Generally they have regularly scheduled trips throughout most of the year and periodically publish newsletters, which are a valuable source of information for the canoeist.

For those who wish to improve their skills in a boat it is almost a necessity to paddle with those of greater experience. In many areas the local club will be the only source of such experience.

Many of us begin paddling to get away from the hustle and bustle of today's busy life; to get back to nature; to see things that few others see; or to engage in an activity that few people do. For this reason joining a club and participating in organized trips might seem alien to us. However, the fact remains, without organizations that are willing to work and fight toward preserving our free-flowing streams, there may be none to enjoy in the future. We don't care to see our rivers become the "L.A. Freeway" at rush hour, but can we afford to be so selfish as to want to keep our favorite streams all to ourselves? How much weight will a handful carry when the "Corps" begins surveying for the best dam site? Your interest may be an occasional quiet float trip down your favorite stream with one or two close friends, but we hope you will see fit to support an organization in your area that may help you save that stream some day. We can save our rivers only if our numbers are large and we are well organized. Not quantity alone, but quantity with quality is needed. A good source for determining whether or not there is a club in your area might be your canoeing outfitter.

LOCAL AND AREA

Carolina Canoe Club
P.O. Box 12932
Raleigh, NC 27605

Western Carolina Paddlers
P.O. Box 8541
Asheville, NC 28814

Catawba Valley Outing Club
c/o Outdoor Supply
774 4th Street Dr. SE
Hickory, NC 28601

Piedmont Paddlers
P.O. Box 11526
Charlotte, NC 28220

Triad River Runners
P.O. Box 11283
Winston-Salem, NC 27116
(Bethabara Station)

Georgia Canoeing Association
P.O. Box 7023
Atlanta, GA 30309

Tennessee Scenic Rivers
Association
P.O. Box 3104
Nashville, TN 37219

Coastal Canoeists
P.O. Box 566
Richmond, VA 23204

NATIONAL

American Whitewater Affiliation
P.O. Box 85
Phoenicia, NY 12464

Composed of boating clubs and individuals interested in white-water paddling, the AWA promotes conservation, cruising, and wild water and slalom competition on national and international levels. *American Whitewater,* the journal of the Affiliation, is published six times yearly.

American Canoe Association
7432 Alban Station Blvd., Suite B-226
Springfield, VA 22150-2311

Comprised of individual members and clubs organized into regional division, the ACA conducts canoe and kayak cruises, promotes canoe sailing, encourages and sanctions competition, and has conservation as one of its prime areas of interest. *Paddler,* the official magazine, is published six times a year.

CONSERVATION ORGANIZATIONS

We are losing our free-flowing rivers and streams one by one in the frantic push for development. Whether that development is by damming, channelization, or dredging, many miles of wild, wonderful water will soon be lost forever. One of our most precious resources is literally going down the drain slowly but surely. We all must stand up and be heard if we are to stem the tide and save some of these waters for our future generations to know and enjoy.

There are many national and local organizations that have as one of their primary objectives the preservation of free-flowing waters. We list only a few of these in hopes the reader might see fit to join in and support the cause.

American Rivers
801 Pennsylvania Ave. SE, Suite 400
Washington, D.C. 20003

Founded in 1973, American Rivers publishes a quarterly newsletter which contains articles about recent action in Congress dealing with wild and scenic rivers and with water resource projects. Also covered are the progress of wild and scenic river studies being performed by federal agencies and state scenic river programs.

In addition to reporting on current events, the newsletter gives suggestions on how individuals can take action to help protect rivers.

Conservation Council of North Carolina
P.O. Box 37564
Raleigh, NC 27627

The Conservation Council of North Carolina is a statewide organization which coordinates activities of the many conservation groups within North Carolina. A monthly newsletter is published commenting on the various environmental concerns in the state. Among the many special committees of CCNC is the River Preservation Committee.

Sierra Club
730 Polk St.
San Francisco, CA 94109

The Joseph LeConte Chapter of the Sierra Club is composed of members in North Carolina and currently has active groups within the chapter in most of the more populous areas of the state. Many of the groups have canoeing activities throughout the year.

North Carolina Natural and Scenic Rivers

A Natural and Scenic Rivers System was created by the North Carolina General Assembly in 1971 to preserve and protect certain free flowing rivers in their natural state. A 13-mile segment of the Linville River and some 26.5 miles of the New and the South Fork of the New became the first rivers to be included in the system in 1976. Currently, the state is treading lightly around the troubled waters of establishing scenic rivers. Opposition, primarily from landowners, has arisen in every case that has come up for study in the recent past. However, progress is being made toward studying the Dan for inclusion in either the state or federal system.

Information regarding trips on these streams can be quite useful. Such information as: date of trip, put-in and take-out, length of trip (time and distance), number of participants, and other details can prove important. Jot it down on a card and send it to the author. Such reports will be tabulated and forwarded to the North Carolina Department of Natural Resources and Community Development. This type of data can be most helpful in making decisions that impact these streams.

State Water Trails

In 1973 a state trails committee was established by the General Assembly to represent the citizen's trail interests. Included in the area are trails for hikers, ORVs, horseback riders, bicyclists, and canoeists. Out of this committee and from interest by the North Carolina Department of Natural Resources and Community

Development has grown the North Carolina Trails Association. This organization is composed of individuals and groups interested in the promotion of trails and trail-related activities. In 1978 some 62 miles of the Lumber River received recognition as the state's first water trail. Also a stretch of the French Broad received such recognition later that year. In addition to these, approximately 1,400 miles of other streams and lakes are deemed to have potential for establishment as State Water Trails.

If interested in working toward a better system of trails in North Carolina, contact:

North Carolina Trails Association
P.O. Box 1033
Greensboro, NC 27402

Paddler Information

The most widely publicized paddler self-evaluation was created by the Keel-Haulers Canoe Club of Ohio. Their system brings the problem of matching paddlers with rivers into perspective but seems to overemphasize non-paddling skills. A canoe clinic student who is athletically inclined but almost totally without paddling skill once achieved a rating of 15 points using the Keel-Haulers system. His rating, based almost exclusively on general fitness and strength, incorrectly implied that he was capable of handling many Class II and Class III rivers. A second problem evident in the system is the lack of depth in skill category descriptions. Finally, confusion exists in several rating areas as to whether the evaluation applies to open canoes, decked canoes, or both.

To remedy these perceived shortcomings and to bring added objectivity to paddler self-evaluation, Bob Sehlinger* has attempted to refine the paddler rating system. Admittedly the refined system is more complex and exhaustive, but not more so than warranted by the situation. Heavy emphasis is placed on paddling skills, with description adopted from several different evaluation formats, including a non-numerical system proposed by Dick Schwind.**

RATING THE PADDLER

Instructions: All items, except the first, carry points that may be added to obtain an overall rating. All items except "Rolling Ability" apply to both open and decked boats. Rate open and decked boat skills separately.

---

* Sehlinger, Bob, *A Canoeing and Kayaking Guide to the Streams of Kentucky,* Menasha Ridge Press.

1. Prerequisite Skills. Before paddling on moving current, the paddler should:

a. Have some swimming ability
b. Be able to paddle instinctively on non-moving water (lake). This presumes knowledge of basic strokes.
c. Be able to guide and control the canoe from either side without changing paddling sides.
d. Be able to guide and control the canoe (or kayak) while paddling backwards.
e. Be able to move the canoe (or kayak) laterally
f. Understand the limitations of the boat
g. Be practiced in "wet exit" if in a decked boat

2. Equipment. Award points on the suitability of your equipment to whitewater. Whether you own, borrow, or rent the equipment makes no difference. Do not award points for both Open Canoe and Decked Boat.

Open Canoe

0 Points: Any canoe less than 15 ft. for tandem; any canoe less than 14 ft. for solo
1 Point: Canoe with moderate rocker, full depth, and recurved bow; should be ≥ 15 ft. in length for tandem and ≥ 14 ft. in length for solo and have bow and stern painters
2 Points: Whitewater canoe. Strong rocker design, full bow with recurve, full depth amidships, no keel; meets or exceeds minimum length requirements as described under "1 Point"; made of hand-laid fiberglass, Kevlar, Marlex, or ABS Royalex; has bow and stern painters. Canoe as described under "1 Point" but with extra flotation
3 Points: Canoe as described under "2 Points" but with extra flotation

Decked Boat *(K-1 or 2, C1 or 2)*

0 Points: Any decked boat lacking full flotation, spray skirt, or foot braces
1 Point: Any fully equipped, decked boat with a wooden frame
2 Points: Decked boat with full flotation, spray skirt and foot braces; has grab loops; made of hand-laid fiberglass, Marlex, or Kevlar
3 Points: Decked boat with foam wall reinforcement and split flotation; Neoprene spray skirt; boat has knee braces, foot braces, and grab loops; made of hand-laid fiberglass or Kevlar

---

** Schwind, Dick; "Rating Systems for Boating Difficulty," *American Whitewater Journal*, Vol. 20, Num. 3, May/June 1975.

3. Experience. Compute the following to determine preliminary points, then convert the preliminary points to final points according to the conversion table

Number of days spent each year paddling:

Class I rivers	x 1 =	_____
Class II rivers	x 2 =	_____
Class III rivers	x 3 =	_____
Class IV rivers	x 4 =	_____
Class V rivers	x 5 =	_____
Preliminary Subtotal	=	_____
Number of years paddling experience	x	_____
Total Preliminary Points		_____

Conversion Table

Preliminary Points	Final Points
0–20	0
21–60	1
61–100	2
101–200	3
201–300	4
301-up	5

Note: Experience is the only evaluation item where it is possible to accrue more than 3 points.

4. Swimming
0 Points: Cannot swim
1 Point: Weak swimmer
2 Points: Average swimmer
3 Points: Strong swimmer *(competition level or skin diver)*

5. Stamina
0 Points: Cannot run mile in less than 10 minutes
1 Point: Can run a mile in 7 to 10 minutes
2 Points: Can run a mile in less than 7 minutes

6. Upper Body Strength
0 Points: Cannot do 15 push-ups
1 Point: Can do 16 to 25 push-ups
2 Points: Can do more than 25 push-ups

7. Boat Control
0 Points: Can keep boat fairly straight
1 Point: Can maneuver in moving water; can avoid big obstacles

2 Points: Can maneuver in heavy water; knows how to work with the current

3 Points: Finesse in boat placement in all types of water; uses current to maximum advantage

8. Aggressiveness

0 Points: Does not play or work river at all

1 Point: Timid; plays a little on familiar streams

2 Points: Plays a lot; works most rivers hard

3 Points: Plays in heavy water with grace and confidence

9. Eddy Turns

0 Points: Has difficulty making eddy turns from moderate current

1 Point: Can make eddy turns in either direction from moderate current; can enter moderate current from eddy

2 Points: Can catch medium eddies in either direction from heavy current; can enter very swift current from eddy

3 Points: Can catch small eddies in heavy current

10. Ferrying

0 Points: Cannot ferry

1 Point: Can ferry upstream and downstream in moderate current

2 Points: Can ferry upstream in heavy current; can ferry downstream in moderate current

3 Points: Can ferry upstream and downstream in heavy current

11. Water Reading

0 Points: Often in error

1 Point: Can plan route in short rapid with several well spaced obstacles

2 Points: Can confidently run lead through continuous Class II; can predict the effects of waves and holes on boat

3 Points: Can confidently run lead in continuous Class III; has knowledge to predict and handle the effects of reversals, side currents, and turning drops

12. Judgment

0 Points: Often in error

1 Point: Has average ability to analyze difficulty of rapids

2 Points: Has good ability to analyze difficulty of rapids and make independent judgments as to which should not be run

3 Points: Has the ability to assist fellow paddlers in evaluating the difficulty of rapids; can explain subtleties to paddlers with less experience

13. Bracing

0 Points: Has difficulty bracing in Class II water
1 Point: Can correctly execute bracing strokes in Class II water
2 Points: Can correctly brace in intermittent whitewater with medium waves and vertical drops of 3 feet or less
3 Points: Can brace effectively in continuous whitewater with large waves and large vertical drops (4 feet and up)

14. Rescue Ability

0 Points: Self-rescue in flatwater
1 Point: Self-rescue in mild whitewater
2 Points: Self-rescue in Class III: can assist others in mild whitewater
3 Points: Can assist others in heavy whitewater

15. Rolling Ability

0 Points: Can only roll in pool
1 Point: Can roll 3 out of 4 times in moving current
2 Points: Can roll 3 out of 4 times in Class II whitewater
3 Points: Can roll 4 out of 5 times in Class III and IV whitewater

Winter Canoeing

Winter canoeing can be beautiful but it can also be quite dangerous unless certain precautions are taken. Some rules that should be followed by open boaters are:

1. Canoe those streams on which you can walk to shore at any point. It is best to stay off the larger rivers and those nearing flood stage.
2. Always have at least three boats in the party.
3. Everyone should have a complete change of clothing in a waterproof container that will withstand pressures of immersion.
4. Each paddler should carry on his person a supply of matches in a waterproof container.
5. Remember that the classification of any particular river is automatically upgraded when canoeing in cold weather. This is due to the extreme effects on the body upon immersion in cold water.

COLD WEATHER SURVIVAL

With more and more paddlers going out in the cold weather to engage in their sport, a basic knowledge of cold water and cold weather survival is necessary. When immersed in water, the loss of

heat from the body becomes much more rapid and survival times without suitable clothing in cold water become very short. For instance, wet clothes lose about 90 percent of their insulating value and lose heat 240 times faster than dry clothing

The following table gives the approximate survival times of humans immersed in water at various temperatures.

Water Temp (F.)	Exhaustion or Unconsciousness	Survival Time
32.5	0–15 min.	0–45 min
32.5–40	15–30 min	30–0 min
40–50	30–60 min	1–3 hrs
50–60	1–2 hrs.	1–6 hrs
60–70	2–7 hrs.	2–40 hrs
70–80	3–12 hrs	3 hrs–???

The greatest change in survival time occurs as the water temperature drops below 50 degrees.

Swimming in cold water increases the flow of water past the body, pumping heat out of the clothing so that heat production is outpaced by heat loss. If there is no prospect of getting out of the water immediately, survival time will be longer if one does not swim but relies on a life jacket for flotation. Better still, assume the HELP position (Heat Escape Lessening Position) in which the knees are tucked close to the chest. This allows one to retain body heat longer. It is, therefore, imperative that a life jacket with adequate flotation be worn. Swim only if there is danger downstream.

In recent years a number of new materials have been developed that make cold weather paddling more comfortable and certainly safer. Materials such as polypropylene, pile, and fleece tend to wick wetness away from the body and dry very quickly. Wool has the ability to provide warmth when wet, but the newer materials do it better. Worn under a paddling jacket and pants, they can be very effective. For the decked boater who is more likely to get wet, a wet or dry suit is highly recommended. Also, a polypro or wool cap can help tremendously because a great deal of body heat is lost through an unprotected head or neck.

Dry clothing should definitely be carried in a waterproof bag on all winter trips and changed into if one gets wet. Quite often you must insist that the victim change clothing and render assistance in changing because of his lack of coordination. The victim more than likely will be totally unaware of his poor reactions.

Symptoms of exposure occur generally as follows: uncontrollable shivering; vague, slow, slurred speech; memory lapses;

slowing of reactions, fumbling hands, and apparent exhaustion. Unconsciousness will follow and then death. The mental effects will be similar to those observed in states of extreme fatigue.

In cases of extreme exposure, build a fire and give the victim a warm drink, if he is able to swallow; strip him and put him into a sleeping bag with another person who is also stripped. Remember that the victim must be warmed from an outside heat source since he cannot generate his own body heat. Do not give the victim any form of alcohol.

Legal Rights of the Canoeist

In any discussion of the legal rights of canoeists the question of navigability arises. It is generally assumed that if a stream is navigable one has the legal right to float a canoe on it. Basically this is correct in the state of North Carolina.

However, the question remains as to what constitutes "navigability" under the laws of the state. One old case defined a stream which loggers used to float their timber down to be navigable; but it is believed that this case defined a limited type of navigable purpose. The general idea seems to be that if a waterway is suitable as a "highway" of commerce it is navigable and the public has a right to use it. When a navigable stream crosses an owner's land the state owns the bottom and the owner cannot legally block use of the stream for navigation or fishing.

In a recent decision, when a land owner attempted to block a waterway, declaring it non-navigable, the California Court of Appeals determined that the test of navigability is met if the stream is capable of boating for pleasure. In making his decision the judge pointed out that the streams of California are a vital recreational resource of the state. Perhaps this case may set a precedent that will be followed in the future in determining the rights of the paddler. Although, with the strong laws protecting the property rights of the individual owner in North Carolina the recreation precedent may never float there.

When a person owns land over which a "non-navigable" stream flows, he owns the land under the stream and has the right to control the surface of the water. For this reason when canoeing on streams of questionable navigability, it is best to observe one's manners to the fullest. If you must cross private property for any reason request the owner's permission before doing so. Generally speaking, the land owner will be a reasonable person if approached courteously and respectfully. More often than not the unreasonable property owner is one whose property rights have been abused in the past.

With the popularity of canoeing growing tremendously, travel on our streams is increasing also. Prime examples of such heavy usage can be found on the Nantahala and the Chattooga. Be sure that you aren't the proverbial straw that breaks the camel's back; by committing some careless act you may cause a landowner along a stream of questionable navigability to block access to it, or perhaps take the next guy to court for trespass. Make sure that you leave the door open for the next paddler.

Safety

A section on safety has been included because of the great interest in whitewater paddling and rafting among the uninitiated. The fact is there are potential hazards involved in the sport, which in many instances is the very reason many are attracted to it. However, with normal precautions and good judgment in determining one's level of skill, it can be a safe sport under normal conditions.

A few tips for the paddler to follow to insure that his trip is an enjoyable one, and above all a safe one, are listed. If each and every one of these rules is followed while on the river, you won't become the proverbial "accident looking for a place to happen."

1. Never boat alone. Three boats are generally considered a minimum on anything but small low-water streams.
2. Always carry a life jacket. Wear it unless you are a capable swimmer and even then have it on when in difficult water.
3. Know your ability and don't attempt water beyond this ability. In considering whether or not to run a particular rapid ask:
   a. Is it much greater in difficulty than anything I've attempted before?
   b. If I try it and don't make it will I place others in a difficult or dangerous situation in order to rescue me or my boat?

If the answer to either one is yes, don't try it. No experienced paddler will ever accuse you of being "chicken" when you back off, but he will respect your good judgment.

4. Be adequately equipped. Have an extra paddle in the canoe, if not an extra one for each paddler. Have bow and stern lines 8–15 feet long tied on securely to the ends of the craft.

Never tie the ends of these lines in the boat. At the same time be sure no lines are positioned so that they might entangle the canoeist's feet. The author observed a canoe swamp in Nantahala Falls, which in itself was certainly not too unusual nor was it very dangerous. But, the paddler came in for what was a terrifying moment when he came up wearing his bailer line around his

neck—with the other end still tied onto the boat. He simply had far too much line tied to his bailer.

A good standard First Aid Kit should be carried in a waterproof container, and a throw line at least 3/8ths-of-an-inch thick, 60–70 ft. long, preferably polypropylene, can become a necessity on all except the small shallow streams.

5. If traveling with a group, or club, know the plans of the group, the organization of the trip, and follow the decisions of the leader. Most clubs have standard trip rules established that determine the trip leader's responsibilities as well as those of each paddler. One rule generally followed on the river is that each canoe is responsible for keeping the canoe following in sight. This same rule should apply when a caravan or cars are traveling to or from the put-in or take-out.

6. Scout unfamiliar rapids before running them. Even those that are familiar can change considerably at different water levels.

7. Stay off flooded streams. The great increase in drownings from paddling and rafting accidents has resulted almost entirely from mishaps on swollen rivers.

8. Do not attempt to run dams or abrupt ledges. Quite often a hydraulic jump is formed in which the surface water flows back upstream, causing a rolling action. This rolling action tends to hold a boat or a person in, tumbling them around and around. The only escape is to swim out to the end or dive toward the bottom into the downriver current.

9. If you spill, get to the upstream end of the boat and if possible, stay with it. Don't risk the possibility of being pinned against a rock. If others spill, rescue the boaters and then go after the boat and equipment.

10. If you get broadside on a rock or other obstacle, lean toward the obstacle, downstream from the direction of the current. It is the unnatural reaction, but the correct thing to do in order to prevent the upstream gunwale from dipping into the current and swamping the boat.

In running smaller low-water streams, the possibility of personal danger is usually not as great as in large-volume rivers, but there are many things to watch for that might prove dangerous if not approached with caution. Some of the most common things that the paddler needs to beware of are logs and trees blocking the passage, barbed wire fences that can prove difficult to see, and low-water bridges that may be just high enough to lure the unwary paddler into attempting a run under them. If in doubt when approaching the latter, pull to shore well above it and check out the clearance. The American Whitewater Affiliation has a

safety code that is quite inclusive, and the aspiring boater should become familiar with it.

Explanation of Terms

DESCRIPTION: A brief description of the stream as a whole or of the particular section is given.

TOPOGRAPHIC MAPS: "Topo Maps" are listed in the order in which the river flows. Unless otherwise noted all maps are located on the North Carolina Index. If there is not a local source for maps they are available on order from:

Branch of Distribution
U.S. Geological Survey
Box 25286
Denver Federal Center
Denver, CO 80225

COUNTIES: Each stream will have the county in which a particular section is located, and where it flows through more than one they will be listed in the order in which the river flows.

PUT-IN: The exact put-in is listed, such as a particular highway or secondary road bridge. Where more than one section is listed, the put-in for the following section will be the take out for the preceding section.

GRADIENT: The total gradient of a section, e.g. "40", has been given rather than breaking it down into an average number of feet per mile. This has been done since quite often on a long stretch the gradient might be rather great in one portion and not on another. Where the drop is quite rapid it will be listed, e.g "1@300", which indicates the section will drop at the rate of 300 feet per mile.

DIFFICULTY: This refers to the rating of difficulty of the rapids located within the particular section of the stream. The rating system used below is based on that of the International Scale for Grading the Difficulty of River Cruising Routes. The first column gives the river/rapid rating and characteristics, the second shows the minimum required experience

Smooth Water

A Pools, lakes, rivers with velocity under 2 mph.

B Rivers, velocity 2–4 mph

C Rivers, velocity above 4 mph., (max. back paddling speed). May have some sharp bends or obstructions.

Whitewater

1 EASY—sand banks, bends without difficulty, occasional small rapids with waves regular and low. Correct course may be easy to find but care is needed with minor obstacles like pebble banks, fallen trees, etc., especially on narrow rivers. River speed less than hard back paddling speed.

2 MEDIUM—fairly frequent but unobstructed rapids, usually with regular waves, easy eddies, and easy bends. Course generally easy to recognize. River speeds occasionally exceeding hard back paddling speed.

3 DIFFICULT—maneuvering in rapids necessary. Small falls, large irregular waves covering boat, numerous rapids. Main current may swing under bushes, branches, or overhangs. Course not always easily recognizable. Current speed usually less than fast forward paddling speed.

4 VERY DIFFICULT—long extended stretches of rapids, high irregular waves with boulders directly in current. Difficult broken water, eddies, and abrupt bends. Course often difficult to recognize and inspection from the bank frequently necessary. Swift current. Rough water experience indispensable.

5 EXCEEDINGLY DIFFICULT—long rocky rapids with difficult and completely irregular broken water which must be run head on. Very fast eddies, abrupt bends, and vigorous cross currents. Difficult landings increase hazard. Frequent inspections necessary. Extensive experience necessary.

6 LIMIT OF NAVIGABILITY—all previously mentioned difficulties increased to the limit. Only negotiable at favorable water levels. Cannot be attempted without risk of life.

It is important to know the difficulty rating of a particular river before setting out on it. The ratings used here are based on normal or ideal water heights. The ratings will vary somewhat as the water level in the stream fluctuates.

The authors have attempted to be as objective as possible in declaring whether or not a rapid is Class III or Class IV. Such a judgment will vary considerably from person to person according to his skill or experience.

Where a section has only one rapid of a higher difficulty than others it is listed II–III (IV), with the final number representing the one more difficult rapid as a Class IV.

For the past several years, whitewater cruising has witnessed an ever-expanding willingness and ability, by top experts, to tackle increasingly difficult rapids. There are individual drops, as well as extended stretches, being run that were thought doable only in some abstract sense as recently as five years ago. Welcome to the hardwater boating scene of the present! Many factors have played a part in bringing the sport to this juncture. There are three areas that stand out:

1. EQUIPMENT—Today decked boats are being built and marketed with primary design functions that aid paddlers on steep, technical descents. These boats are generally short, high-volume, and heavily rockered in the bow, with large cockpits—all helpful performance and safety features. Open boats are shorter, narrower, dryer, and more maneuverable. Many experts can roll open boats in difficult water because they are essentially outfitted as C-1s and chock-full of flotation. Drysuits and synthetic undergarments, vast improvements over wetsuits and wool, allow the paddler more comfort and freedom of movement in cold weather (when the steep stuff normally runs). Life vests with exotic safety features, while not widely seen in the US, are becoming commonplace in Europe. Skirts are dryer and more bombproof, with rubber gaskets gripping the cockpit rims. Paddles are lighter and stronger. Helmets with chin and face guards are being used by more paddlers. Hand and elbow armor will not be far behind.

2. EXPERIENCE—The experts paddling hair runs today often have an experience backlog of 10, 15, and 20 years on difficult water. Whitewater sport being the relatively recent phenomenon it is, we can look back to the 1970s and find very few expert hardboaters with the experience level that so many have today. These days more informed decisions can be made on marginal runs because there is more information (prior probing) available. A certain psychological edge is developed from years of paddling difficult water. This mental toughness is a very real aid in making cool, objective decisions on the river. Instruction is more effective and efficient, allowing paddlers to get on more difficult water sooner. The Class V rapids of the 1970s will not feed the adrenaline rat of the veteran hair-head today.

3. AVOCATIONAL BOATING—There are increasing numbers of paddlers who look upon the sport as more than a weekend pastime. These folks tend to put more energy, time, and effort into the sport than the weekend warrior, eschewing "real" jobs and "normal" lifestyles to pursue whitewater paddling full time. Much as surfing, rock climbing, and other sports have their devotees, these acolytes of the boating subculture are often on, or creating, the "edge" of the sport.

4. UNSPOKEN COMPETITION—Finally, there is a good deal of unspoken competition at this level of paddling. While this is not new to the sport, it has certainly had an effect on it. This one-upmanship, if you will, has a much larger ante today than 10 years ago.

For years the terms "hard" and "easy" have been used as adjuncts in describing whitewater difficulty. We've all heard "easy Class V" or "hard Class IV" used as a means of further delineating differences between rapids. Largely as a result of the more extreme water being paddled nowadays, rapids graded at the Class IV and V level have by far a broader range of difficulty, within and between them, than the other classes. The much more difficult Class V water of today is put in the same category as rapids that were considered extreme 10 years ago. Sometimes this results in shoving the "old" Class V rapid down into a lesser category. More often, rapids with large difficulty differences are placed in the same category. With the current ICF scale, this "crowding" is inevitable, and it can be very confusing. There is a need for further, and more precise, delineation in classifying rapids at the Class IV and V level. The old "measuring stick" needs a new coat of paint, one that shows the inch, as well as the foot, markers.

The mechanics of such a scale are relatively simple. It has been suggested to expand the ICF's I–VI scale by adding Class VII, Class VIII, etc.—similar to what was done on many western rivers years ago. This seems too radical a departure, though, because rivers would have to be re-rated. A simpler method would be to add gradations within the Class IV and V levels of difficulty. There is a precedent. Rock climbing has seen an explosion of increasingly difficult moves and routes. Climbers have answered this by steadily upgrading the scale of difficulty to correspond to the more gymnastic or aid-requiring moves that are becoming the new standards. Why not follow the rock climbing lead?

What we've done with the rating system in the book is to break Class IV and V rapids down into three sub-classes. Starting with Class IV and moving into Class V in order of increasing difficulty, the scale reads: 4, 4.1, 4.2, 5, 5.1, and 5.2. Three sub-classes within each class, at this time, seems to satisfy the variance of difficulty of the rapids.

We understand the subjectivity involved in rating whitewater, with one man's Class III being another man's Class V. However, we have tried to maintain as objective a stance as possible in rating the rivers contained in this book against each other. The reader can be reasonably certain, by the ratings reflection, that Linville Gorge is a tougher run than the Broad River Gorge, and Watauga Gorge is a stiffer paddle, on the whole, than the North Fork of the

French Broad (but the North Fork has one rapid tougher than anything in the Watauga Gorge).

The current ICF system does not allow for such delineation and doesn't give the reader as much information as this revamped scale does. This is certainly not an ideal solution, but hopefully a step in the right direction. For instance, we have not attempted to define a Class 5.2 rapid, but will rely on the ICF definition of a Class V rapid and only suggest that a 5.2 drop is at the extreme end of what is considered Class V. We have not broken down Class I, II, III, or VI rapids. We feel there isn't much variation of difficulty within Class I, II, or III rapids. What most experts consider Class VI is run so infrequently that there is too little basis to make valid comparisons or quality differences between them. We welcome any dialogue or criticism toward realizing a more informative and realistic scale of difficulty in today's brave, new whitewater world.

DISTANCE: Measured in miles from county and USGS maps; generally rounded off.

TIME: This is actual paddling time on the river including time for scouting when necessary. When paddling with a group larger than two or three boats, or when a lunch stop will be made, additional time should be planned for.

SCENERY:
AA Unusually beautiful even to the spectacular, generally remote, and wild.
A Generally remote and wild. Perhaps some signs of civilization but mostly uninhabited.
B Most pastoral type of country with more settled areas.
C Fair amount of development, general signs of civilization such as garbage dumps, autos left on the side of the stream, visual pollution.

WATER QUALITY:
AA Where watershed is protected and water generally remains "clear as crystal."
A Where some small amount of sediment appears but on the whole the water would be considered clean.
B Heavier sediment in stream but no evident pollution.
C Signs of human or industrial pollution to the extent water is actually discolored.

GAUGE: Where there is a USGS gauge located close enough to the put-in or take-out on a particular section, readings have been taken from it. Wherever possible a minimum level for solo

paddling has been established. Generally a reading of 0.20 or two tenths of a foot above that listed for solo would be enough for tandem paddling. (Example: 1.54 minimum solo level; 1.74 for tandem). On streams where a high level can be extremely dangerous, a maximum reading is given whenever one has been established.

Where no USGS gauge is available, gauges have been painted, usually on a bridge, at a put-in or take-out. Generally a level of 6" below "0" can be considered a minimum for solo paddling. There has been some confusion over how to interpret the gauge levels. We consider the level to be "0" when the waterline is even with the bottom of the "0."

GAUGE ILLUSTRATION

```
——6"——2
——6"——
——6"——1
——6"——
——6"——0
——6"——
```

WATER SURFACE: Whenever information can be obtained by phone, such as dam controlled streams and those entering into the Tennessee Valley, a telephone number has been given that can be called.

A recorded message giving stream flow in the Valley can be obtained by calling (800) 238-2264.

DIFFICULTIES: A brief description of specific points that might present problems for the paddler are listed, hopefully in enough detail to recognize them, but not so much as to take away the thrill of running a new river.

DIRECTIONS: Detailed directions have been given to find the put-in and the take-out. Where there are several sections of a particular stream included, only the put-in on the first section and the take-out on the last section are described. It is assumed that one who intends paddling a good bit of a river will obtain county road maps. These maps are available from the local county office of the State Highway Engineer or from:

Head of Location and Survey Unit
N.C. Department of Transportation
Division of Highways
P.O. Box 25201
Raleigh, N.C. 27611

Where a river flows through several counties, reference will be made to a county route by name and number (Burke Co. Rt. 1100) initially. Thereafter only route number will be referred to until another road in the next county is introduced.

The authors will appreciate any pertinent comments, corrections, or suggestions which might prove valuable in any future editions.

Exertion brings vital physiological reactions when there are worthwhile goals to achieve. Without weariness there can be no real appreciation of rest, without hunger no enjoyment of food, without the ancient responses to the harsh simplicities of the environment that shaped mankind, a man cannot know the urges within him. Having known this during a period of life when I could satisfy the needs, I think I understand what wilderness can mean to the young men of today.

—Sigurd F. Olson

part**One**

Hiawassee & Little Tennessee Watershed

TUSQUITEE CREEK

Tusquitee Creek heads up in Nantahala National Forest and runs along south of the Tusquitee Mountains. It flows primarily through a pastoral region before confluencing with the Hiawassee River downstream from Hayesville. The trip can be extended 2.5 mi. by continuing on to the Hiawassee and paddling downstream to the second bend, coming close to Rt. 1300. Take out at the junction of Rt. 1345 with Rt. 1300.

MAPS: Shooting Creek, Hayesville (USGS); Clay (County)

RT. 1330 BRIDGE TO RT. 1300 BRIDGE

CLASS	I–II
LENGTH	5.2
TIME	2.5
GAUGE	VISUAL
LEVEL	-5 IN.& ABOVE
PERMITS	No
GRADIENT	27
SCENERY	A–B

DESCRIPTION: There are no difficulties. This is primarily a series of small rock gardens interspersed with an occasional ledge; however, be on the lookout for downed trees blocking the passage.

SHUTTLE: Take Tusquitee St. north out of Hayesville across the Hiawassee and bear northeast on Rt. 1307 to the Gauge. Go beyond the Gauge approximately 3.5 mi. to Rt. 1330 and south to the bridge. To reach the take-out, take Tusquitee St. across the Hiawassee and bear northwest on Rt. 1300 approximately 1 mi. to the take-out bridge.

GAUGE: It's located on the southwest side of the Rt. 1307 bridge at the junction of Rt. 1326. Minimum level for solo: 5" below the bottom of "0." The river can be run most all year except during dry spells.

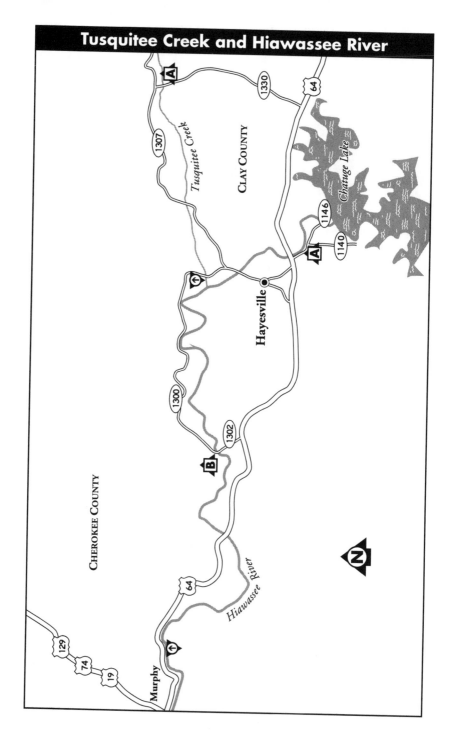

Tusquitee Creek and Hiawassee River

HIAWASSEE RIVER

The Hiawassee heads up in the vicinity of Unicoi Gap in the Chatta-hoochee National Forest in north Georgia and runs north until the impoundment at Lake Chatuge, where it enters North Carolina. It flows generally west to the backwaters of Hiawassee Lake west of Murphy.

MAPS: Hayesville, Peachtree (USGS); Clay, Cherokee (County)

RECREATION AREA ON CLAY CR 1140 (MEYERS CHAPEL RD.)
TO CLAY CR 1302 BRIDGE

CLASS	I–II
LENGTH	11.5
TIME	2.5
GAUGE	VISUAL
LEVEL	N/A
PERMITS	No
GRADIENT	11
SCENERY	A–B

DESCRIPTION: There is some fairly heavy water at the shoals about 0.5 mi. below the mouth of Fires Creek. This spot can swamp the unwary paddler quite easily. At lower levels there are many rock and boulder gardens throughout the stretch. The trip can be extended 1.5 mi. by continuing on Rt. 1140 south to Rt. 1146, putting in at Barnard Bridge below the dam.

SHUTTLE: Take US 64 east from Hayesville and turn right into the recreation area on Clay CR 1140. The take-out is reached by going west on US 64 from Hayesville and turning right on Clay CR 1302 to the bridge.

GAUGE: None. The TVA plant at Lake Chatuge is generally in operation throughout the week and under certain conditions runs on weekends. This can easily be recognizable if there are no mud flats along the river. The operation schedule is not known until after 8 p.m. the night before. Call (704) 644-5121 after that time to check for the following day. The paddling times given on both sections are estimates for when power is being generated. When it is not, add at least 2.5 hrs. to 1 and 1.5 hrs. to 2.

CLAY CR 1302 (SHALLOWFORD) BRIDGE
TO US 64 WEST OF PEACHTREE

CLASS	I–II
LENGTH	9.5
TIME	3
GAUGE	VISUAL
LEVEL	N/A
PERMITS	No
GRADIENT	14
SCENERY	A–B

DESCRIPTION: Mission Dam, located about 1.5 mi. below the put-in, should be approached cautiously. There is a log boom below sand flats on the right, which can be crossed to a fairly easy take-out. Portage about 75 yds. down the old road to a well-worn path, and then another 50 yds. below the fence, to a short path

to the dam race. The dam, operated by Alcoa, only runs when power is being generated at Lake Chatuge. The shoals below the dam can best be scouted at this time. The trip can be extended 2.8 mi. by taking out at the access area above the Frank Forsyth Bridge on Hiawassee St. in Hayesville.

SHUTTLE: Take out alongside US 64, about 0.5 mi. west of Rt. 1550, west of Peachtree.

GAUGE: See Section A.

CULLASAJA RIVER

The Cullasaja rises in the Nantahala National Forest and drops over many falls and cascades before slowing down and entering the Little Tennessee. Three of the better known falls are Bridal Veil, Dry Falls, and Cullasaja. The latter drops some 400 spectacular ft. to a point about 0.5 mi. above the put-in. US 64 follows alongside the river throughout most of this area. It is well worth a drive up through the gorge toward the resort village of Highlands.

MAPS: Scaley Mtn., Corbin Knob (USGS); Macon (County)

RT. 1678 BRIDGE TO RT. 1668

CLASS	II–III
LENGTH	5.3
TIME	2.5
GAUGE	VISUAL
LEVEL	2.3 FT.
PERMITS	No
GRADIENT	23
SCENERY	B–C

DESCRIPTION: Watch for a fairly steep cut through a rock garden, about 150 yds. down from the put-in, which is followed by a series of ledges. At higher water levels it would be best to scout this stretch.

SHUTTLE: From Franklin, drive east on US 64 to Rt. 1678 (Peeks Creek Rd.) and go south to the bridge. To reach the take-out, travel on Rt. 1668 west off US 64 (just south of the US 64 bridge) 0.4 mi. to Rt. 1698.

GAUGE: USGS is on Rt. 1524 (Sugar Fork Rd.) about 40 yds. above US 64 on the east bank. Minimum for solo is a reading of 2.30.

LITTLE TENNESSEE RIVER

The Little Tennessee first appears to the traveler on US 23/441 south of Franklin as a small creek. One will wonder how such a small stream can grow to a full size river between here and Iotla. It flows

generally north between the Nantahala Mountain Range to the west and the Cowee Range to the east before reaching the impoundment at Fontana.

The riverside alternates between farmlands and woodlands in Section A, while below Lost Bridge it becomes heavily forested, except where Rt. 1114 occasionally hits it. The area near Franklin and around much of Macon County is widely known for its great mineral deposits and is certainly a rock hound's heaven.

The "Little T" is one of the few rivers in North Carolina that lends itself to overnight canoe camping. Generally speaking, there is enough water to carry gear, while the rapids aren't so formidable that

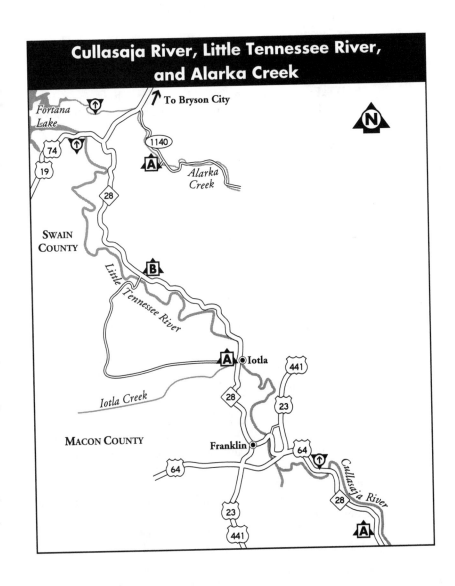

the paddler is likely to finish the day with wet provisions. Unfortunately there aren't many streams remaining that can claim both of these qualities. The good ones have either been dammed, leaving nothing but flat water, are too shallow to carry the necessary equipment, or are too rough to maneuver through rapids with the extra weight in the boat.

MAPS: Franklin, Alarka, Wesser (USGS); Macon, Swain (County)

NC 28 BRIDGE AT IOTLA TO LOST BRIDGE

CLASS	I–II
LENGTH	10
TIME	4.5
GAUGE	VISUAL/PHONE
LEVEL	N/A
PERMITS	No
GRADIENT	5
SCENERY	A–B

DESCRIPTION: There are no difficulties. The first several miles are flat with an occasional riffle. There are a few shallow ledges in the latter part of the section.

SHUTTLE: Drive north on NC 28 to bridge at Iotla, about 4 mi. north of Franklin. To get to the take-out, continue on NC 28 to Lost Bridge.

GAUGE: The USGS Gauge is on the left bank 0.8 mi. north of Needmore and approximately 6.8 mi. below the Lost Bridge Rd. bridge. The "Little T" is very seldom too low to run. Only following extreme dry periods would it be too low to run.

LOST BRIDGE, OFF NC 28, TO US 19 BRIDGE

CLASS	II–III
LENGTH	13
TIME	4.5
GAUGE	VISUAL
LEVEL	350–2,000 CFS
PERMITS	No
GRADIENT	14
SCENERY	A

DESCRIPTION: There are several ledges which should be approached cautiously at higher levels. When Fontana is quite low, there is a series of ledges which runs for close to 250 yds. At the end of this rapid, the river, which previously has been up to 300 ft. wide, narrows down to rush through an area no wider than 20 ft. Before Fontana Dam flooded the river, this part was known as The Narrows.

The Narrows should definitely be scouted before attempting to run, especially in higher waters when the entire rapid can be quite formidable. The standing wave created at the bottom of The Narrows is as high as 5 ft. at higher levels. At lower levels scout on the left; at higher levels, scout on the right.

The water level of Lake Fontana is generally lowered during the winter in preparation for the spring rains. Paddle beyond the US 19/NC 28 bridge to the right bank, to a small "goat path" which cuts back up under the bridge. This steep path isn't recommended

for potential coronary victims, but even paddlers with healthy hearts may second guess their decision to work this section.

SHUTTLE: From Lost Bridge, continue north on NC 28 to US 19/NC 28; turn left and park at the bridge over the Little Tennessee.

GAUGE: See Section A. The lower section can become dangerous with high water levels when Lake Fontana is low. To check on the stream flow, call (800) 238-2264. Minimum reading is about 350 cfs, while the maximum will be approximately 2,000 cfs.

ALARKA CREEK

Description: Alarka Creek heads up in Nantahala National Forest on the slopes of the Alarka Mountains. It is a small, fast stream flowing over ledges under low-hanging branches. It might carry through a backyard and seconds later through impenetrable laurel thickets that completely enclose the paddler.

On one trip a copperhead dropped into the bow of a canoe passing downstream, so the heavy foliage also bears watching. This is the only hitchhiking snake the authors have observed or heard of, so don't let it discourage what can be a most delightful trip.

MAPS: Alarka, Bryson City (USGS); Swain (County)

RT. 1140 BRIDGE TO OLD RT. 1309 BRIDGE

CLASS	II–III
LENGTH	4.5
TIME	2
GAUGE	VISUAL
LEVEL	2.5 FT.
PERMITS	No
GRADIENT	44
SCENERY	A–C

DESCRIPTION: The narrow passages and low overhanging branches can present problems. There are two ledges that should be scouted. They are easily recognized. As with all small streams of this nature, watch for strainers. For those into running waterfalls, there are two located in the next three or so miles to the backwaters of Lake Fontana. The first, a 12-footer, is about 200 yds. below the recommended take-out. The banks are extremely steep, making it very difficult to carry. At a level approaching 3.0, one may well be committed to run it without the option of scouting. If so, enter left of center, moving to the right immediately, then stay right. The fall is located at the rear of a private home, so do not trespass to scout. J. Johnson Falls, an 8-footer, is 1.5 mi. below the Rt. 1307 bridge. It can be scouted on river left.

SHUTTLE: From Bryson City, drive south on US 19 to Rt. 1140 and turn left (southeast) onto the first bridge crossing the creek

west of the community of Alarka. Return to US 19 and turn left; then drive 0.1 mi. and turn right (northwest) on Rt. 1309 to the old Rt. 1309 bridge and take-out.

GAUGE: The USGS Gauge is below the Rt. 1307 bridge (0.8 mi. below the take-out). Minimum for solo run is a reading of 2.50. The creek can be run in later winter, spring, and early summer except after an unusually dry spring.

WHITEOAK CREEK

Whiteoak Creek is born high in the Nantahala National Forest between Split Whiteoak Ridge and Rocky Bald Ridge, a few miles west of Nantahala Lake. From its origin it tumbles steeply for a few miles, slows (somewhat) through a short valley, then picks up steam once more before joining the Nantahala. This last section is described below. Due to its small watershed, this run is available only after a long, heavy rainfall.

MAPS: Topton, Hewitt (USGS); Macon (County)

CLASS	IV–VI
LENGTH	4.5
TIME	1.5
GAUGE	VISUAL
LEVEL	N/A
PERMITS	NO
GRADIENT	216
SCENERY	A

WHITEOAK DAM ON SR 1310 TO
JUST ABOVE CONFLUENCE WITH NANTAHALA RIVER

DESCRIPTION: You'd better be strapped in tightly and extremely focused before slipping out of the put-in eddy, because you're about to dance a 2.4 mi. waltz with Captain Gravity. With vital statistics including a 216 fpm drop, a stream width of 30 ft., deadfalls and/or overhanging branches every 50 ft., small to nonexistent eddies, and two huge, kidney-reducing drops, Whiteoak Creek has everything the jaded hair-head could want. Actually, the gradient is very steady and generally unblocked and boat-scoutable, with a few exceptions.

You'll often find yourself going a little faster than your comfort level allows as you paddle into a semi-blind turn, with little hope of catching an eddy. About two-thirds of the way into the run, watch for a 10-ft. drop that is best run in the center. Just downstream is a 25-ft., Class 5.2 drop consisting of four ledges practically piling on top of each other. None have particularly clean landings, though a route down the right center is barely feasible. Serious full-contact boating. Hospital air. Scout or carry on the right. Below here the river resumes its steady downhill gradient for about 0.5 mi. The last drop above the confluence with the

Nantahala is 28 ft. of mega-gnarl that we'll call Mean Mistreater. Make sure to take out at least 50 yds. above this, as there isn't much of an eddy to depend on any closer. Then tiptoe carefully around and put in for a sane run down the Cascades, if you've got the energy. Mean Mistreater has been run, but not by people who put their skirts on like you and I do.

SHUTTLE: From Nantahala Outdoor Center, take US 19/74 south to SR 1310. Take a left onto SR 1310 and go 6.6 mi. to Whiteoak Dam on the right. Take out just above the confluence with the Nantahala River on SR 1310.

GAUGE: None. Assuming a normal dam release, a level of 4.5 ft. on the Nantahala River Gauge may be a good indicator of enough water.

NANTAHALA RIVER

The Nantahala heads up in the edge of Nantahala National Forest before entering Nantahala Lake, reportedly the highest lake in North Carolina. From there some water is piped down the mountain to the power plant 0.25 mi. above the Section C put-in. Sections A and B only run after heavy, extended rainfall, which results in dam spillover from Nantahala Lake and heavy feeder stream influence up high. The piped water meets the natural flow just above Section C, one of the most popular whitewater runs in the country. The water temperature on this stretch is generally 45 degrees due to the diverted water being pulled from the bottom of the lake. While Section A is recommended only for experts, Section B is challenging for high intermediate/advanced boaters. Section C is suitable for intermediate level paddlers and ends just above Class V Wesser Falls. Below is Lake Fontana. Nantahala, meaning "land of the noon-day sun," was the name given by the Cherokee Indians because the deep gorge shuts out the sun for most of each day.

The cold water can create an unusual phenomenon on a very warm day. A fog rises about 3 ft. above the water, sometimes cutting visibility down to a few feet. There is continuous whitewater from Patton's Pool to the take-out below Nantahala Falls. A bailer—make that a big bailer—is a necessity for the canoeist running the Nantahala.

Nantahala Outdoor Center is located at the take-out below Nantahala Falls, and they conduct paddling clinics and raft trips down the river beginning in the spring and continuing into the fall. This is an excellent way for the uninitiated to try the river for the first time. NOC also has restaurants, stores, and motel accommodations. For those who wish to camp, Lost Mine Campground, which is privately owned, is located on SR 1103 only 1 mi. from Wesser.

MAPS: Topton, Hewitt, Wesser (USGS); Macon, Swain (County)

CLASS	IV–V
LENGTH	I
TIME	I.5
GAUGE	VISUAL
LEVEL	4.2 FT.
PERMITS	NO
GRADIENT	210
SCENERY	A

SR 1310 (GRAVEL ROAD TURN OUT 4.2 MI. ABOVE FOREST SERVICE PUT-IN) TO FIRST BRIDGE DOWNSTREAM ON SR 1310

DESCRIPTION: This section, known to the local boaters as the Cascades, is user-friendly only for confident experts. Though not in the top echelon of hard water runs, this 1-mi. stretch will test anyone's skills. After a brief 0.3-mi. warm-up, you come to the

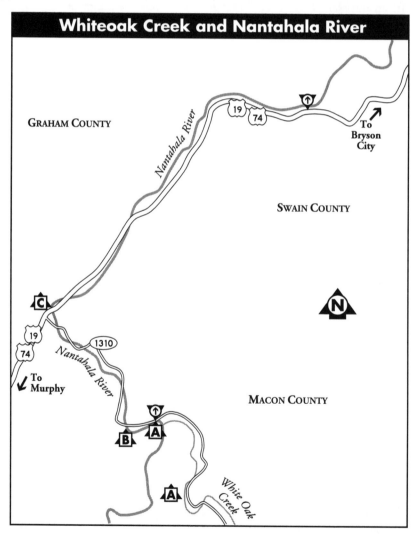

Whiteoak Creek and Nantahala River

first Class V rapid. First Falls is a two-stage drop of 16 ft. The upper drop has one obvious slot while the second ledge has a bit more margin for error. Shortly downstream is the largest, most difficult rapid on this run. Big Kahunah has a total drop of 22 ft. The line is down the right, blasting off the 9-ft. ledge to finish. Almost immediately downstream is Chinese Feet, the last major rapid. Chinese Feet (the name has to be blotter influenced) is best run by hammering into the eddy on the left at the top and then running the 8-ft. slot to the left of the boulder that splits the river. From here to the bridge, there is a lot of interesting, though less significant, whitewater. The run can only be done after extended rainfall and generally has a window of two days at best. The road parallels the river on this section allowing for easy scouting, portaging, and aborted trips.

SHUTTLE: From Nantahala Outdoor Center, take US 19/74 south to SR 1310. Take a left onto SR 1310 and go 4.2 mi. to a small dirt road on the right where you can park. Take out at the first bridge downstream.

GAUGE: The USGS Gauge located just upstream of Ferebee Park on Section C should read 4.2 for a minimum level. This assumes a normal release of 3.2 ft. from the power plant. See gauge for Section C below.

B

SR 1310 BRIDGE TO FOREST SERVICE PUT-IN
FOR STANDARD (SECTION C) RUN

CLASS	III
LENGTH	3.2
TIME	2.5
GAUGE	PHONE
LEVEL	N/A
PERMITS	No
GRADIENT	100
SCENERY	A

DESCRIPTION: This section is solid, continuous, boat-scoutable Class III water. There are no major difficulties for the boater who can handle those conditions. The road, as on Section A, follows the river pretty closely.

SHUTTLE: From Nantahala Outdoor Center, take US 19/74 south to SR 1310. Take a left onto SR 1310 and go to the fifth bridge across the river. Take out at the Forest Service access area at the intersection of SR 1310 and US 19.

GAUGE: See Section A.

CLASS	I–II (III)
LENGTH	8
TIME	2.5
GAUGE	PHONE
LEVEL	N/A
PERMITS	YES
GRADIENT	33
SCENERY	A–B

POWER PLANT TO WESSER

DESCRIPTION: Below the put-in at the forks, Patton's Run begins. The rapid is named after Charlie Patton of Brevard, NC. He was an avid paddler of the Nantahala despite the fact that he had practically no use of one arm. He died, following a trip down his beloved river.

Patton's Run is a long Class III, requiring the paddler to stay to the inside of the bend. This is heavy, fast water. It, as well as most of the river, can be scouted from US 19, which follows the river very closely throughout the run. Scout this one from the pull-off on the highway before launching.

The river continues along its fast course with little letup for the next 7.5 mi.

Nantahala Falls, which is about 400 yds. above Nantahala Outdoor Center, is a Class III, which at higher levels easily becomes a Class IV. There is a short quiet pool above it where one can pull over easily—either to scout the falls or to pull out. Look for a small section of flat land on the right with a well-marked path. The entrance and approach to the falls is rather difficult and can put a lot of water in the boat before one hits the falls. Be sure to empty the boat before attempting to run. The entrance is generally where the novice or low-intermediate skilled paddler gets in trouble, only to be finished off in the falls.

The falls consist of two ledges. The top one doesn't extend all the way across the river, and the passage is just on the left end of it. The paddler then must cut hard back to the right to catch the tongue on the lower drop. With higher water the upper ledge can be run straight through on the right, therefore lining up for the tongue below. This is about 3 ft. off the large boulder on the right.

In the event one swamps or dumps in the falls, get control of the craft immediately. Wesser Falls, which is 0.25 mi. downstream, will only spew out little pieces.

SHUTTLE: Go north on US 19 from Wesser and NOC to Macon CR 1310 on the left; turn left into the NFS access area. Take out just above the NOC store.

GAUGE: This section can be run only when the power plant is operating, which is generally the case during the week and more often than not on weekends. Phone (704) 321-4504 or NOC (704) 488-2175 to determine whether or not the plant is in operation (see "Explanation" section in Introduction).

SNOWBIRD CREEK

Snowbird Creek has its origin high in the Unicoi Mountains, and within Nantahala National Forest, which ensures excellent water quality. The Snowbird Mountains form the southern rim of the gorge. The upper portion of the creek is very remote and flows through three sections of falls named Upper, Middle, and Big, all of which are well upstream of the sections described. The river becomes less remote as Snowbird winds its way to its inundation at Santeet-lah Lake. The creek is only runnable after heavy rainfall and has at best a two-day window.

MAPS: Santeetlah Creek, Robbinsville (USGS);
Graham (County)

JUNCTION TO FIRST BRIDGE DOWNSTREAM

CLASS	III–IV
LENGTH	2.8
TIME	1.5
GAUGE	VISUAL
LEVEL	N/A
PERMITS	No
GRADIENT	143
SCENERY	A

DESCRIPTION: This section of Snowbird Creek is extremely tight and technical, but there are no major drops. Extreme hazards exist if the water is very high (read Class V screamer) and/or you are any less than an expert boater. This creek has more moves than a downtown street hustler. Be aware of several boulder and log strainers. Creek Meister Jim Holcombe has carried in and run as high as 3 mi. above Junction where it is steeper. You may want to consider this ageless Bob Dylan lyric before following suit: "How far do you want to go? Not too far, but just enough so's we can say we been there."

SHUTTLE: From Robbinsville, drive north on US 129 and turn left onto SR 1116. At the next intersection, turn right onto SR 1127. Turn left at SR 1115 and continue to SR 1120. Go right on SR 1120 to the dead end. This is known as Junction. Take out at the first bridge over the creek downstream of Junction.

GAUGE: None. Runnable only after extended rainfall.

B

FIRST BRIDGE DOWNSTREAM OF JUNCTION TO SR 1127 BRIDGE

CLASS	II–III
LENGTH	8.5
TIME	3
GAUGE	VISUAL
LEVEL	N/A
PERMITS	No
GRADIENT	42
SCENERY	A–B

DESCRIPTION: There are no difficulties. Watch out for the 3-ft. lowhead dam on the lower part of this section.

SHUTTLE: See Section A for put-in. The take-out is located at the first bridge over the creek on SR 1127, just past SR 1116.

GAUGE: None. Runnable only after extended rainfall.

CHEOAH RIVER

The Cheoah River is normally a dry streambed that runs from Santeetlah Dam to the Little Tennessee River. It enters the Little Tennessee within spitting distance of the Cheoah Dam. TVA pipes water from Santeetlah Lake into the Little Tennessee/Lake Cheoah inundation for the obvious reasons, leaving the resultant dry stream bed. The Cheoah below Santeetlah Lake is just west of the Cheoah Mountains in southwestern North Carolina. The river runs only after extended rainfall. If the lake is spilling over the dam, there may be more water on the last 2 mi. than most paddlers want. Most of the run can be seen from US 129 north of Robbinsville.

MAPS: Tapoco (NC/TN), Fontana Dam (USGS); Graham (County)

CLASS	III–IV
LENGTH	9.2
TIME	4.5
GAUGE	VISUAL
LEVEL	N/A
PERMITS	No
GRADIENT	70
SCENERY	A

SANTEETLAH DAM TO US 129 BRIDGE
(JUST BELOW CHEOAH DAM)

DESCRIPTION: The first 7 mi. of this run are primarily Class II–III. The water here is flowing over small to moderate boulder fields and through shrubs and small trees, as the riverbed is normally dry. There is one 4-ft. ledge just downstream of the overhead pipe carrying water to Lake Cheoah. The more enjoyable run for advanced boaters is to put in 3 mi. above the take-out. This section picks up volume (due to several creeks entering) and gradient quickly. The action here is more continuous, with only a few flat stretches. The boulders are larger and the view is often blocked. At moderate levels, everything can be boat-scouted, with the exception of one 10-ft. drop, best run on the far right. The last 2 mi. drop at a rate of 100 fpm. At higher levels (water spilling over the dam), the extra push would make for some Class V drops.

SHUTTLE: There are any number of places to put in on this run, as US 129 follows the river for most of its length. For those wanting to do the entire run, take US 129 north of Robbinsville to the Cheoah Point Recreation Area and scramble down to the

base of the dam. To take out, follow US 129 north of Robbinsville to the bridge over the Little Tennessee River (just downstream of the Cheoah Dam).

GAUGE: None. Runnable only after heavy, extended rainfall.

SANTEETLAH CREEK

Santeetlah Creek originates in the Nantahala National Forest, just south of the pristine, virgin woods of Joyce Kilmer Memorial Forest. It springs from the Unicoi Mountains a few miles east of the NC/TN

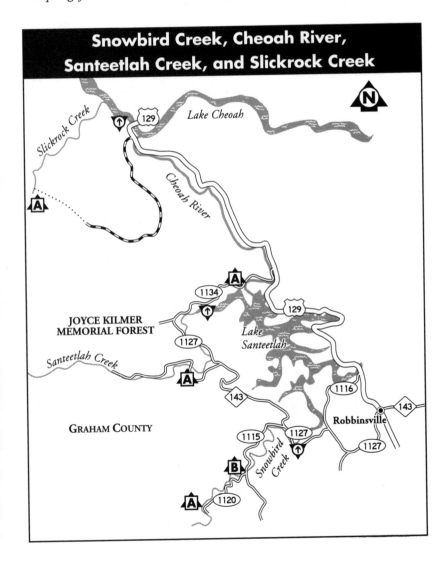

state line. *The upper section of this run is easy Class II water with the more interesting stuff towards the end. In 1973, Jim Holcombe and I did this run, and I remember rolling over and drinking from this fine creek. The water still appears to be drinkable, although we certainly can't advise it! This run is an option only after heavy rainfall and has at best a two-day window of runnability.*

MAPS: Santeetlah Creek (USGS); Graham (County)

CLASS	III–IV
LENGTH	4.2
TIME	2
GAUGE	VISUAL
LEVEL	N/A
PERMITS	No
GRADIENT	66
SCENERY	A

GOVERNMENT RD. 81 TO SANTEETLAH LAKE

DESCRIPTION: This section has lots of fun, boat-scoutable Class III and easy Class IV water. Most of the action is below the SR 1127 bridge. There is a 5-ft. natural dam that needs to be looked at closely, especially at high water. Shortly before entering the lake, there is an 8-ft. low head dam that can be run on the right at moderate levels. Paddle 100 yds. down the lake to take out.

SHUTTLE: From Robbinsville, drive north on US 129 and turn left onto SR 1116. At the next intersection, turn right onto SR 1127, then go 1.7 mi. to FR 81. Turn left and follow this to the bridge over the creek. For take-out, return to SR 1127, turn left, and continue north of Rattler Ford Campground. Take the first right onto SR 1134 and go to the lake.

GAUGE: None. Can be run only after extended rainfall.

SLICKROCK CREEK

Slickrock Creek originates in the Unicoi Mountains of southwestern North Carolina and southeastern Tennessee. It forms part of the state line between North Carolina and Tennessee for its entire length. There are 4.8 mi. of runnable creek above its inundation/confluence with the Little Tennessee River. Slickrock meets the Little Tennessee 2 mi. below the Cheoah Dam, whereupon one must paddle upstream (uplake) to the take-out. The creek flows between Nantahala National Forest (NC) and Cherokee National Forest (TN), where it enjoys a pristine environment and excellent water quality.

MAPS: Tapoco (NC/TN) (USGS); Graham; Monroe (TN) (County)

BIG FAT GAP TRAIL TO ACCESS RD. OFF US 129
(JUST BELOW CHEOAH DAM)

CLASS	IV
LENGTH	5.2
TIME	2.5
GAUGE	VISUAL
LEVEL	3 FT.
PERMITS	YES
GRADIENT	888
SCENERY	B

DESCRIPTION: With an average gradient of 162 fpm, Slick-rock Creek is one of the most demanding runs in the Southeast. It is extremely technical, very steep, and next to impossible to catch with enough water to paddle. The run starts off with continuous, steep boulder gardens. Slightly over 1 mi. into the trip is a series of ledge drops of 10, 8, and 22 ft. The big one has a short pool separating drops of 8 and 14 ft., respectively. Water levels will dictate the routes on these falls. Below this section there are alternating stretches of fun and slam dance gradient. About 1.5 mi. above the take-out is a 15-ft. ledge best run in the middle or off the far right. Below this ledge the creek continues its quick descent into the Little Tennessee River. Due to the amount of time one will spend out of the boat scouting and carrying dead-falls, it is suggested not to make this run in colder temperatures. A hypothermic paddler would have a long walk to find help.

SHUTTLE: From Robbinsville, go approximately 14.3 mi. north on US 129 to Slickrock Rd. Take a left (across Cheoah River) onto Slickrock Rd. and go 7.1 mi. to the dead-end at Big Fat Gap. Walk 30 minutes down Big Fat Gap Trail to the creek. For take-out, continue past the Slickrock Rd. turnoff on US 129, cross the bridge over the Little Tennessee River below Cheoah Dam, and take a left on the access road to where it dead-ends.

GAUGE: None. The creek can only be run after heavy, extended rainfall. Since the run is unobservable except by hiking (almost 2 mi. to the put-in) or paddling (about 1.7 mi. to the take-out), it is advisable to put in at the take-out and paddle to the creek's confluence with the Little T (first left downlake) to check the flow. This bit of trouble will be worth the effort, as too much or too little water will make for an extremely long, hard trip.

CANEY FORK CREEK

The Caney Fork has its headwaters in the Nantahala National Forest and is joined by many smaller rivulets as it cuts between Coward Mountain to the north and Shelton and Rich Mountains to the south and southeast. It drops over many ledges before confluencing with the Tuckasegee River at the community of East Laport.

One may want to take a short side trip here to Judaculla Rock just north of the creek. The Rock has elaborate American Indian hieroglyphics which to this time have not been interpreted. Simply follow the signs from NC 107. This run can be extended 2.1 mi. with a reading of 3.20 on the Gauge. Put in at the gauging station.

MAPS: Tuckasegee, Sylva South (USGS); Jackson (County)

CLASS	II
LENGTH	4.5
TIME	2
GAUGE	VISUAL
LEVEL	3.1 FT.
PERMITS	NO
GRADIENT	32
SCENERY	A

JACKSON COUNTY RT. 1737 BRIDGE (THE SECOND BRIDGE ABOVE NC 107) TO 107 BRIDGE

DESCRIPTION: There is a cable just below the second bridge which can present problems at higher water levels. At normal levels one can easily pass under it. Also, there are a couple of ledges that drop off gradually, which could present stoppers at just slightly higher water levels. This in effect would increase the run to good Class II–III. Beware of strainers.

SHUTTLE: From Sylva, drive south on NC 107. After crossing Caney Fork Creek on NC 107 (the take-out), immediately take a left on Rt. 1737. Go to the second bridge across the creek.

GAUGE: The USGS Gauge is located alongside Rt. 1737 approximately 2.1 mi. above the put-in. Minimum for solo is 3.10. The creek is generally runnable December through the middle of May and following rains.

TUCKASEGEE RIVER

The Tuckasegee begins in the Nantahala National Forest, at the confluence of the East Fork and the West Fork of the Tuckasegee. From there it meanders through a valley with a highway following along its entire length, except for about 4 mi. It flows through Bryson City before entering Lake Fontana.

The river primarily runs over gravel bars until it reaches the gorge below Dillsboro, where it begins to drop over ledges. After leaving the gorge it resumes its original character, with a few ledges and shoals interspersed.

The water quality down from Dillsboro was very poor due to industrial pollution prior to late 1974, when the culprit responsible for it closed down. Since then the river has steadily improved. When the Thorpe Power Plant is operating, the trip can be extended 1.5 mi. by putting in on the West Fork. The put-in is found by driving

up NC 107 along the West Fork, where the water enters the streambed. This is a very narrow run down very fast water. If the Main Plant is operating on the East Fork, the run can be extended about 2 mi. by driving up Rt. 1135 to River Park Campground, which is located immediately below the dam on Lake Cedar Cliff. Information on whether the Main Plant is operating can be obtained by calling Nantahala Power in Sylva, (828) 369-4533.

MAPS: Tuckasegee, Sylva South, Green's Creek, Whittier, Bryson City (USGS); Jackson, Swain (County)

A

NC 107 BRIDGE AT THE COMMUNITY OF TUCKASEGEE TO LENA DAVIS LANDING IN CULLOWHEE

CLASS	I–II (III)
LENGTH	9.5
TIME	3
GAUGE	VISUAL
LEVEL	N/A
PERMITS	No
GRADIENT	9
SCENERY	B

DESCRIPTION: There is a low Class III rapid beyond East Laport, where the river bends away from the highway. It runs continuously for over 100 yds. Approach it in the center.

The Lena Davis Landing is above a 10-ft. dam. It should be approached cautiously. Take out or carry on river left on the

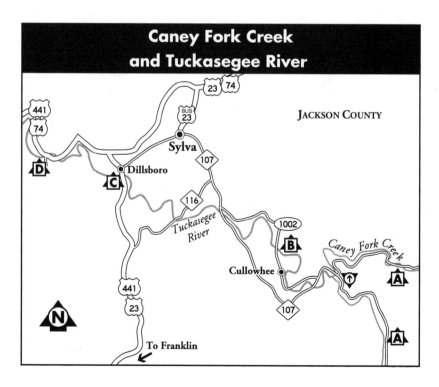

Caney Fork Creek and Tuckasegee River

portage trail. To reach the landing, take the first road on the southeast side of the old Cullowhee bridge (down from Hardees).

For those wishing a shorter run, put n at East Laport. Access at the mouth of the Caney Fork. The area, developed by TVA and the Jackson County Recreation and Parks Department, has rest rooms. The gate is closed at dark. This will make a run of 6.5 mi.

SHUTTLE: From Sylva, drive south on NC 107. Pass the Caney Fork Creek take-out and put in at the bridge crossing the East Fork of the Tuckasegee in the community of Tuckasegee. Take out on Rt. 1002 at the dam in the community of Cullowhee.

GAUGE: The USGS Gauge is on the left bank at the foot of River St. in Bryson City, or about 150 yds. below the old bridge in the center of town. No reading is available for a minimum level. Generally the river can be run all year except during extremely dry spells. A better run is likely if the power plants on the East Fork and West Fork are in operation.

CLASS	I–II
LENGTH	11
TIME	4.5
GAUGE	VISUAL
LEVEL	N/A
PERMITS	No
GRADIENT	8
SCENERY	B

DAM AT CULLOWHEE TO DAM AT DILLSBORO

DESCRIPTION: Watch for small riffles and gravel bars, primarily. The take-out at Dillsboro is above a 15-ft. dam. An easy take-out can be made about 50 yds. above the dam on the right.

For those who wish to continue the trip into Section C, take-out should be made on the left in the flats, about 75 yds. above the dam. This will require a portage of about 250 yds. to the road and back down a steep path to a sandy beach below the dam.

SHUTTLE: From the dam in the community of Cullowhee, take Rt. 1002 north to NC 107 and turn right. Continue on NC 107 through Sylva to the dam in the community of Dillsboro.

GAUGE: See Section A.

CLASS	II–III
LENGTH	5
TIME	1.5
GAUGE	VISUAL
LEVEL	N/A
PERMITS	No
GRADIENT	15
SCENERY	A–C

DILLSBORO RIVER ACCESS TO RT. 1392 BRIDGE

DESCRIPTION: The river drops through a steep gorge while running through rock gardens and over ledges, several of which may require scouting. To put in, cross the first bridge going south on US 441 to the shops on the east side. Turn onto River St. then

immediately left onto Webster St. and left again beneath the bridge.

SHUTTLE: Put in below the dam in Dillsboro. To reach the take-out, drive north on US 441/23 and head west on US 74/441. Turn left on Rt. 1392 (Barkers Creek Rd.) to the bridge across the river.

GAUGE: See Section A.

RT. 1392 BRIDGE AT BARKERS CREEK TO THE INTERSECTION OF SHOAL CREEK RD. AND US 19, WEST OF WHITTIER

CLASS	I—II
LENGTH	8
TIME	3
GAUGE	VISUAL
LEVEL	N/A
PERMITS	No
GRADIENT	7
SCENERY	B

DESCRIPTION: No difficulties.

SHUTTLE: From the put-in on Rt. 1392 (Barkers Creek Rd.), go across the bridge and turn left (west) on US 74/441 toward Bryson City. Where 441 heads north, continue west on US 74 to Whittier and take US 19 A north to Shoal Creek Rd. and put in.

GAUGE: None. Can be run all year.

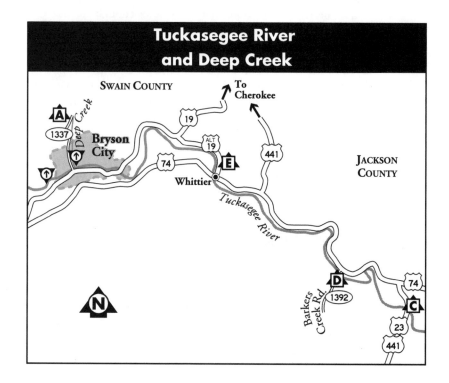

Tuckasegee River and Deep Creek

CLASS	IV
LENGTH	5.2
TIME	2.5
GAUGE	VISUAL
LEVEL	3 FT.
PERMITS	YES
GRADIENT	888
SCENERY	B

INTERSECTION OF SHOAL CREEK RD. AND US 19
WEST OF WHITTIER TO BRYSON CITY

DESCRIPTION: Shortly after leaving the put-in, the river runs through an area of shoals, which at medium-high water levels, can kick up some pretty good waves. This can be best run by staying to the right most of the way. Also, it will keep the paddler from being swept over a double ledge at the bottom. It can be recognized by the first short flat stretch as the river bends right, below the longest continuous shoals. The river drops about 7 ft. in 15 yds. It can be run in several different ways, depending on the water level. Scout from the right bank.

Just after passing under the railroad bridge below Ela, there is a rapid on the right that will have a large hydraulic in medium-high water levels.

A series of shoals begin just above the US 19 bridge in Bryson City. These should be approached carefully.

The last rapid above the take-out consists of a long run down the left, and ends in a right-angle turn. This is known as Devil's Dip. The right turn should be made soon enough to miss the rather nice souse hole that waits to gobble up the paddler who lets his canoe drift too far to the outside of the turn.

SHUTTLE: Take out on the left bank downstream from the first bridge in Bryson City. Go north on the road to Deep Creek Campground off Main St. (US 19), and take a left into the parking lot. On Sunday an automobile can be left here, but on weekdays try the Federal Building parking lot, which is west on Main St.

GAUGE: This section is runnable all year except during extremely dry periods. A reading of 3.75 on the Bryson City Gauge would be the suggested maximum level for intermediate paddlers. At this level, some of the shoals can get quite heavy. Call Blue Ridge Outing Company (800) 572-3510.

DEEP CREEK

Deep Creek has its headwaters below Indian Gap (elevation 5,286 ft.) and flows through the valley between Noland Divide and Thomas Divide, which rise above it. The watershed is completely within the Great Smoky Mountains National Park, thus providing it with excellent water quality. Deep Creek continues as a small, fast-moving stream with a steady gradient until just before joining the Tuckasegee River, when it flattens out somewhat.

Tubing is one of the main forms of recreation for campers— young and old—at Deep Creek Campground, as well as for the local populace. The run is short but delightful for the experienced open boater.

MAPS: Bryson City (USGS); Swain (County)

GOVERNMENT ROAD ON WEST SIDE OF CREEK AT GATE
ABOVE CAMPGROUND TO RT. 1340 BRIDGE

CLASS	II
LENGTH	2
TIME	I
GAUGE	VISUAL
LEVEL	-5 IN.
PERMITS	NO
GRADIENT	33
SCENERY	A–B

DESCRIPTION: There are many hazards, but none that are dangerous. At low water this creek requires the utmost in skill to read the small passages, to push, pull, lean, and anything else to squeeze through. This is definitely not a trip for the heavy-water lover. One should be on the alert for tubers during the summer.

SHUTTLE: Follow signs out of Bryson City to Deep Creek Campground (Rt. 1337). Continue on the west side of the creek to the gate and put-in. If the gate is open, proceed to the first or second bridge, depending on the water level. If you're putting in at the second bridge, cross it and put in about 50 yds. above it. This bridge crosses Indian Creek. Deep Creek is on your left after crossing the bridge. The 0.5 mi. through the gorge drops at a rate of 50 fpm. For take-out, cross the bridge entering into the main entrance of the campground from Rt. 1337 and turn right on Rt. 1339. Proceed approximately 2 mi. to Rt. 1340 and the take-out. Ask permission at the residence behind the Baptist Church before taking out on the west bank.

GAUGE: It's located on the northwest corner of the Rt. 1340 bridge. 5" below "0" is minimum for solo paddling. With a reading of 3" below "0," put in 0.5 mi. farther upstream, above the next bridge, for a run through a small but beautiful gorge. It can be run all year except after long dry spells.

OCONALUFTEE RIVER

The Oconaluftee heads up between Indian Gap (elevation 5,286 ft.) and Newfound Gap (elevation 5,048 ft.) and generally flows beside US 441 through the Great Smoky Mountains National Park, until it confluences with the Tuckasegee River east of Bryson City. The run above Cherokee is one through many rock gardens in crystal clear water. Below Cherokee, the water quality diminishes considerably due to sewage being dumped in. A distinct odor may be noticeable below the US 441 bridge, but it doesn't continue for long.

The river enters the Cherokee Indian Reservation 0.5 mi. below its confluence with the Raven Fork River, and from this point to the take-out is designated as "Enterprise Waters." As of press time, the Cherokee Indian Reservation has banned all boating on waters passing through its land. This may change, though, in the future.

The approximately 4.5 mi. stretch above the reservation boundary can be paddled at any time. In order to do so, one should check in at the ranger station at Park Headquarters, which is located at Pioneer Structures on US 441 north of Cherokee, to inform them of plans to canoe the river. This might save one from being "pulled" off the river by park rangers. This actually happened to a friend of mine several years ago. It could not only prove embarrassing, but could also lead to a rather long hike.

Note: Trout season on the reservation is year-round except for the three weeks preceding the opening of the state-wide season on the first Saturday in April.

MAPS: Smokemont, Whittier (USGS); Swain (County)

CLASS	II–III
LENGTH	11.5
TIME	4.5
GAUGE	VISUAL
LEVEL	1.7 FT.
PERMITS	No
GRADIENT	27
SCENERY	A–C

SMOKEMONT CAMPGROUND TO BIRDTOWN

DESCRIPTION: There are many tight runs over ledges and through gravel bars that require fast thinking and faster maneuvering.

After entering Cherokee, there are the remains of an old washed-out dam along US 441. Iron rods protrude from some of the rocks and it is best to run on the far right directly behind the trailer. This is located about 80 yds. above the Cherokee Information Station and picnic area.

For anyone wishing to extend the trip into the Tuckasegee, or on to Bryson City, there is a 30 ft. dam 3 mi. below Birdtown. It can be portaged on the right.

SHUTTLE: From Cherokee, go north on US 441 toward Gatlinburg, TN, to the entrance of Smokemont Campground; cross the bridge. The take-out is west of Cherokee on US 19 at Birdtown; cross the Rt. 1359 bridge (at the Cherokee Recreation Park Campground sign) to the Gauge.

GAUGE: The USGS Gauge is on the south bank 200 ft. upstream from the Rt. 1359 bridge below Birdtown. Minimum for solo run is 1.70. It can be run at 1.32 from Ravensford Bridge (above Pioneer Structures), which cuts about 4 mi. off the total trip. A Gauge directly across on the opposite bank (along US 19) will read approximately 0.05 lower than the opposite Gauge, so estimate accordingly.

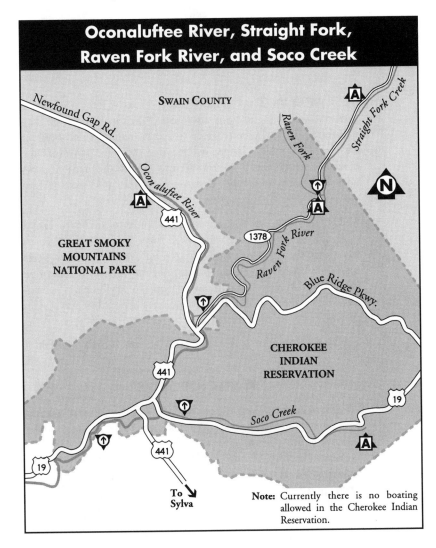

Oconaluftee River, Straight Fork, Raven Fork River, and Soco Creek

SWAIN COUNTY

Newfound Gap Rd.

Straight Fork Creek

Raven Fork

Oconaluftee River

441

GREAT SMOKY MOUNTAINS NATIONAL PARK

1378

Raven Fork River

Blue Ridge Pkwy.

441

CHEROKEE INDIAN RESERVATION

19

Soco Creek

441

19

To Sylva

Note: Currently there is no boating allowed in the Cherokee Indian Reservation.

STRAIGHT FORK

The Straight Fork originates between Balsam Mountain and Hyatt Ridge in the Great Smoky Mountains National Park. The stream is pristine as is the area through which it flows. Although a dirt road parallels the creek, it feels like a wilderness run. The put-in is immediately downstream of the Hyatt Creek confluence. With an average drop of 141 fpm, the gradient is deceptively high. It doesn't seem that steep except for one short stretch in the middle portion of the run. This run has a small, densely-vegetated watershed and will need considerable rainfall to bring it to a runnable level.

MAPS: Bunches Bald (USGS); Swain (County)

CLASS	II–IV
LENGTH	2.2
TIME	2
GAUGE	VISUAL
LEVEL	N/A
PERMITS	No
GRADIENT	140
SCENERY	A

LOW WATER BRIDGE ON GOVERNMENT ROAD
TO NATIONAL PARK BOUNDARY

DESCRIPTION: The Straight Fork is an extremely tight, twisty run that will demand your attention from top to bottom. The streambed primarily consists of stubblefields and small boulder gardens. The major danger will be tree strainers that cross the creek in several spots. About 1 mi. into the run the gradient picks up and it becomes a solid, demanding Class III–IV trip and requires excellent boat control.

SHUTTLE: Take US 441 north of Cherokee to SR 1378. Take a right on SR 1378 and go to where the two government roads fork. Take the right fork and go to the only low-water bridge (actually under the water). Go 0.6 mi. beyond the fish hatchery on the same road as the put-in. Taking out here will keep the paddler within the National Park and allow for paddling any day of the week. Below the fish hatchery are "Enterprise Waters."

GAUGE: None. Runnable only after extended, heavy rainfall.

RAVEN FORK RIVER

The Raven Fork comes off Breakneck Ridge, often at just that speed. It flows through the Cherokee Indian Reservation to a point just above the town of Cherokee, where it joins the Oconaluftee River.

Raven Fork runs through boulder fields and rock gardens, to present one of the most delightful trips a paddler can find anywhere. The Cherokee have designated the river as "Enterprise Waters." As of press time, the Cherokee Indian Reservation has banned all boating on wa-

ters passing through its land. *This may change, though, in the future.*

MAPS: Bunches Bald, Smokemont (USGS); Swain (County)

A

CONFLUENCE WITH THE STRAIGHT FORK TO
THE BRIDGE AT THE JOB CORPS CENTER

CLASS	II–III
LENGTH	8
TIME	4
GAUGE	VISUAL
LEVEL	1.5– 2.5 FT.
PERMITS	No
GRADIENT	51
SCENERY	A–B

DESCRIPTION: There is a rapid with a large hydraulic just below the put-in that may encourage one to start below it. It makes for a rather unpleasant trip to take two strokes and find oneself out of the boat. The river drops at a rate of 75 fpm through the first 0.5 mi. Fortunately, this stretch, as well as much of the rest of the trip, can be scouted from the road, and it will be wise to do so through here.

There are numerous Class II rapids before reaching the first Class III, which cannot be seen completely from the road. This rapid is in the bend of the river behind Smith Memorial Pentecostal Holiness Church. With a higher water level it requires a great deal of difficult maneuvering to prevent swamping the canoe.

After passing Sherries Cove Creek bridge, the river enters a 900-ft.-deep gorge and makes a large bend around River Valley Camp, a private campground. There are three Class III rapids in the gorge, all of which should be scouted. The gradient increases to over 60 fpm. The approach to the first two rapids will vary somewhat with the water level, but both can be scouted from the right. The third, Crack-in-the-Rock, can be scouted on the left and run on the left. It is located just beyond the campground and just above the National Park boundary sign. There is fairly heavy water above the rapid, so care should be taken in the approach.

SHUTTLE: Take Government Rd. east of the US 441 bridge over the Oconaluftee in Cherokee for approximately 10 mi. For take-out, turn west on the first paved road south of the Government Rd. bridge crossing the Raven Fork. This road goes into the Job Corps Center. Take-out can be made at this bridge or at the first one (Government Rd.) for a slightly shorter run.

GAUGE: The USGS Gauge is at Sherries Cove Creek bridge. Minimum for solo: 1.50. Maximum for a safe run through the gorge: 2.50. At a level of 1.50, it would be best to cut the trip shorter and put in at the confluence of Bunches Creek.

SOCO CREEK

Soco Creek heads up in Soco Gap (elevation 4,345 ft.), where the Blue Ridge Parkway crosses US 19, east of Cherokee at the Qualla Reservation line. It flows to its confluence with the Oconaluftee River just below the take-out. It presents the skilled paddler with a real roller-coaster ride. Although it never strays more than a few yards from US 19, and runs through many backyards, one has little opportunity to view the scenery—good or bad.

Soco is wholly within the reservation and has been designated as "Enterprise Waters." As of press time, the Cherokee Indian Reservation has banned all boating on waters passing through its land. This may change, though, in the future.

MAPS: Sylva North, Whittier (USGS); Jackson (County)

SOCO CREEK RD. AND US 19 TO US 441 BRIDGE

CLASS	II–IV
LENGTH	8.5
TIME	3
GAUGE	VISUAL
LEVEL	-6 IN.
PERMITS	NO
GRADIENT	67(1.8 @106)
SCENERY	B

DESCRIPTION: This is a natural slalom course with no big drops, but several rapids might require scouting, especially in the upper 1.75 mi. which drops at the rate of 106 fpm. Much of the run can be scouted from the highway. Below Bluewing Rd., the channel is being changed due to dredging. Stay to the left here, although this may get into a rather shallow stretch due to rechannelization.

SHUTTLE: Use Soco Creek Rd. where it leaves US 19, going up the creek across from Soco Trail Campground. Take out at the US 441 bridge, 1 mi. south of Cherokee.

GAUGE: It is located at the US 19 bridge on the southwest side, across from El Camino Restaurant. A reading of 6" below "0" is minimum for a run from US 19 bridge, while a reading of 2" below "0" will allow a run from the first put-in. Dredging is still being done in some stretches, which will possibly affect the level through those areas.

EAST FORK PIGEON RIVER

The East Fork of the Pigeon is a shallow, low-water stream meandering through farm land as it courses back and forth under US 276 before finally joining the West Fork.

MAPS: Cruso (USGS); Haywood (County)

RT. 1887 BRIDGE (PISGAH CREEK RD.) TO NC 110 BRIDGE

CLASS	II–III
LENGTH	8.7
TIME	4
GAUGE	VISUAL
LEVEL	-6 IN.
PERMITS	NO
GRADIENT	30
SCENERY	B

DESCRIPTION : There are no difficulties. The river has a fairly constant gradient with no abrupt drops. At one point the river flows through a gravel pit, which gets rather shallow. This area is evident from the highway. There are two or three posted signs through this area, which primarily refer to fishing.

SHUTTLE: From Canton, drive south on NC 110 to where it crosses the West Fork/East Fork confluence. This is the take-out. Continue 1 m. south to the intersection with US 276 and turn left. At the community of Cruso, turn left onto Rt. 1887 and put in at the bridge.

GAUGE: It is located on the n northwest side of the NC 110 bridge. Minimum for solo: 6" below "0." You must go down to water level in order to read the Gauge. The river is generally runnable during wet seasons or early spring.

WEST FORK PIGEON RIVER

The West Fork of the Pigeon heads up in the Pisgah National Forest, then flows through Champion Papers' property at Lake Logan before confluencing with the East Fork. The put-in is about 0.25 mi. below the dam at Lake Logan. From there down it is a fast-moving, low-water stream flowing over a series of gravel beds.

MAPS: Waynesville (USGS); Haywood (County)

JUNCTION OF NC 215 AND RT. 1129 TO
CONFLUENCE WITH EAST FORK OF THE PIGEON

CLASS	II–III
LENGTH	6.3
TIME	2
GAUGE	VISUAL
LEVEL	1.8 FT.
PERMITS	No
GRADIENT	32
SCENERY	B

DESCRIPTION: There are several fast runs through long gravel bars. In addition to these, there is one hard S turn dropping over two ledges, which is located just beyond a high undercut clay bank as the river bears to the left.

SHUTTLE: From Canton, drive south on NC 110 to where it crosses the West Fork/East Fork confluence. This is the take-out. Continue 1 mi. south, cross US 276, and drive down NC 215 to

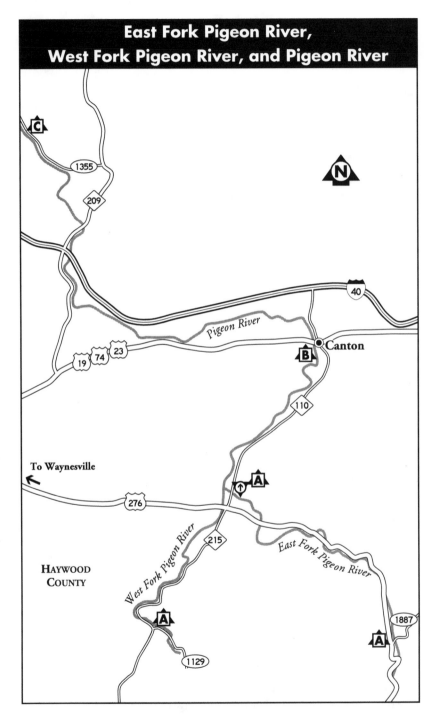

East Fork Pigeon River, West Fork Pigeon River, and Pigeon River

the bridge at the junction of NC 215 and Rt. 1129 (Little East Fork Rd.), below Champion Papers' property line.

GAUGE: The USGS Gauge is on the east bank, downstream at the Rt. 1111 bridge. Minimum for solo: 1.80. The river is generally runnable during wet seasons or early spring.

PIGEON RIVER

Used to be you took your life in your own hands if you paddled the Pigeon. Just 40 miles upstream is the town of Canton, the Champion International Plant—a pulp and paper mill—dumped toxic wastewater into the Pigeon, leaving the river the color of coffee (no cream please) and smelling quite bad. Thanks to the work of the State of Tennessee, the EPA, and others, Champion cleaned up its act. As a result, the rafting industry on the Pigeon blossomed in the early 1990s, bringing an increase in paddling (not to mention tourist dollars) to the area.

The Pigeon originates in the hills surrounding Canton, flowing through farmland. Several miles below Canton the river flows through a deep gorge with I-40 running along high above it. The "Dry Gorge" between Waterville Lake and the Walters Plant is just that, except in periods of extremely high water. The distance is approximately 13 mi.

The river below Walters Plant becomes a natural slalom run through a rock-strewn course. This could be made into one of the finest slalom courses in the East except for the amount of pollution.

MAPS: Waynesville, Cruso, Canton, Clyde, Fines Creek; Waterville, Hartford, Newport (TN) (USGS); Haywood, Cocke (TN) (County)

CONFLUENCE OF EAST AND WEST FORKS
OF THE PIGEON TO US 19/23 BRIDGE

CLASS	I–II
LENGTH	5
TIME	2
GAUGE	VISUAL
LEVEL	-6 IN.
PERMITS	NO
GRADIENT	12
SCENERY	B

DESCRIPTION: There are no difficulties.

SHUTTLE: From Canton, drive south on NC 110 to where it crosses the West Fork/East Fork confluence, 1 mi. north of US 276. Take out at the US 19/23/74 bridge across the Pigeon in Canton.

GAUGE: It is located on the west side of the NC 110 bridge at the put-in. Minimum for solo: 6" below "0." The river can be

run from here down most of the year, except during long dry spells.

US 19/23 BRIDGE IN CANTON TO FERGUSON BRIDGE

CLASS	I–II
LENGTH	15.6
TIME	6.5
GAUGE	VISUAL
LEVEL	-7 IN.
PERMITS	No
GRADIENT	10
SCENERY	B–C

DESCRIPTION: There are no difficulties. Primarily, the difficulty will be with the olfactory nerves.

SHUTTLE: From the put-in at the US 19/23/74 bridge in Canton, travel west on I-40 to the NC 209 Exit. Go north on NC 209 and turn left onto Rt. 1355 (Riverside Rd.). Take out at the first bridge (Ferguson Bridge) across the Pigeon on the left.

GAUGE: Minimum level for solo: 7" below "0."

FERGUSON BRIDGE TO NEW HEPCO BRIDGE

CLASS	II–IV
LENGTH	6.1
TIME	2.5
GAUGE	VISUAL
LEVEL	-7 IN.
PERMITS	No
GRADIENT	26
SCENERY	B

DESCRIPTION: There is a boulder garden, which drops 8 ft. in 20 yds., with standing waves at the bottom (Class IV). This can be recognized by a long stretch of flat water after having paddled along I-40 for some distance. A short rapid just above the boulder garden tends to lead into the fast water before the danger is apparent. Passage at a normal water level is through the second chute from the right. Scout on the right.

A second long flat stretch precedes the Class IV, which is 600 yds. above the take-out. An old, 4-ft.-high dam with a heavy hydraulic is followed by 60 yds. of rather heavy water. The paddler must move from far right to far left through here if attempting to run the dam, or even below it. This hydraulic held a C-1 paddler in for a few anxious moments before he got out. However, his boat tumbled for some 30 minutes before a tandem team was able to hook a grab loop and pull it out. One break in the old wall may be run on the far right. Do not attempt to run straight down on the right all the way. Cut to the left above the large rock at the bottom of the run.

SHUTTLE: From Ferguson Bridge on Rt. 1355, return west to NC 209 and turn right (south) to I-40. Turn right (west) on I-40 and go to the Fines Creek Rd. Exit. Turn left at the bottom of the ramp to reach the river.

GAUGE: Minimum level for solo: 7" below "0."

Pigeon River, Jonathans Creek, and Cataloochee Creek

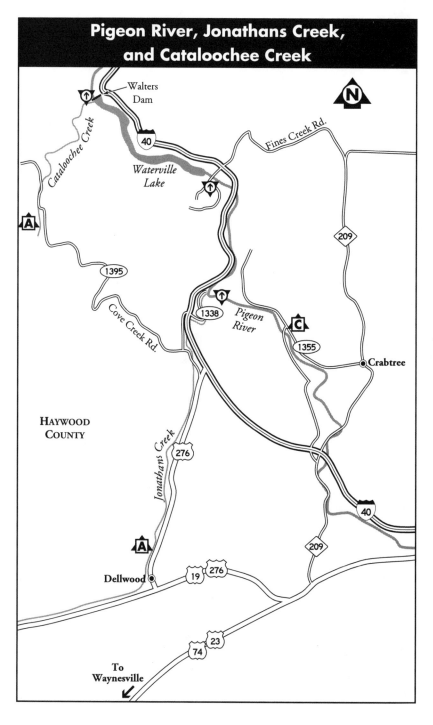

CLASS	III–IV
LENGTH	4.5
TIME	2.5
GAUGE	PHONE
LEVEL	N/A
PERMITS	No
GRADIENT	18
SCENERY	A–B

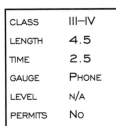

BELOW THE WALTERS PLANT OF CAROLINA POWER
AND LIGHT TO THE BRIDGE AT HARTFORD, TN

DESCRIPTION: There are several rapids that should be scouted. Most of these can be seen from the road or highway. The water volume is generally large and presents many large standing waves and souseholes to give any but the most advanced paddlers trouble galore. At a run of 50,000 kw, one has all the water he'll care to see from an open boat.

SHUTTLE: Take I-40 to the Waterville Rd. Exit. Follow SR 1332 to Walters Plant. For take-out, return to I-40 and drive west. After you pass into Tennessee, take Exit 447 (Hartford).

GAUGE: None. Call (704) 486-5965 and ask for the water flow from Walters Plant. It is generally in operation. A reading of 50,000 kw is maximum for solo open boats.

CLASS	I–II+
LENGTH	8
TIME	3.5
GAUGE	VISUAL
LEVEL	N/A
PERMITS	No
GRADIENT	16
SCENERY	A–C

BRIDGE AT HARTFORD (TN) TO COCKE CR 2484 BRIDGE

DESCRIPTION: There are no difficulties. However, there are many ledges on the section between the two I-40 bridges. At higher water levels this stretch can be fairly turbulent.

For those who might like to extend the trip, a run of 7.5 mi. to the US 25/70 bridge north of Newport (TN) (an easy take-out) can be made. This stretch is fairly flat, but has enough riffles scattered along the way to be interesting, plus there is good scenery.

SHUTTLE: For take-out, take the I-40 Exit 440 and go west to the first right; proceed to the CR 2484 bridge. An easier take-out may be made along the road on the west side of the river 0.25 mi. above the bridge. Put-in located at Hartford, TN. Return to I-40, drive east and take Exit 447 into town.

GAUGE: None. Runnable most of the year, except during dry spells.

JONATHANS CREEK

Jonathans Creek heads up at Black Camp Gap (elevation 4,522 ft.) just off the Heintooga Overlook Rd. from the Blue Ridge Parkway at Soco Gap. It plunges down through Maggie Valley before turning north along US 276 and joining the Pigeon below I-40. It is primarily a fast run over gravel bars through farm lands above Cove Creek. Below, it changes to more of a ledge-type stream, cutting a small gorge as it rushes to the Pigeon. This is a good trout stream, so the paddler should be as considerate as possible of the trout fishermen encountered along the way.

Note: At a water level of 2.50 on the Gauge, a run of about 3 mi. from the Rt. 1306 bridge (off US 19) to the second bridge of Rt. 1307 can be made. However, about 0.25 mi. of posted property is just downstream from this take-out, so a run on down to the put-in point on Rt. 1394 might present problems. This 3 mi. stretch is quite fast and narrow with a gradient averaging almost 75 fpm.

MAPS: Dellwood (USGS); Haywood (County)

HAYWOOD CR 1394 BRIDGE TO THE END OF RT. 1338
JUST ABOVE THE CONFLUENCE WITH THE PIGEON

CLASS	II–III
LENGTH	8.8
TIME	4
GAUGE	VISUAL
LEVEL	1.5 FT.
PERMITS	No
GRADIENT	40
SCENERY	A–C

DESCRIPTION: About 1 mi. below the put-in, there is a chute on the right blocked off by an overhanging tree limb. This is recognizable by a small channel running to the left toward a large silo. This can be carried or lined easily on the small island there.

In the area down from the US 276 bridge, there is a ledge that presents a fair-sized hydraulic at levels above 2.0. This is about 0.25 mi. below a broken foot bridge and at higher levels should be scouted. Approximately 0.4 mi. below the I-40 bridge, there is a series of ledges where a drop of about 15 ft. occurs within some 100 yds. Strainers are possible here, so be sure to scout before committing. The entire stretch can be easily scouted on the left bank.

SHUTTLE: Drive north on US 276 off US 19 at Dellwood for approximately 5 mi. to the Rt. 1394 bridge on the left. The creek runs beside US 276 at this point. For take-out, go north on US 276. Just before the second bridge across the creek (just south of I-40), turn left toward Cover Creek and follow along the creek's south side. Follow the Rt. 1338 bridge across Cove Creek and continue on Rt. 1338 along Jonathans Creek to its end, and take out about 100 yds. above the old house at the end of the road.

GAUGE: The USGS Gauge is located on Rt. 1338 approximately 0.5 mi. above the confluence with the Pigeon. Minimum reading for solo is 1.50.

BIG CREEK

Big Creek is born in the Great Smoky Mountains National Park, which ensures excellent water quality. The creek's origins are northwest of Mt. Sterling and Big Cataloochee Mountain. It confluences with the Pigeon River at Walters Plant. The Big Creek watershed is a very popular hiking and horseback riding area. The streambed has

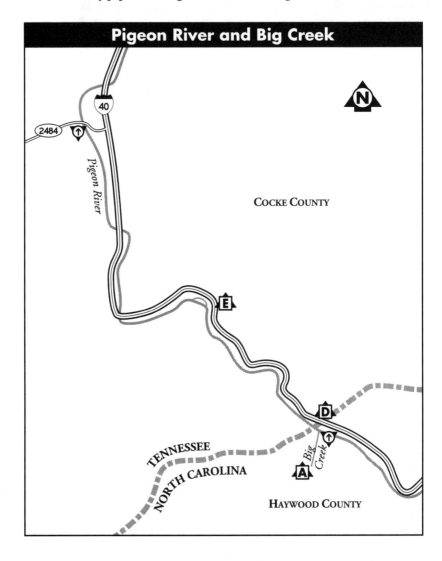

a constant gradient and is full of medium-sized boulders. When this is combined with adequate water levels, it provides for an exciting, expert-level trip. This section is available only after heavy, extended rainfall and has a small window of runnability.

SR 1332 TO WALTERS PLANT

CLASS	IV
LENGTH	2
TIME	3.5
GAUGE	VISUAL
LEVEL	N/A
PERMITS	No
GRADIENT	165
SCENERY	A—B

DESCRIPTION: Big, in body-building parlance, means extreme muscularity. Big Creek maintains a fully-flexed, muscular pose for the duration of the run. Although the authors' view is slightly warped due to having run this at near flood state, it's clear enough to know that with less water this would still be a bang-up run. At high levels this is hard Class IV water, typical of steep western rivers. The creek is essentially one long rapid. With 165 fpm gradient, 500–1,000 cfs, and a narrow streambed, it begets predictably unpredictable results. If the creek is running high, you'll find yourself dodging a myriad of sticky holes, pour-overs, and barely submerged boulders, while traveling at speeds that scarcely allow you time to make decent choices on good lines.

SR 1332 parallels the river most of the way. The run can be made longer by carrying your boat beyond the SR 1332 gate. The road continues to follow the creek for some ways. Be aware of the concrete weir where Big Creek tumbles into Pigeon River. Give yourself plenty of room to take out above it.

This run, at medium and high water, is for confident experts with bullet-proof rolls. A failed roll here is probable grounds for permanent paddler-boat separation.

SHUTTLE: Take I-40 to the Waterville Rd. Exit. Follow SR 1332 to Walters Plant and continue for 2 mi. to the gate across the road. Take out at the Pigeon River put-in.

GAUGE: None. Runnable only after extended rainfall.

CATALOOCHEE CREEK

Cataloochee Creek originates on the western slope of the Cataloochee Divide. From there it runs through a beautiful valley for several miles before entering a small gorge below and flowing into Waterville Lake. The entire watershed is within the Great Smoky Mountains National Park. It is one of the most pristine runs in the state. There

is a reasonably good watershed that should allow for dependable water levels for much of the wet part of the year.

MAPS: Cove Creek Gap (USGS); Haywood (County)

SR 1397 TO WATERVILLE LAKE DAM

CLASS	II–III (IV)
LENGTH	6.3
TIME	4.5
GAUGE	VISUAL
LEVEL	2.7
PERMITS	No
GRADIENT	51
SCENERY	A+

DESCRIPTION: This is a busy, entertaining piece of water. At high water the run can be made by starting at the dead-end of the government road. You have to do some quick maneuvering and dodging of occasional strainers and overhanging branches. Things open up considerably 1 mi. into the run with easy Class II rapids down to the SR 1397 bridge. From here, both gradient and volume increase as Little Cataloochee Creek joins the fun. The creek maintains a fast Class II–III pace for 2 mi. before reaching a Class IV drop of 10 ft. Scout on the left. Enter the rapid far right with a sharp left angle and finish far left. Immediately downstream is a 7-ft. slide ending just above a 15-ft. unrunnable cascade. The slide can be run far right or far left; just don't miss the eddy at the bottom. Portage the cascade on the left. Paddle another 0.5 mi.; pristine Cataloochee Creek enters sewage-laden Waterville Lake. The take-out is 0.5 mi. up the lake at the dam. When setting shuttle do not drive to the dam, as the CP&L people don't want a lot of traffic on their road. Park up the hill at the gate and carry your boat up so we can maintain good will with these folks.

SHUTTLE: Take the Maggie Valley US 276 Exit off I-40. Take SR 1395 (Cove Creek Rd.) to Cataloochee. Take SR 1397 approximately 0.5 mi. above the ranger station. Traveling west on I-40, look for the 11-mi. marker and turn right through an opening in the fence. You can only get on or off this road traveling west. Drive under the interstate to the gate at the top of the hill and park. To get back on I-40 east you must drive to the next exit (Harmon Den).

GAUGE: The USGS Gauge is located beside the SR 1397 bridge. Minimum level is 2.7 ft.

part**Two**

BROAD & FRENCH BROAD
RIVER SYSTEM/WATERSHED

WEST FORK FRENCH BROAD

*The West Fork of the French Broad forms as drainage between
Round Mountain and Big Pisgah Mountain in Pisgah National
Forest. It runs quietly through a valley for several miles before entering a short, steep gorge below where it confluences with the North,
East, and Middle Forks to form the French Broad. This run starts off
with a bang—the three largest rapids come in the first mile of the
run. Below the first mile, the river settles into a fun Class II–III
pace. This section is only runnable after extended rainfall.*

MAPS: Lake Toxaway, Rosman (USGS); Transylvania (County)

SR 1309 BRIDGE TO US 64 BRIDGE

CLASS	III–V
LENGTH	3.4
TIME	2.5
GAUGE	VISUAL
LEVEL	-4 IN.
PERMITS	No
GRADIENT	100
SCENERY	A–B

DESCRIPTION: Approximately 0.25 mi. below the put-in is a
13-ft. Class IV–V (depending on the water level). Bow pin potential looms large at the base of this drop. The only route is obvious. Scout or carry on the left. Around the bend is another
rapid dropping 14 ft. in a cascading slide. During a solo exploratory run, a bow pin did occur in the middle of this drop
causing the C-1 to fill instantly and ripping both thigh straps
out. It was just a split second pin, but the potential for worse is
there. Scout or carry on the left. Two hundred yds. downstream
is a cascading Class V with a total drop of 22 ft. Scouting this
drop is tough because the rhododendron is very thick. Last seen,
this rapid had a large tree in the middle bottom. Scout or carry
on right. After these three major drops the river can be boat-
scouted down to the confluence.

SHUTTLE: From Brevard, take US 64 west to SR 1309. Take a
right and go 2.4 mi. to the bridge. Take out at the confluence of
the West and North Forks at the junction of US 64 and NC 215.

GAUGE: It is located on the river left piling of the SR 1309 bridge. Minimum is 4" below bottom of "0." For a reading, call Headwaters Outfitters at (828) 877-3106.

NORTH FORK FRENCH BROAD

The North Fork of the French Broad heads up on the eastern edge of the Nantahala National Forest. The stream originates in the vicinity of Devil's Courthouse, off the Blue Ridge Parkway. Its protected watershed ensures excellent water quality. High in the mountains it

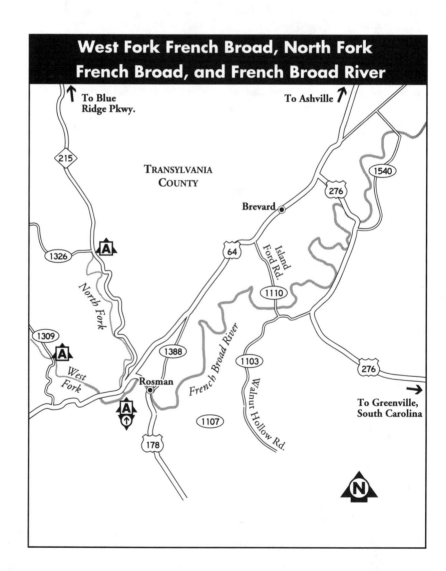

West Fork French Broad, North Fork French Broad, and French Broad River

tumbles over Courthouse Falls, a stunning 50-ft. drop. Below the falls it remains a steep mountain rivulet for some miles before entering the flat valley at Balsam Grove. Downstream of Balsam Grove there are several beautiful falls—most notably Birdtown Falls, a runnable 20-footer. Flatwater follows Birdtown Falls down to the section described. The North Fork drains a small area, so extended rainfall is necessary to be able to paddle it.

MAPS: Rosman (USGS); Transylvania (County)

SR 1326 BRIDGE TO US 64 BRIDGE

CLASS	IV–V
LENGTH	7
TIME	3.5
GAUGE	VISUAL
LEVEL	-6 IN.
PERMITS	NO
GRADIENT	55 (1 @145)
SCENERY	A+

DESCRIPTION: At the end of the first mile, there is a slide dropping 12 ft. followed by a Class III rapid. Scout on the left. The next rapid of consequence, Boxcar Falls, is so named because of a mishap which occurred when the narrow gauge railroad was in operation. Legend has it a boxcar fell in the narrow, deep sluice at the base of the falls. Boxcar Falls drops about 22 ft. into a narrow rock trough. There are two obvious routes over the drop, neither pleasant, both with a reasonable degree of potential for injury. Scout or portage on the old railroad bed on the right. Below here is good Class IV gradient for several hundred yds. Razorback comes at the end of this stretch. Below Razorback is the Clog, a steep Class V boulder garden of a hundred yds. Scout or carry on the left. More interesting Class IV rapids follow, leading into Submarine, a 9-ft. slide on the far left. The gradient starts to slow progressively from Submarine to the take-out. For those interested in cutting some flatwater out of the run, take out at Alligator Rock. Alligator Rock (so named because of a jaws-like formation above the road on the right) pull-off is 1.7 mi. north on NC 215 from the intersection at US 64.

SHUTTLE: From Brevard, take US 64 west to NC 215, then go north toward the Blue Ridge Parkway. Turn left on SR 1326 and put in at the bridge. Take out at the confluence of the West and North Forks at the junction of US 64 and NC 215.

GAUGE: It is located on the center piling of the US 64 bridge. 6" below bottom of "0" is a minimum level. For a reading, call Headwaters Outfitters at (704) 877-3106.

FRENCH BROAD

The French Broad is formed in the vicinity of Rosman, NC, where the North Fork, West Fork, Middle Fork, and East Fork join together. The upper reaches of the river are primarily flat, flowing over shallow shoals alternating between farm lands and wooded areas. It is ideal for quiet float trips. Beautiful views of the Biltmore Estate can be had between NC 280 and Riverbend Park on Amboy Rd. in west Asheville

It was in the area of Johnson Bridge, below US 64, that the "Mountain Lily" (hailed as "the highest steamboat in the world") was constructed to run between Asheville and Brevard (ca. 1878). It had a short life due to floodwaters that destroyed the channel, as well as the "plantings" of the "Lily."

MAPS: Rosman, Brevard, Pisgah Forest, Horseshoe, Skyland, Asheville, Weaverville, Leicester, Marshall, Spring Creek, Hot Springs, Paint Rock, Needy Mtn. (TN) (USGS); Transylvania, Henderson, Buncombe, Madison, Cocke (TN) (County)

CLASS	I–II
LENGTH	75
TIME	31.5
GAUGE	VISUAL
LEVEL	N/A
PERMITS	No
GRADIENT	8
SCENERY	A–C

CHAMPION PARK ON US 64 TO DAM AT NC 251

DESCRIPTION: The river is primarily flat, running over shallows and shoals throughout. There is a 10-ft. dam at the end of this section. Take out on the left and carry around, then ferry across to the right bank if taking out.

SHUTTLE: There are any number of places to begin and end a trip along this section of the French Broad. In addition to where the West and North Forks come together, access can be had at the Transylvania CR 1110 bridge (Island Ford Rd.), Hap Simpson Riverfront Park on US 276, Blantyre Park on Henderson CR 1202, US 64 (McLean Bridge, just east of Blantyre), Henderson CR 1419 (Fanning Bridge), Sandy Bottoms Park Access off NC 280, Riverbend Park Access on Amboy Rd. in west Asheville, and North Carolina Electric Power dam on NC 251.

GAUGE: None. The river is runnable all year, except during periods of extreme dryness and even then the lower section can be run. See section E for maximum safe level.

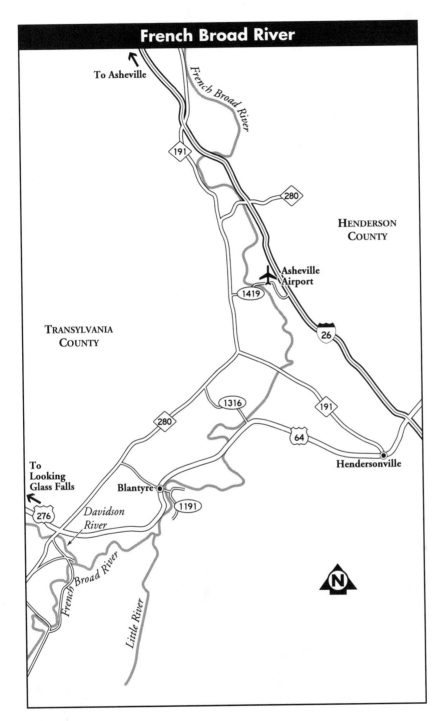

French Broad River

To Asheville

French Broad River

191

280

HENDERSON
COUNTY

Asheville
Airport

1419

TRANSYLVANIA
COUNTY

26

1316

191

280

64

Hendersonville

To
Looking
Glass Falls

Blantyre

1191

276

Davidson
River

French Broad River

Little River

N

CLASS	II–III
LENGTH	6.5
TIME	2
GAUGE	VISUAL
LEVEL	N/A
PERMITS	No
GRADIENT	20
SCENERY	A–B

DAM AT NC 251 AT WOODFIN TO BUNCOMBE CR 1634 BRIDGE

DESCRIPTION: From Asheville down to Hot Springs, the river cuts through a more mountainous area and changes complexion greatly as the volume and gradient increase. It becomes a wide powerful force, flowing through scenic gorges, over series of ledges, and around large boulders. The river here requires a much higher level of skill from the paddler.

Below Hot Springs, the river slows down to flat stretches interspersed with rapids, along with some outstanding rock formations, such as Paint Rock and Chimney Rock.

Below the dam the current picks up speed as the river begins to drop over a series of ledges and heavier shoals. On the far right about 1 mi. below the dam, a Class III chute with heavy water presents the experienced paddler with an exciting run. This can be bypassed by working through the rock gardens in the center. With the increased gradient and widening of the river, this section can become quite difficult in higher water. The Metro Sewage Treatment Plant empties just below the put-in, which might give one added incentive to stay upright.

A fine detailed map of the river from Rosman, NC, to Newport, TN, has been prepared by the Land-of-Sky Regional Council. It is available from the French Broad River Foundation, 70 Woodfin 19, Suite 327, Asheville, NC 28801; (704) 252-1097.

SHUTTLE: To reach the put-in, drive north on NC 251 from Asheville to the dam. Continue on NC 251 to reach the take-out. After you pass SR 1727 on your right, look for the Rt. 1634 bridge on the left.

GAUGE: See Section A.

CLASS	I–II
LENGTH	11.5
TIME	4.5
GAUGE	VISUAL
LEVEL	N/A
PERMITS	No
GRADIENT	12
SCENERY	A–B

RT. 1643 BRIDGE TO DAM IN MARSHALL

DESCRIPTION: The 8-ft. dam at the end of this section can present problems, so if taking out, it would be best to pull out on the right bank in the vicinity of the intersection of NC 213 and US Business 70/25, which will cut about 0.5 mi. off the trip. If continuing, a carry of some 400 yds. to below the Rt. 1001

bridge will be necessary due to the bulkhead built along the banks below the dam.

SHUTTLE: To reach the put-in, drive north on NC 251 from Asheville. After you pass SR 1727 on your right, look for the Rt. 1634 bridge on the left. For take-out, continue north on NC 251 to Marshall just above the dam.

GAUGE: See Section A.

RT. 1001 BRIDGE IN MARSHALL TO RT. 1151 BRIDGE

CLASS	II
LENGTH	6.5
TIME	3
GAUGE	VISUAL
LEVEL	N/A
PERMITS	No
GRADIENT	15
SCENERY	A

DESCRIPTION: About 1.5 mi. below Marshall, a 25-ft. dam should be approached quite cautiously. A carry of some 200 yds. on the right side is necessary. Beyond the dam the river continues with a constant gradient presenting the paddler with steady Class II water and practically no flat water. Those running this section, who don't wish to portage the dam, can put in below the dam and above the Rt. 1135 bridge, at Redmond Park on the right bank. This leaves a trip of some 5 mi.

SHUTTLE: Cross the river on the Rt. 1001 bridge in Marshall for put-in. For take-out, drive north on US Business 70/25 to US 70/25. Continue west to the town of Walnut, then turn left on Rt. 1151 and go to the bridge.

GAUGE: See Section A.

RT. 1151 BRIDGE AT BARNARD TO
US 70/25 BRIDGE IN HOT SPRINGS

CLASS	III–V
LENGTH	7.5
TIME	3
GAUGE	PHONE
LEVEL	N/A
PERMITS	No
GRADIENT	28
SCENERY	A

DESCRIPTION: The increased gradient combined with greater width and heavier water makes for an exciting trip through this section. Scouting becomes very difficult but quite necessary. For those who don't have a very dependable eddy turn in their repertoire, this simply "ain't the place to be." Generally the rule to follow is to stay to the left of all islands of any size. There are seven major rapids in this section, all of which should be approached cautiously. The third of these rapids, Big Pillow, will be found on the left side. The main flow of the river runs left, as the right side is clogged with boulders. The entrance rapid, a fast chute, flows

diagonally left and requires the boater to fight to get back to the right in order to get by the large pillow and souse hole below it. There is, however, a narrow chute on the immediate left of the pillow, which can be negotiated in the event one ends up too far to the right. Both the entrance and the pillow should be scouted carefully. Big Pillow is located approximately 1.5 mi. below the put-in. The next two rapids should be scouted on the left and right, respectively.

The community of Stackhouse, located approximately halfway through the section, can be recognized by the second island on the right. From this island a row of iron rods extends diagonally

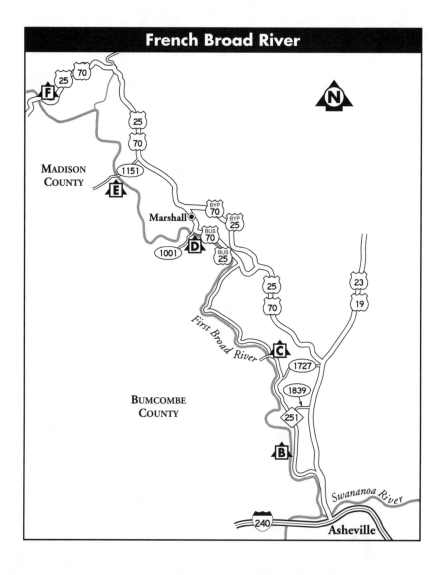

upstream about two-thirds of the way across the river. Move to the far left as soon as the island is observed. These rods can be seen at levels below 4,000 cfs.

Big Laurel Creek joins the French Broad about 0.25 mi. downstream from Stackhouse. Another 0.75 mi. downstream is Needle Rock, a sliver of shining rock located on the left bank high above the island separating the main channel. The main channel, which is on the left, has big standing waves which can easily swamp an open boat. It can be best scouted from the island. A small protected chute just left of the island drops rather quickly but can be run without too much danger. To the right of the island is Kayak's Ledge, a 6-ft. vertical drop that dumps into a pool. Scout on river right.

The next large island in the middle of the river below Needle Rock will indicate the Class V and the last rapid of any consequence on the section. The rapid on the right has become known as Frank Bell's Rapid* by canoeists in the area. It consists of three concentric ledges which funnel the river into a giant whirlpool at the bottom. The passage to the left of the island is safest but certainly not unexciting. Both sides can be best scouted from the island.

SHUTTLE: From the town of Walnut, turn left off of US 70/25 onto Rt. 1151 and go to the bridge. Take out at the US 70/25 bridge in Hot Springs.

GAUGE: Call (800) 238-2264 (TVA). A reading of 4,000 cfs is maximum for open boats.

US 70/25 BRIDGE TO US 70/25 BRIDGE IN TENNESSEE

CLASS	II–III
LENGTH	I 3
TIME	4.5
GAUGE	VISUAL
LEVEL	N/A
PERMITS	No
GRADIENT	I 2
SCENERY	A–A+

DESCRIPTION: At normal water levels there are several rapids where standing waves build up enough to give tandem paddlers problems. All can be "sneaked" by, scouting carefully and generally staying to the inside on the bends. Below the second railroad bridge there is a 4-ft. ledge that can be best run on the far left. Around the next bend, there is a rapid running some 75 yds. which one should approach cautiously on the right, and run on the right. At medium to high water levels, a giant eddy is formed

---

* The late Frank Bell of Camp Mondamin, NC, was fortunate enough to be a paddler at a time before dams were the answer to all problems. He ran the French Broad from its headwaters to the Gulf of Mexico. An attempt to run down the right side of this particular rapid ended with his canoe trapped in the whirlpool for some ten minutes. His escape was difficult.

between this rapid and the next ledge downstream, which is a natural dam. It should be scouted—left or right—and be given the same respect one should give any dam. There are breaks that can be run, but hydraulics are formed at higher levels.

For those wishing to continue farther down, a run of 11.4 mi. can be made to US 705/25 (Bridgeport Bridge). Take out on river left. About 3 mi. below Del Rio Bridge (TN 107), the river begins dropping again, presenting some 3 mi. of rapids ending in a 4-ft. ledge called the Falls. Scout on the right and run on the right.

SHUTTLE: Put in at the US 70/25 bridge in Hot Springs. Take out on the east bank beneath the US 70/25 bridge in Cocke County, TN.

GAUGE: See Section A.

DAVIDSON RIVER

The Davidson is formed in northern Transylvania County by Shuck Ridge, Daniel Ridge, and Right Fork Creeks. Its headwaters are in the Nantahala National Forest, assuring the paddler of clean, clear water. The upper Davidson must be caught at the crest of high water to ensure a decent run. An outstanding point of interest in the area is Looking Glass Mountain, a large granite dome that presents many challenging routes for the rock climber.

MAPS: Shining Rock, Pisgah Forest (USGS); Transylvania (County)

CLASS	II–III
LENGTH	3.5
TIME	2.5
GAUGE	VISUAL
LEVEL	2 FT.
PERMITS	No
GRADIENT	66
SCENERY	A

FS 475-A TO US 276 BRIDGE

DESCRIPTION: Approximately 0.5 mi. below the put-in is an easy Class III drop of 7 ft. Scout on the left and run on the right. Less than 0.25 mi. below this drop is another long Class III rapid dropping 10 ft. The run here is obvious because there is only one clear channel. Scout on the left. If you make it through these two in good shape, you'll do fine on the remainder of the run. This is a very busy and technical piece of water and everything below the second Class III rapid can be boat-scouted. The scenery is great although you won't have much time to notice. Be aware of the 3.5-ft. fish weir adjacent to the fish hatchery.

SHUTTLE: Take US 276 north out of Brevard to Looking Glass Creek bridge and take a left onto FS 475-A. Go 3.6 mi. to the

put-in on the side of the road. Take out at the Looking Glass Creek bridge on US 276.

GAUGE: The USGS Gauge is located 50 yds. above the US 276/64 bridge on the west bank. Minimum reading should be "2.0."

B

CONFLUENCE OF DAVIDSON AND
LOOKING GLASS CREEK TO US 276 BRIDGE

CLASS	I–II
LENGTH	6.1
TIME	2
GAUGE	VISUAL
LEVEL	1 FT.
PERMITS	No
GRADIENT	22
SCENERY	A

DESCRIPTION: There are no difficulties

SHUTTLE: Travel northwest of Brevard on US 276 to Looking Glass Creek bridge. Pull off to the left on the forest road. Take out at the US 276/64 bridge northeast of Brevard.

GAUGE: The USGS Gauge is located 50 yds. above the US 276/64 bridge, on the west bank. Minimum reading for solo run is "1.0."

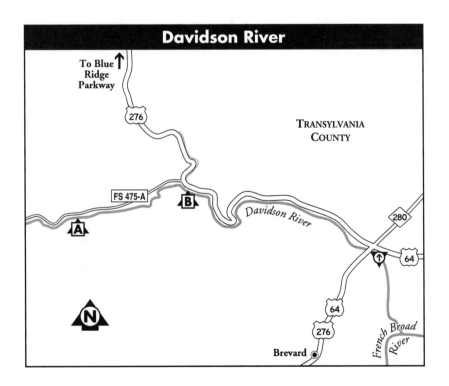

SWANNANOA RIVER

The Swannanoa drops off the western slopes of the Blue Ridge at Swannanoa Gap just east of the town of Black Mountain. It remains fairly small and narrow until joined by the North Fork, east of Swannanoa.

It flows through wooded areas and farmland, much of which is owned by Warren Wilson College, before passing under US 70 and through an industrial area in Asheville. It joins the French Broad in the city limits.

Bob Watts, of Black Mountain, has been a one man "Save the Swannanoa" gang in trying to clean up the river and keep it clear for canoeing. Every stream needs a friend like Bob.

MAPS: Oteen (USGS); Buncombe (County)

MAIN BRIDGE IN SWANNANOA TO
THE US 70 BRIDGE AT AZALEA

CLASS	I–II
LENGTH	8.6
TIME	4
GAUGE	VISUAL
LEVEL	-4 IN.
PERMITS	NO
GRADIENT	16
SCENERY	A–C

DESCRIPTION: Always be on the lookout for downed trees.

There is a sewer pipe across the river at the upper end of Charles D. Owen Park. At water levels at the bottom of "0" and above, the paddler won't be able to run under it. Move right quickly and portage.

Just below the park there are several small islands with narrow channels. The one main channel can easily be blocked by downed trees. Proceed carefully.

SHUTTLE: Go to the north side of the river about 50 yds. below the bridge. There is adequate parking along the shoulder here. Please don't use the lot at Mr. Zip for parking.

To Charles D. Owen Park (Buncombe County Parks and Recreation Dept.) bear right on Farm School Rd. off old US 70 from the main bridge in Swannanoa. Put in at the lower end of the park. A small road runs to within a few yards of the river. It would probably be best to park cars at the main lot after unloading. Putting in here will shorten the trip by about 2 mi.

Take out on the southeast side of the US 70 bridge at Azalea, opposite Azalea Methodist Church.

GAUGE: It's located on the southwest side of the main bridge in Swannanoa. Minimum for solo is 4" below "0." Can be run at 6" below "0" from Charles D. Owen Park. Generally there is adequate water to run during the spring through mid-June and during wet seasons.

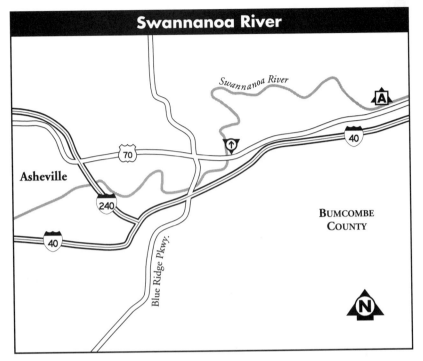

Swannanoa River

Swannanoa River

Asheville

BUMCOMBE COUNTY

BIG LAUREL CREEK

This is a fast wild water stream cutting a gorge 1,200 ft. deep between Mill Ridge on the north and Walnut Knob on the south. This is truly a most spectacular scenic run. Unfortunately, as with many trips of this type, one isn't able to raise his eyes from the job at hand long enough to be able to enjoy nature's wonders to the fullest.

Big Laurel flows into the French Broad 3.5 mi. above Hot Springs. This section must be run unless the paddler goes upstream 0.25 mi. to the community of Stackhouse (see the French Broad River, section E).

MAPS: White Rock, Hot Springs (USGS); Madison (County)

US 70/25 BRIDGE TO US 70/25 BRIDGE
OVER THE FRENCH BROAD IN HOT SPRINGS

CLASS	III–IV
LENGTH	4
TIME	3
GAUGE	VISUAL
LEVEL	-6 IN.
PERMITS	NO
GRADIENT	50
	(0.5 @ 80)
SCENERY	A+

DESCRIPTION: There are many rapids that should be scouted, the first of which is 0.25 mi. below the put-in. An innocuous looking 2 ft. ledge that is run on the left pushes the bow squarely into a pointed rock at the bottom of the chute. This ledge can

be recognized by the cottage just below it on the left bank, which is the last sign of habitation until the railroad bridge 100 yds. above the confluence with the French Broad. This ledge is a warning of bigger and better things to come.

Some other rapids worth mentioning are: The Stair Steps, a tightly constricted series three drops of 3 ft. each, which becomes quite hairy at even 2" below "0" Gauge. Suddy Hole, an 8 ft. ledge that can be run on the left at water levels above the bottom of "0," and on the right by those with suicidal tendencies. The Narrows, easily recognized, certainly should be scouted to determine the best passage. The bed of an old railroad runs on the south side the entire length of the creek, which can help one in scouting.

The previously mentioned railroad bridge marks the end of the Big Laurel run and the beginning of big water on the French Broad (see section E of the French Broad River).

SHUTTLE: Put in on the east side of US 70/25 bridge over the Big Laurel. Take out on the west side beneath the US 70/25 bridge.

GAUGE: It's located at the US 70/25 bridge on the east side. A

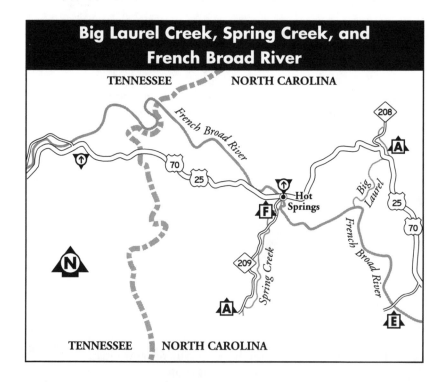

reading of 6" below "0" is minimum for solo run. At this level two rapids must be carried. A reading of 3" above the bottom of "0" is the maximum level recommended. The great increase in difficulty with the slight increase in level is due to the constricted course. It can be run except during extremely dry seasons.

SPRING CREEK

Spring Creek cuts a deep, scenic gorge between Long and Deer Park Mountains on the west and Spring Creek Mountain on the east. Its drainage lies within Pisgah National Forest. The put-in is just downstream of the confluence of the Meadow Fork of Spring Creek and Spring Creek. Rarely would there be adequate water to run above the confluence, because the creek itself is only runnable after fairly extensive rainfall.

MAPS: Spring Creek, Hot Springs (USGS); Madison (County)

NC 209 TO TOWN OF HOT SPRINGS

CLASS	III–V
LENGTH	6.8
TIME	3
GAUGE	VISUAL
LEVEL	9 IN.
PERMITS	NO
GRADIENT	77
SCENERY	A

DESCRIPTION: Spring Creek introduces itself in a brisk manner. With the exception of one drop, the toughest water comes in the first mile. The run starts off with several interesting boulder gardens. Two of the three Class IV drops on the trip come within the first 0.5 mi. After the first mile the run eases up just a bit, though it remains very busy down to the take-out. The creek primarily intersperses ledge drops with small boulder gardens. In the second mile there is a 6-ft. drop that can be run left center or far right (the more interesting line) at higher water. The steepness of the gorge that Spring Creek cuts can't be as fully appreciated from the water as it can from the road to the put-in. As the river starts paralleling the road, you will soon come under the first NC 209 bridge. Approximately 0.5 mi. downstream of the bridge is a nasty 10-ft., Class V drop. Scout and/or carry on the right. The main chute is inundated with rock and leads into a rock wall. At higher levels this rapid can be cheated on the left, which is the only advisable place to run at any level. Be aware of the occasional well-placed log or tree sweeper throughout the trip. This is a suitable trip for the high intermediate/advanced boater.

SHUTTLE: Take NC 209 south of Hot Springs to the intersection with SR 1173. Continue on NC 209 for 50 yds. and take

another left onto the dirt road, which leads to the river. The take-out is at the US 70/25 bridge in downtown Hot Springs.

GAUGE: It's located on the river right bridge piling of the US 70/25 bridge in downtown Hot Springs. Minimum level is 9" above "0."

GREEN RIVER

The Green River has its origins southwest of Tuxedo where it runs quietly for several miles before its inundation at Lake Summit. The Saluda Mountains are the southern border of this upper section. Below the dam at Lake Summit, the river drops through a short gorge, flattens for a few miles, and then enters the Narrows, a world-class stretch of whitewater. Downstream of the Narrows, it levels out into a delightful fast-flowing stream cutting between Cove and Chimney Top Mountains to the south and McCraw Mountain to the north. Through this area, it is a fairly small stream dropping over easy ledges and flowing through mild rock gardens. The area is sparsely settled, but evidence of encroaching civilization is growing fast.

MAPS: Zirconia, Hendersonville, Cliffield, Lake Lure, Rutherfordton South (USGS); Henderson, Polk, Rutherford (Broad) (County)

CLASS	II–IV (V)
LENGTH	1.3
TIME	1.5
GAUGE	VISUAL
LEVEL	N/A
PERMITS	NO
GRADIENT	123
SCENERY	A

LAKE SUMMITT DAM TO TUXEDO HYDRO PLANT

DESCRIPTION: Except during extreme flood conditions, this section of the Green remains dry. This section has been bypassed due to Duke Power diverting the water from Lake Summitt to the Tuxedo Hydro Plant.

If paddling conditions occur, carry up the river left side 0.4 mi. to the dam. Class II water will be encountered until you reach the two large slides that can be seen from the US 176 bridge. Run generally left center on the first and right center on the second.

Downstream of the bridge is the meat of the run, with 0.25 mi. of steep, boulder-strewn drops. Below here is easy Class II water to just above the hydro plant. The last rapid on this section, Powerhouse Falls, is a 12-ft. vertical fall best run left of center off a slight rooster tail at the lip of the drop.

SHUTTLE: Take US 176 west of Saluda to the bridge over the Green River. Carry up on river left 0.4 mi. to the base of Lake Summitt Dam. For take-out, take US 176 west of Saluda 300 yds.

beyond the bridge over the river. Take a right onto SR 1836 and go approximately 1 mi.

GAUGE: None.

B

THE UPPER GREEN, TUXEDO HYDRO PLANT
TO BIG HUNGRY RD. TRAIL

CLASS	II–III (IV)
LENGTH	3.6
TIME	1.5
GAUGE	VISUAL
LEVEL	N/A
PERMITS	No
GRADIENT	50
SCENERY	A

DESCRIPTION: With the exception of two drops, this section has no real difficulties, just pleasant, semi-continuous Class II water. The first large rapid, Bayless' Boof (Class IV), comes about 1 mi. into the run and consists of a slide into a vertical ledge with about 10 ft. total drop. The run is generally far left (about 8 ft. off the left bank), angling left off the ledge. There is a rock just underwater at the bottom to the right of the preferred line, where boats have been known to front end. Downstream of the I-26 bridge is the second Class II-rapid, Pinball. It consists of consecutive drops of 4 and 6 ft. Enter about 20 ft. off the left bank and angle left across the first drop, which generally puts you on line for the next ledge.

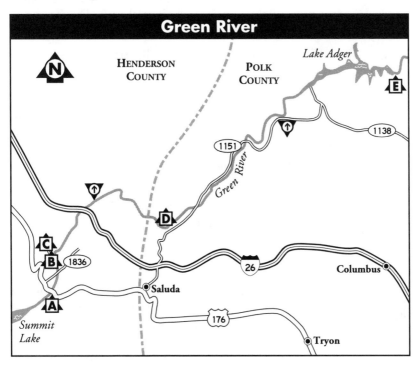

Approximately 0.6 mi. downstream of this rapid is the take-out trail. Look for an easy Class II sluice with a fun play wave at the top. The trail is on the left at the bottom of this rapid. If you see the Hungry River confluencing on the left, you've gone too far. The hike out is 0.6 mi. up to Gallimore Rd. One note of caution about the take-out: this is private property with "No Trespassing" signs posted where paddlers park. Apparently there have been some problems with drunks and litterbugs. The landowner has given paddlers permission to park here and haul out boats. Try to keep shuttle vehicles to a minimum on this end. Pick up any litter lying around. This is a tenuous situation that needs to be approached with respect and care by the paddling community or we may lose it.

Note the overlapping of Sections B and C. They are presented in this manner because this is the way they are paddled. The expert-level paddlers running the Narrows generally put in at the hydro plant because of the good, long warm-up it provides.

SHUTTLE: Take I-26 to the Upward Rd. Exit. Go northeast on Upward Rd. (SR 1722) to Big Hungry Rd. (SR 1802) and take a right. Once on SR 1802 take the left fork at the first intersection and the right fork at the second intersection, then take a right onto SR 1956 (this road is numbered 1154 on the Polk County map) and go 0.8 mi. to the pull off on the left. The river is 0.6 mi. down a jeep track.

GAUGE: None. This is a dam-controlled stream and is runnable only when the plant in Tuxedo, NC, is operating. Generally under normal conditions the plant operates during the week. The water normally takes 3–4 hours to reach section D. Call (800) 829-5253 to check the schedule of operations on weekends, holidays, or during extreme dry spells. All sections can run with two turbines operating. The Narrows (Section C) should be approached with extreme caution if Hungry River is thought to be dumping in above-average quantities of water from run-off.

THE NARROWS, TUXEDO HYDRO PLANT TO GREEN COVE RD.

CLASS	IV–V (VI)
LENGTH	6.6
TIME	4
GAUGE	VISUAL
LEVEL	N/A
PERMITS	No
GRADIENT	106 (1 @ 350)
SCENERY	A+

DESCRIPTION: There is a somewhat contorted adage which applies here: "the bigger they fall, the harder they are." The Narrows of the Green begin approximately 0.25 mi. downstream of the Hungry River confluence. The entrance to the Narrows is quite evident as the river constricts to half its former width and

crashes off a complex 8-ft. ledge. The next 5,280 ft., known as the Monster Mile, drops 350 ft. Though everything on this stretch has been run numerous times by many paddlers, there is a sense of ominous possibility on many of these rapids. The Narrows generally has a zero tolerance policy on missed lines. The list of major and minor mishaps and injuries incurred by the best paddlers in the country is growing month by month. The outstanding rapids (in the order met as one descends) include Frankenstein, Boof or Consequence, The Slot, Zwink's Backend, Chief, Gorilla, Power Slide, Rapid Transit, Nutcracker, Sunshine, and Fishtop Falls (a.k.a. Hammer Factor). At this point, Gorilla is generally considered the most bodacious rapid ever run by the elite eastern hair-heads. It is a runnable, legitimate Class VI rapid. Sunshine Falls, the second most feared drop, marks the end of the Narrows.

If problems arise in the Narrows and an evacuation or aborted trip is in order, one can walk out a trail that originates in the vicinity of Nutcracker (the next to last major drop in the Narrows). This trail is steep and will take an unhindered person at least 45 minutes to walk out. The trailhead is 4.8 mi. down Big Hungry Rd. from the Upward Rd. intersection. Below Sunshine the river eases up to hard Class IV for 1.3 mi. Fishtop Falls comes at the end of this stretch and brooks no relaxation. The take-out is just downstream.

Due to the Green being a dam-controlled stream, paddlers in the East will enjoy a certain familiarity with it as they have no other extreme run. (It is indeed the hardest dam-controlled stream in the East, if not the country.) Hopefully this familiarity will not breed contempt, either with the truly exceptional hardboater who handles this water with relative ease or with the hair boating wanna-bes who have little business being there. Be extremely confident on every other high-caliber run around before attempting this—your reputation might not be the only thing you make or break, or you may end up walking through a lot of impossible-to-avoid poison ivy on the way "down the river."

SHUTTLE: See Section B for the put-in. For take-out, take Saluda Exit off I-26, go east approximately 300 yds. to Green Cove Rd. (SR 1151), and then left down a series of hairpin turns to where the road straightens. Turn into the first pull-off on the left.

GAUGE: See Section B.

CLASS	I–II
LENGTH	6
TIME	2.5
GAUGE	VISUAL
LEVEL	N/A
PERMITS	NO
GRADIENT	21
SCENERY	A–B

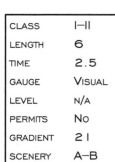

THE LOWER GREEN, RT. 1151 (GREEN COVE RD.) TO
WHERE THE RIVER LEAVES THE ROAD

DESCRIPTION: Next to the Nantahala, this section of the Green is paddled more than any river in North Carolina. During the summer months, hardly a day passes without two or three groups of canoeists from various summer camps holding classes there. It is an excellent stretch for teaching the basics of river canoeing.

This popularity has created problems for people who live in the Cove. On summer weekends dust hangs in the air as shuttles race up and down the river road, litter is strewn about, and nudity is flaunted. This is a nice place to visit, but not as nice to live. At this time there is limited parking on the side of the road through the Cove. It is patrolled regularly—especially on weekends.

Green Cove Rd. follows the river the entire distance, making scouting rather easy. The first rapid of any consequence is Big Corky (1.3 mi. below the first bridge), which can be recognized by the quiet pool above it and the sandy beach on the left below it. When both turbines are running it presents a nice standing wave to douse the bowman in.

A second rapid about 0.25 mi. below Big Corky can present problems to the unwary paddler. It bears to the left and drops over a rock bed for about 75 yds. Farther downstream a series of ledges running for some 200 yds. should be approached cautiously. The road is high above the river at this point.

The approach to Little Corky, a low Class II, occurs just beyond a point where the road has dropped down to the river and a sizable island separates the main stream. The more difficult run is on the left of the island. It drops fast with an apparent straight chute off the right bank. One rock barely under water is the grabber awaiting the straight shooter. A slight movement to the left will shoot the canoe between it and a similar rock on the left. They are little more than a canoe width apart. Scout on the left.

Below Little Corky the river continues to drop fast for 0.5 mi., then it slows down somewhat. Primarily fun water following the last Corky.

SHUTTLE: From Mill Springs, NC, take NC 9 north about 100 yds., then go west on Rt. 1138 to Silver Creek Baptist Church. Turn left on Rt. 1151 to the river. Proceed to the point where the road starts up the mountain and turn right into the parking lot. Go 6.3 mi. from the put-in parking area to the second parking

area, located just beyond a point where one loses sight of the river for the take-out.

GAUGE: See Section B.

E

NC 9 BELOW LAKE ADGER DAM TO
NC 1004 ON THE BROAD RIVER

CLASS	I–II
LENGTH	24
TIME	10
GAUGE	VISUAL
LEVEL	N/A
PERMITS	NO
GRADIENT	5
SCENERY	A

DESCRIPTION: This section of the Green has been included for those who might like to take a more leisurely float trip, or who might be looking for quieter waters for overnighters. If one wishes for an extended trip beyond the reaches of the Green, see the description for the Broad elsewhere in the book.

We used to joke occasionally about setting the shuttle on the wrong river—always considering such below our level of intelligence. In this area the impossible can happen. On the first trip by the author on Section B of the Broad we arrived at the take-out only to find no vehicle. Same story at the next bridge. Here we

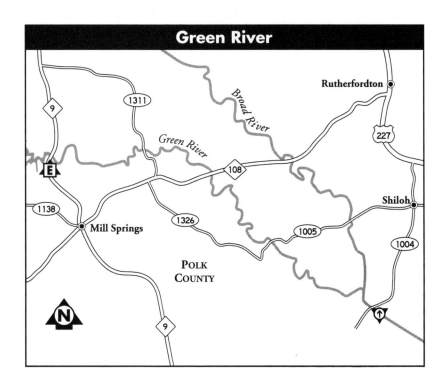

were, mid-March and cold, and getting more so with the sun setting and no transportation. Well, logic finally prevailed and we found our shuttle after a 5 mi. walk in the dark—not on the Broad, but on the Green.

There are no difficulties on this section, but beware of downed trees.

SHUTTLE: There are several places along this stretch where you can access the river. To reach the put-in, drive west on NC 108 from Rutherfordton to the community of Mill Springs and NC 9. Turn right (north) to Lake Adger Dam. Other access points include Polk CR 1311, NC 1005, and NC 108 itself. The last take-out on the Green is just past its confluence with the Broad; drive south on US 227 to Rt. 1004 and go south toward Shiloh until you reach the bridge across the Broad.

GAUGE: None. When the upper Green is running, generally the dam at Adger will be generating, thus providing a very nice water level.

BROAD RIVER

The Broad begins just south of the Tennessee Valley Divide and flows generally southeast above its impoundment at Lake Lure. For the first several miles, it flows through a long, fairly flat valley and can be seen along NC 9. The river then tumbles down two steep gorges, most notably Hickory Nut Gorge, and courses by the towns of Bat Cave and Chimney Rock. Downstream of Lake Lure, most of the rapids are found between the dam and the first river bridge at Uree. Beyond Uree the Broad follows US 64/74 closely before cutting away through a heavily wooded and rather remote area to the take-out.

MAPS: Bat Cave, Lake Lure, Rutherfordton South, Cowpens, Boiling Springs South, Blacksburg North (NC/SC); Blacksburg South, Kings Creek, Hickory Grove, Lockhart, Leeds, Carlisle, Blair, Pomaria, Jenkinsville (SC) (USGS); Rutherford, Cleveland (NC); Cherokee, Union, Newberry (SC) (County)

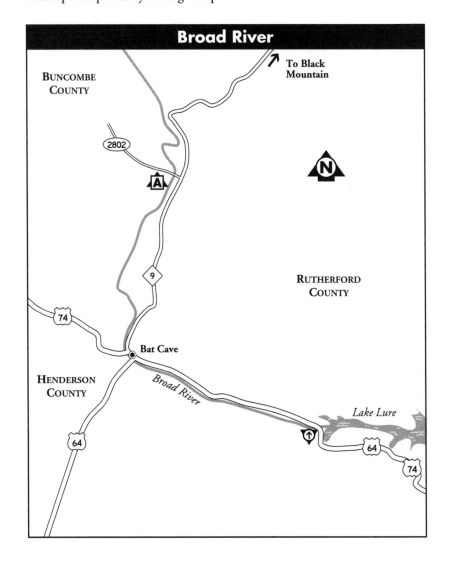

A

SR 2802 (LOWER FLAT CREEK RD.) TO
VOLUNTEER FIRE DEPARTMENT AT CHIMNEY ROCK

CLASS	III–V
LENGTH	6.3
TIME	5.5
GAUGE	VISUAL
LEVEL	-4 IN.
PERMITS	No
GRADIENT	146
SCENERY	A

DESCRIPTION: The Broad starts off with a bang. After a short warm-up of 0.5 mi., you enter the first gorge with consecutive waterfalls of approximately 10, 16, 8, and 13 ft. None are clean at the bottom, though all have marginally runnable slots at favorable levels. With some interesting boulder gardens, the first 3 mi. is comprised primarily of ledge drops.

Broad River

To Black
Mountain

BUNCOMBE
COUNTY

2802

A

9

RUTHERFORD
COUNTY

74

Bat Cave

HENDERSON
COUNTY

Broad River

Lake Lure

64

64

74

Once reaching Bat Cave (where the river parallels the road to the take-out), the streambed abruptly changes to boulder-strewn. If you were thinking things were going to ease up, think again. The next 3 mi. are some of the most technically difficult you'll find anywhere. There are two mandatory portages (10 yds. each) in this section where the river chokes down with boulders. Everything else is runnable, though at times questionable. One Class V drop, Geek Peek, drops 12 ft. through a tight maze with the final drop harboring a strainer tree that is tough to dodge. This stretch that parallels the road has a small allowance for varying water levels. Too little or too much water will either be impossible to get down or impossible to get down and tell about it later. This is a super run. Large-volume creek boats are a must. The proximity of the road along the lower part of this run, though comforting, should not encourage any less-than-expert paddlers.

SHUTTLE: Take NC 9 south of Black Mountain to SR 2802 (Lower Flat Creek Rd.). For take-out, continue on NC 9 south to Chimney Rock Volunteer Fire Department.

GAUGE: It's located on the center piling of the SR 2802 bridge. Minimum level should be 4" below "0."

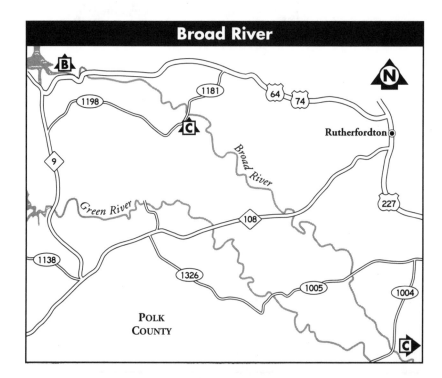

Broad River

DAM AT LAKE LURE TO RUTHERFORD CR 1181

CLASS	I–II
LENGTH	7.4
TIME	2.8
GAUGE	VISUAL
LEVEL	-6 IN.
PERMITS	No
GRADIENT	12
SCENERY	A–B

DESCRIPTION: When the water is coming through the dam, the section between the dam and the bridge at Uree can be run, otherwise the water level will be too low. There are several ledges through here that require some fast maneuvering. Another short set of ledges is located beyond the confluence of Cove Creek. Watch for logs blocking the passages below the Uree bridge, where the river splits into several channels.

SHUTTLE: Travel north off US 64/74, 1 mi. east of the bridge at Uree to the dam. You must carry the boat down steps on the south end of the dam. For take-out, go 6.8 mi. east on US 64/74 from the bridge at Uree to Rt. 1181, then south to the Rt. 1181 bridge.

GAUGE: It's located on the US 64/74 bridge at Uree, on the southeast pillar. A reading of 6" below "0" is minimum for a solo run. The entire section can only be run when water is coming through the dam.

RUTHERFORD CR 1181 BRIDGE TO SC 34 BRIDGE

CLASS	I–II
LENGTH	112.5
TIME	VARIES
GAUGE	VISUAL
LEVEL	N/A
PERMITS	No
GRADIENT	3
SCENERY	A–B

DESCRIPTION: Below Section B, the Broad winds its way east across southern North Carolina before bending sharply south into South Carolina. Although several dams have been constructed on the river, there are no long stretches of slack water behind them. Approximately 16 mi. from the put-in, paddlers will note the Green entering on the right.

Note: On certain days about halfway down this section, those with keen ears may hear the startling scream of the "Wild Flat Chested Broad Bird," although the more discerning paddler of the wild will recognize this unusual sound as the call of the Pea Fowl.

Watch for downed trees. About 1.5 mi. below the US 221-A bridge, paddlers will encounter a Duke Power dam. Begin moving right after passing under the bridge at the power plant. Pull out on the right and carry to the bottom of the hill. Watch the backwash below the dam, being sure to put-in well below it. A few small shoals will be encountered occasionally from here on down to NC 150.

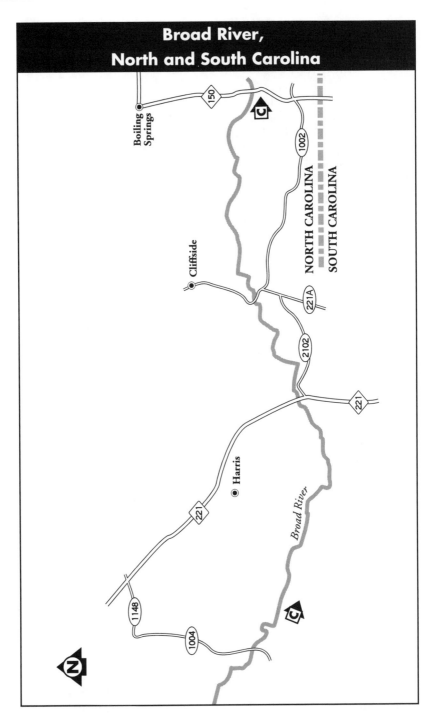

Broad River,
North and South Carolina

Between the NC 150 bridge and SC 18 bridge near Gaffney, SC, paddlers will find Gaston Shoals or Gravo Dam after paddling through some 40 minutes of slackwater. The dam is constructed in three sections, with the easiest portage to the left of the section on the right (the first section to be approached). Pull out about 30 ft. upstream from the highest concrete. Carry into the small ravine, up to the top, and directly down the trail (total carry of 100 yds.). There is an excellent campsite on the right bank below the dam. In low water there will be slow going for some distance below the dam, due to sand deposits.

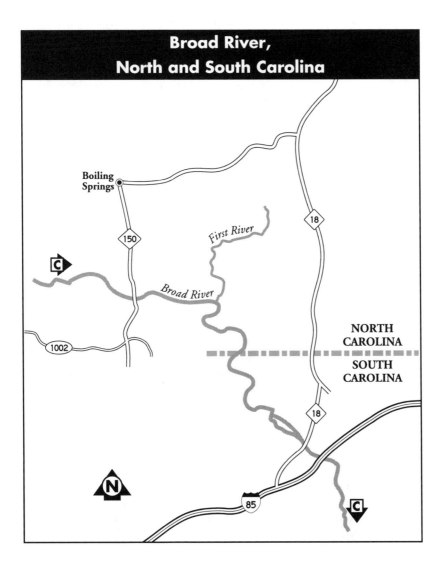

Broad River, North and South Carolina

Between the SC 18 bridge and SC 211 bridge, approximately 1 mi. below the US 29 bridge, there is an area of shoals running for 200 yds., which should be approached rather cautiously—especially at levels even slightly higher than normal. There is a launching ramp on the right at the head of the shoals.

Cherokee Falls Dam is downstream a short distance from the two islands with the old bridge pilings. Water runs over the top, so move to the right as quickly as possible and take-out far enough above the dam to prevent being caught by the current. The carry here is fairly short. Following is a series of ledges interspersed among rock gardens, which can prove quite difficult at higher water levels. At normal to lower levels it is best to work to left center and down. Keep to the right channel after the rapids. *Note:* Cherokee Nuclear Power Plant is a short distance west of the river and some 2 mi. downriver from Cherokee Falls.

There are many large sand bars suitable for camping between Cherokee Falls and the up-coming No. 99 or Ninety-nine Island Dam. The dam can be recognized by the high, narrow, rocky dam on the left. Paddle around the island to the right of this rock dam while staying as close as possible to the island. Bear left around the island and above the face of the dam. Water flows over the dam so hug it closely. Proceed to the left bank, behind the rock dam, to the dock. If the Duke Power staff is on duty, arrangements may be made for a shuttle around the dam and power plant. Otherwise a 600–700 yd. portage along the fence to the side road on the left of the entrance gate and then down the road to the riverside will be necessary.

Between the SC 211 bridge and the dam at Lockhart, paddlers will encounter no difficulties until arriving at Lockhart. Move to the extreme right and take out above the log boon. Carry along the fence. The pool and sluice running along the right here is closed for any water traffic. There is a distance of 1.4 mi. from here to the next point below the Lockhart Power Company Plant where one can re-enter the river. One alternative, which is questionable as far as ease of accomplishment, is to stay to the left of the dam. This will require a carry through a boulder field below the dam. Paddle the pool below and then carry across the boulders at the opposite end, and paddle the left side of the island from the power plant. Whatever the decision, the character building session for the day will begin here and now.

Eleven miles downstream of Lockhart Power Company is Neal Shoals Dam. Approach on the far left, where a good 60-yd. portage can be made. Watch the slippery rocks! Be sure to put-in far enough below the backwash from the dam, and work your way carefully back into the main current. *Note:* Get permission to

Broad River

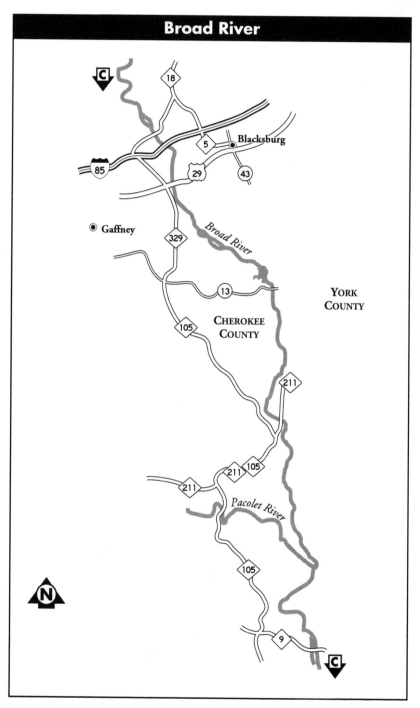

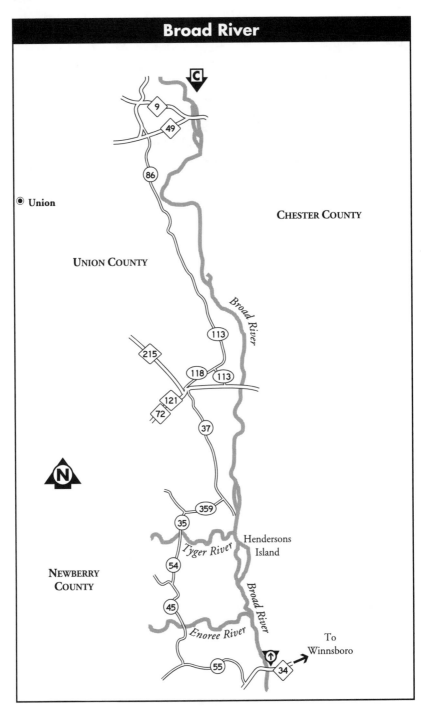

Broad River

C

9
49

86

⊙ **Union**

CHESTER COUNTY

UNION COUNTY

Broad River

113

215

118   113

121

72

37

N

359

35

Tyger River   Hendersons
Island

**NEWBERRY
COUNTY**

54

Broad River

45

Enoree River

To
Winnsboro

55

34

drive onto Lockhart Power Company property. Put in about 90 yds. below the power plant at a break in the wall, where a small sand bar is located.

Woods Ferry Recreation Area in Sumter National Forest is 8 mi. below the put-in on the east bank. In fact, the National Forest boundary is just below Lockhart, and the paddler will be within its boundaries down to SC 34.

Paddlers will encounter some riffles along the Shelton Island area 4 mi. below the SC 121/72/215 bridge (located southeast of Union, SC). They aren't difficult, but one may become complacent after a few miles of fairly flat water. Approximately 7.5 mi. past the SC 121/72/215 bridge, the Tyger enters, just above Henderson Island. The Enoree enters 12.4 mi. below the SC 121/72/215 bridge.

Below the Enoree the flow slows appreciably, especially so if power isn't being generated at Parr Shoals. The wind then becomes the only difficulty to be encountered on the remainder of the trip.

SHUTTLE: There are any number of access points to allow the paddler trips of any length. See a state road map or consult USGS topos for possible put-ins and take-outs. The description above ends at the SC 34 bridge northwest of Columbia, SC. Take out at a small launching area about 100 yds. below the SC 34 bridge on the left bank. To reach here, take the first right after crossing the bridge going east. Go down the hill and bear hard right across the railroad tracks.

GAUGE: None. This section is runnable year round, except possibly following an extremely long dry spell.

FIRST BROAD RIVER

The First Broad rises on the slopes of South Mountain and flows easterly through Golden Valley below the South Mountain range before cutting south through central Cleveland County and joining the Broad River below Shelby.

The upper stretches meander through the foothills, many of which are filled with mountain laurel and rhododendron.

MAPS: Benn Knob, Shelby (USGS); Rutherford, Cleveland (County)

CLASS	I–II
LENGTH	14.9
TIME	5.5
GAUGE	VISUAL
LEVEL	1.52 FT.
PERMITS	No
GRADIENT	12
SCENERY	A

RUTHERFORD CR 1726 BRIDGE TO CLEVELAND CR 1529 BRIDGE

DESCRIPTION: There are no difficulties. Paddlers will encounter primarily pebble fields with occasional ledges. The stretch below Rt. 1734, which is filled with laurel and rhododendron, is particularly scenic. The lower quarter of the run has many trees down, presenting a natural slalom for the paddler.

SHUTTLE: Travel southeast on NC 226 from US 64 to Rutherford CR 1726 (50 yds. west of the river bridge), then southwest for 1.1 mi. to the put-in bridge. For take-out, take NC 226 south of the Rutherford-Cleveland County line to Cleveland CR 1529, then northeast 0.5 mi. to the take-out bridge. By using the Rutherford CR 1737 bridge, the section can be divided into trips of 8.8 or 6.1 mi.

GAUGE: The USGS Gauge is located 75 yds. above the Cleveland CR 1530 bridge on the south bank. Minimum level for solo run is "1.52."

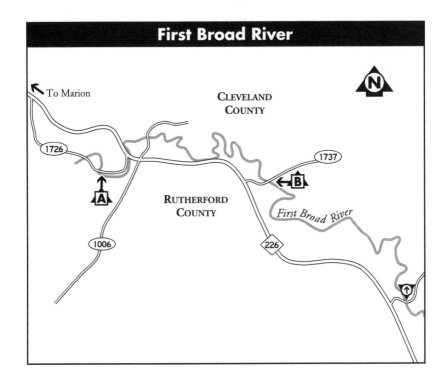

part**Three**

Watauga, New River, & Catawba Watershed

NORTH TOE RIVER AND TOE RIVER

The North Toe heads up east of Minneapolis in the vicinity of New-land. It moves south through a mountainous area until it turns west entering the Toe Valley, which is widely known for its mineral deposits. Below the junction with the South Toe, the river gets considerably wider and becomes known as the Toe. From the Toe's confluence with the Cane the Nolichucky is born.

There are several areas of outstanding scenic beauty, in particular the rock formations between the US 19 E. bridges just north and south of Ingalls. Unfortunately much of the natural beauty is marred by the grayish color of the water from Spruce Pine down the rest of the river. This is the result of many mica mines and feldspar plants in the area. Although the quality of the water is rather poor, it has improved considerably.

MAPS: Newland, Carvers Gap, Spruce Pine. Linville Falls, Micaville, Bakersville, Burnsville, Huntdale (USGS); Avery, Mitchell, Yancey (County)

AVERY CR 1164 BRIDGE AT MINNEAPOLIS TO SPRUCE PINE

CLASS	I–III
LENGTH	31.5
TIME	14.5
GAUGE	VISUAL
LEVEL	VARIES
PERMITS	NO
GRADIENT	21
SCENERY	A–B

DESCRIPTION: The upper section is runnable only with a good runoff; it drops continuously over many small stubblefields. Watch for low-water bridges and logs. Take out and carry on the left of the dam at Plumtree (15 ft. high), which is located just below the bridge.

If starting at the dam, put in about 400 yds. below the dam on Rt. 1123. There is one broken dam a little over halfway between Rt. 1123 south and the US 19 E. bridge north of Ingalls that should be approached and scouted very carefully. This can be run on the left at a good water level. Difficulty Class III+.

Between the US 19 E. bridge north of Ingalls and US 19 E.

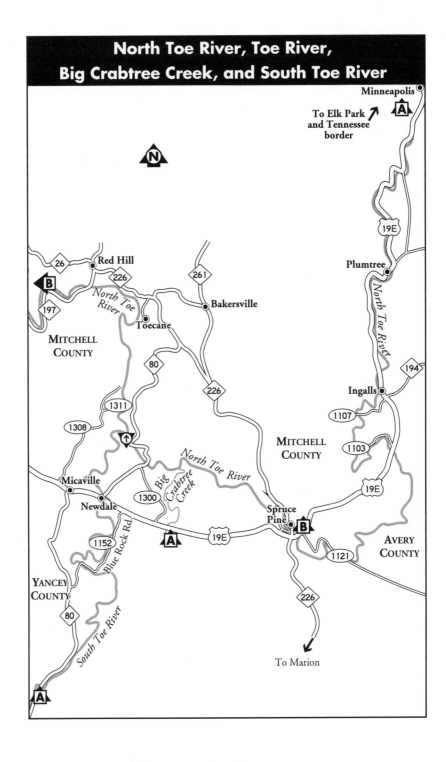

North Toe River, Toe River, Big Crabtree Creek, and South Toe River

bridge south of Ingalls, paddlers will find many gravel bars and one ledge that will require some tight turning in approaching it. This ledge can be scouted on the left, run on the right. This is a most scenic area with many overhanging rocks.

From here on down, watch closely for a broken dam (10 ft. high) approaching the outskirts of Spruce Pine. The river bends to the left and the paddler should stay to the left, inside the bend, where the carry should be made. This can be a very dangerous area with high water, so proceed with caution. This is a scenic run with many high bluffs over the river.

SHUTTLE: From Spruce Pine, drive north on US 19 E. to the community of Minneapolis. There are several access points along this section, including several places where US 19 E. crosses the river. To reach the take-out in Spruce Pine, go west on Greenwood Rd., then turn right onto Stroupe Rd. and take out above the sewage treatment plant.

GAUGE: It's located on the US 19 E. bridge on the southwest side (north of Spruce Pine). The section above the dam at Plumtree can be run only following rain. Minimum level for solo in upper section is the bottom of "1." The section between the Plumtree dam and US 19 E. north of Ingalls can be run year round except following long dry seasons, while the remainder can be run year round.

STROUPE RD., IN SPRUCE PINE, TO NFS PUT-IN AT POPLAR

CLASS	I–III
LENGTH	34.3
TIME	3.5
GAUGE	VISUAL
LEVEL	N/A
PERMITS	No
GRADIENT	14
SCENERY	A–C

DESCRIPTION: Paddlers will find a broken dam about 3 ft. high 1 mi. below the put-in; it should be scouted on the right. This may be run on the far left depending on the water level. If you're doubtful about making it, don't try it! There are two other low-washed dams that can be easily scouted before you reach the NC 80 bridge at Boonfield, 7.5 mi. into this section.

The South Toe River enters on the left about 1 mi. below the NC 80 bridge. One-and-a-half mi. below this confluence, paddlers will find a Class III rapid consisting of a boulder garden; it should be scouted on the left. Enter on the right. Several canoes have broken up here. Below the bridge at Toecane the river begins dropping faster, at the rate of 30 fpm, through a gorge that presents constant whitewater for close to 2 mi. The first ledge below the bridge should be scouted.

The section between the NC 197 bridge south of Red Hill in Mitchell County to the intersection of Yancey CR 1304 and CR

1349 is fairly flat, but wider and faster moving than earlier sections. As you approach Poplar, about 1.5 mi. upstream, paddlers will encounter a series of shoals.

SHUTTLE: From Spruce Pine, go west on Greenwood Rd., then turn right onto Stroupe Rd. to put in above the sewage treatment plant. For take-out, start at the junction of NC 197 and NC 226 at Red Hill, and go west on Mitchell CR 1304 to Mitchell CR 1321, then north to the community of Poplar.

GAUGE: See Section A.

BIG CRABTREE CREEK

Big Crabtree Creek originates in Sugar Cove Gap and then flows through the Crabtree Meadow area along the Blue Ridge Parkway. It drops quickly off the Blue Ridge and runs northerly before entering the North Toe.

MAPS: Micaville (USGS); Mitchell, Yancey (County)

CLASS	I–II
LENGTH	6.2
TIME	2.5
GAUGE	VISUAL
LEVEL	-6 IN.
PERMITS	No
GRADIENT	24
SCENERY	A

OLD US 19 BRIDGE TO NC 80 BRIDGE
OVER THE NORTH TOE AT BOONEFORD

DESCRIPTION: About 1 mi. into the run a downed tree will require a carry on river left. The last 2 mi. of the creek drop at a rate of some 40 fpm, so action will pick up somewhat.

SHUTTLE: Put in at the old US 19 bridge, located just downstream from US 19 E. For take-out, drive west to CR 1300. Turn right and drive to NC 80, then turn right again and stop at the bridge over the North Toe.

GAUGE: It's located on the northeast side of the SR 1102 bridge (first bridge south of the US 19 E. bridge). Minimum for solo is 6" below "0."

SOUTH TOE RIVER

The South Toe has its headwaters on Mt. Mitchell, the highest peak east of the Rockies (elevation 6,684 ft.), which is south from the put-in. It is a delightful stream winding through the mountains over gravel bars and through boulder gardens. The section between the CR

1152 bridge (Bluerock Rd.) to the NC 80 bridge in Newdale flows through a particularly scenic area. The water quality drops considerably around Newdale, due to silt from local mica mines. It meets the North Toe below Newdale to form the Toe River.

MAPS: Celo, Micaville (USGS); Yancey (County)

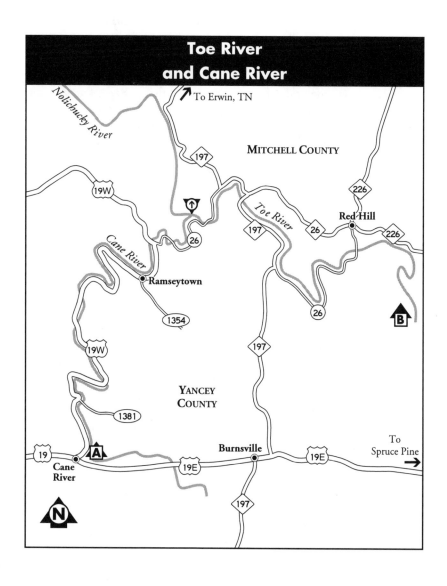

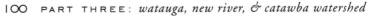

CLASS	I–II (III)
LENGTH	22.5
TIME	10.5
GAUGE	VISUAL
LEVEL	1.09 FT.
PERMITS	No
GRADIENT	16
SCENERY	A–B

NC 80 BRIDGE TO CR 1311

DESCRIPTION: Paddling above the CR 1152 bridge requires a good bit of maneuvering through the gravel bars and over small shoals. Below this bridge, the river cuts through a narrow rocky gorge that has some ledges which will require scouting. The first one has a large flat rock on the left. The second and largest entering the gorge has a series of three drops totaling some 10 ft. in 40 yds. Scout it on the left. Below the NC 80 bridge a lot of maneuvering will be required at low water levels.

SHUTTLE: To reach the upper section from Spruce Pine, go west on US 19 E. and turn left (south) on NC 80 at Micaville. Put in where the bridge first crosses the South Toe River. For take-out, return to US 19 E., turn left, go 0.5 mi., then turn right (north) onto CR 1308. Drive about 5.4 mi., then turn right (east) on CR 1311 until reaching the river opposite Lunday. You must ford the creek three times before reaching the river. The take-out can be recognized from the river by the footbridge just upstream. Several intermediate points can be used as access points, including CR 1152 (Blue Rock Rd.) and the NC 80 bridge just north of US 19 E. in Newdale.

GAUGE: The USGS Gauge is located above the Rt. 1167 bridge alongside Rt. 1168. Minimum level for solo is 1.09. The river can generally be run following periods of wet weather.

CANE RIVER

The Cane forms between Big Pine Mountain and Bearwallow Stand Ridge on the western slope of Mt. Mitchell. It flows north then west from the Burnsville area before turning north again to join the Toe River where the Nolichucky is born.

Below Section A, highways run alongside the river for most of the way. Generally the course is well below the level of traffic.

MAPS: Burnsville, Bald Creek, Chestoa, Huntdale (USGS); Yancey (County)

US 19 E. BRIDGE TO RT. 1354 (0.3 MI. ABOVE THE TOE RIVER)

CLASS	IV
LENGTH	5.2
TIME	2.5
GAUGE	VISUAL
LEVEL	3FT
PERMITS	YES
GRADIENT	888
SCENERY	B

DESCRIPTION: Above the Yancey CR 1381 bridge, watch f or possible strainers and one low footbridge located about 0.5 mi. below the first bridge. Between the CR 1381 bridge and the US 19 W. bridge at Lewisburg, there is a double ledge upstream from the second bridge. It can be scouted from river left. Below the second bridge, a boulder clog in a bend to the left makes it difficult to determine the best passage. Scout on the left. There are three low-water bridges that have to be portaged. Below the US 19 W. bridge at Lewisburg the gradient increases for some 400 yds. downstream from the second bridge. Two low-water bridges have to be portaged.

SHUTTLE: The put-in is located on the US 19 bridge west of Burnsville. For take-out, take US 19 W. to Ramseytown. Take right on Rt. 26/1417 just before US19 W. crosses Cane River. Takeout is located at next bridge.

GAUGE: It's located on the Rt. 1381 bridge on river left downstream. Minimum for solo is 6" below "0." Below Rt. 1381, minimum for solo is 7" below "0." Below US 19 W., minimum is 9" below "0."

NOLICHUCKY RIVER

Below the confluence of the Toe and Cane Rivers the Nolichucky is born—not as a small, gurgling trickle but as a full grown, boisterous, fast-flowing river. Down from Poplar the river enters Cherokee National Forest while cutting a gorge 800–1,000 ft. deep between the Bald Mountains on the south and the Unaka Mountains on the north. The Clinchfield Railroad follows the river through the entire gorge. For those who would like to enjoy the rugged grandeur of the gorge and the river to the fullest, hiking is the way. The paddler can enjoy only the river, as there is little opportunity to view the magnificent scenery above. The river has many long rapids with heavy water, which offer little opportunity for rescue. This is a river for the advanced paddler.

MAPS: Huntdale (NC); Unicoi, Erwin (TN) (USGS); Mitchell (NC); Unicoi, Washington (TN) (County)

CLASS	III–IV
LENGTH	10.5
TIME	7
GAUGE	PHONE
LEVEL	500–
	2,000 CFS
PERMITS	No
GRADIENT	32
SCENERY	A

NATIONAL FOREST SERVICE PUT-IN AT POPLAR, NC, TO
NATIONAL FOREST RECREATION AREA AT CHESTOA

DESCRIPTION: The first rapid below the railroad bridge is about 75 yds. long, over a series of ledges. There is an open passage to the right of center, but two large standing waves tend to swamp open boats in higher water. The next rapid, "On the Rocks," can be easily recognized. An attempt at running it may well prove why it's so named. A line of boulders on the right forces the main current through a narrow chute in the center. A hidden rock left of center blocks what normally appears as an open run through here. At about 1,200 cfs the 4-ft. vertical drop to the immediate left of the chute is runnable. Both of these rapids can be best scouted by pulling in at the railroad bridge and walking down the tracks. The time spent walking here can save a considerable amount that would be required to free a boat.

If the passage on each of the rapids which follow isn't immediately apparent, scout! Generally most of them can be run on the right side.

The third and fourth are series of ledges interspersed with boulders. The fourth, some 250 yds. long, ends up with a 4-ft. ledge. Run the chute on the far right at medium levels. Scout on the left.

The third rapid, "Quarter Mile," contains a series of ledges interspersed with boulders that ends with a 4-ft. ledge. Not a good place to swim, but many do. (If you want to try your time for 440 yds., do it in a pool.) Run the chute on the far right at medium levels. Scout on the left.

There is still plenty of action beyond here, but if the paddler has made it this far without major mishaps he can breathe a little easier. Most of the remaining rapids have passages that are easily recognized.

There is one, however, "The Sousehole," that should be approached very carefully. A creek enters the river through a culvert 10 ft. above the river on the left. Below it the river bears hard right by an island and then back to the left. Stay close to the left bank all the way around these two bends. At the bottom of the left bend one will find "The Sousehole." It's a nice place to pass and look but certainly not to visit.

Downstream the river continues to drop over a few ledges and through some stubblefields until it reaches the take-out.

SHUTTLE: From Spruce Pine, NC, take NC 226 0.1 mi. north of Red Hill; go west on Mitchell CR 1304 to the river, then continue to Mitchell CR 1321, then north and west approximately 5 mi. to Poplar. For take-out, go west from Poplar on 1321, to 1323 (FS 230) over Indian Grave Gap to the state line and TN Rt. 30, into Erwin. Go south on US 19 W. and 23 to Cherokee National Forest Recreation Area at Chestoa.

GAUGE: Call TVA at (800) 238-2264 for a 24 hr. recorded message on stream flow. A flow of 500 cfs is a minimum, while 2,000 cfs can be considered a reasonably high level.

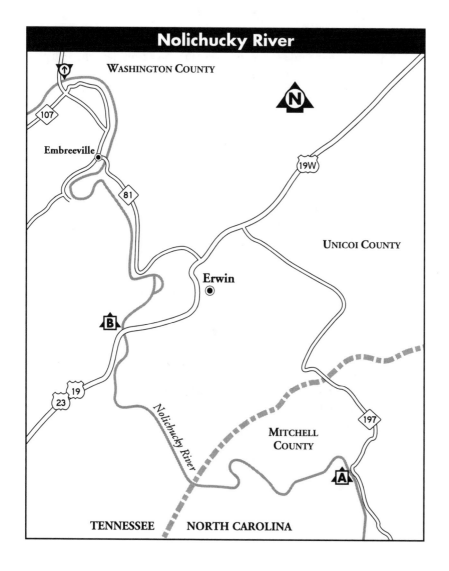

CLASS	II–III
LENGTH	12.8
TIME	5.5
GAUGE	PHONE
LEVEL	500–
	2,000 CFS
PERMITS	No
GRADIENT	14.5
SCENERY	A

NATIONAL FOREST RECREATION AREA AT CHESTOA TO
TN RT. 67 BRIDGE

DESCRIPTION: Although not as spectacular, Section B offers the paddler outstanding scenery with such rock formations as Devil's Looking Glass.

There are several long rapids in this section which require scouting, particularly at levels even slightly above normal, especially in the area of Devil's Looking Glass, about 3.5 mi. below the put-in.

High standing waves will be found on most of these, so following the rule of staying toward the inside of the bend will generally provide the safer passage.

Scout the first rapid, located 0.5 mi. downstream from the TN 81 bridge at Embreeville, on the left bank. The main chute is obvious but difficult.

SHUTTLE: Put-in at the National Forest Recreation Area in Chestoa, just south of Erwin, TN. The take-out can be found at the TN 67/81 bridge. The trip can be shortened some 2 mi. by taking out on the river, left just off Dr. A. J. Willis Rd. The sandy area at this take-out is slightly over 0.5 mi. below the old bridge abutments. Take the first right going west on TN 81 in Embreeville and proceed approximately 1.4 mi. to this spot.

GAUGE: See Section A. There is also a USGS Gauge located on the west side, 100 yds. upstream of the TN 81 bridge at Embreeville. A medium level would be a reading of about 2.40.

BOONE FORK

The Boone Fork rises as a tiny tributary falling off the eastern flank of Grandfather Mountain and then flows a few miles before being backed up by Price Lake. Price Lake is small and man-made with a spill-over dam. This run is available only during, or immediately after, serious rainfall because of its tiny watershed.

MAPS: Boone (USGS); Watauga (County)

CLASS	III–IV
LENGTH	4.5
TIME	2.5
GAUGE	VISUAL
LEVEL	SEE BELOW
PERMITS	No
GRADIENT	102
SCENERY	A+

DESCRIPTION: The first 1.5 mi. of the run is easy Class I–II. After coming to the old washed-out timber bridge, you'll go 200 yds. to the first portage. This section drops 100 ft. in less than 100 yds. Portage on a small trail that appears at the top of this section on river left. After putting back in you'll paddle perhaps 0.4 mi. before coming to the second portage. Take out on the left and

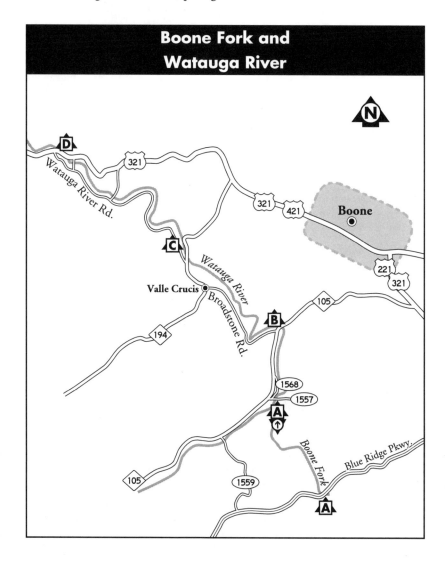

Boone Fork and Watauga River

carry along the Boone Fork Trail for 60 yds. and put in below the second boulder clog. For the next mile there is continuous Class III–IV water and everything is runnable at favorable water levels. The total length of the gorge is about 1.75 mi. Then the rapids slack off to Class II–III down to the confluence with the Watauga River. Paddle 0.5 mi. down the Watauga to the take-out. This is gorgeous country and a highly recommended trip if there is adequate water.

SHUTTLE: Take the Blue Ridge Parkway south out of Blowing Rock to Julian Price Memorial Park. Put in at the small footbridge. For take-out, return to Boone, and take NC 105 south to SR 1568 (Old Shulls Mill Rd.). Follow SR 1568 0.8 mi. to SR 1557. Go left to the bridge.

GAUGE: Check the small foot bridge at Julian Price Memorial Park. The white paint slash on the river left concrete piling should be underwater for a minimum level.

WATAUGA RIVER

The Watauga heads up on the eastern slope of Sugar Mountain. It winds along NC 105 for several miles before entering a short, steep section. After leaving NC 105, it meanders through hilly pasture and then through spectacularly rugged Watauga Gorge before reaching Watauga Lake in Tennessee.

MAPS: Boone, Valle Crucis, Sherwood; Elk Mills, Watauga Dam; Elizabethton (TN) (USGS); Watauga; Johnson (TN) (County)

CLASS	II–IV
LENGTH	2
TIME	2
GAUGE	VISUAL
LEVEL	-2 IN.
PERMITS	No
GRADIENT	90
SCENERY	B

SR 1557 BRIDGE TO NC 105 BRIDGE

DESCRIPTION: This run is Dr. Jekyll/Mr. Hyde in character. The first half, down to the washed-out bridge, is composed of fun Class II water. Then the river changes nature immediately and becomes a Class IV–V (depending on water level) challenge for the best boater. The 1-mi. section down to the dam is recommended as a warm-up for what waits below. Known to the locals as the Red Roofs run, this is a terrific late afternoon adrenaline pumper due to its ease of access and short paddling time. This section must be caught during or shortly after heavy rains for adequate water.

The lower portion of the run is steeper and less forgiving than most anything in the gorge downstream. Well into the hard stuff,

there is one house-sized boulder with a ledge spanning the river. Run far right. Below is a small island which should be run down the left side. Routes through most other drops are fairly obvious, if not pretty. Everything is blind and must be shore scouted. At levels of "0" and below this is hard Class IV water. Above "0" and the extra push increases the intensity to Class V.

SHUTTLE: Take NC 105 south of Boone to SR 1568 (Old Shulls Mill Rd.). Go 0.8 mi. to SR 1557 and take a left onto the bridge over the river. The take-out is located on NC 105 south of Boone; go 4.8 mi. to the bridge over the river.

GAUGE: The gauge is on the river right concrete abutment of the SR 1557 bridge. Minimum level should be 2" below "0."

NC 105 BRIDGE TO NC 194 BRIDGE AT VALLE CRUCIS

CLASS	I–II
LENGTH	4.5
TIME	2
GAUGE	VISUAL
LEVEL	1.95 FT.
PERMITS	No
GRADIENT	39
SCENERY	A–B

DESCRIPTION: This section runs over a bed of rocks with some small ledges that can require a lot of maneuvering.

SHUTTLE: From Boone, take NC 105 south about 4.8 mi. to the bridge over the river. For take-out, continue across the river and take the first right onto Broadstone Rd., which intersects NC 194 in Valle Crucis. Continue north on NC 194 to the bridge across the river.

GAUGE: The USGS Gauge is on the right bank 250 ft. upstream from the Rt. 1121 bridge. Minimum reading for solo is 1.95. The river can be run throughout most of the year below Section A, except during long dry periods.

NC 194 BRIDGE TO US 321 BRIDGE

CLASS	I–II
LENGTH	7.5
TIME	2.5
GAUGE	VISUAL
LEVEL	1.85 FT.
PERMITS	No
GRADIENT	9
SCENERY	B

DESCRIPTION: This section is a very pleasant, easy float trip. There's one low-water bridge. Below the Rt. 1121 bridge there is a 15-ft. dam that can be portaged on the right (50 yds.). Watch for a few other gravel bars as well.

GAUGE: USGS minimum for solo is 1.85.

SHUTTLE: To reach take-out, drive west from Boone on Hwy. 321/421 to where it crosses Watauga River. For put-ins, return to Boone on Hwy. 321/421, turn right at NC 194 and drive to bridge across river.

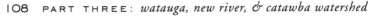

D

CLASS	II–III
LENGTH	4
TIME	2
GAUGE	VISUAL
LEVEL	1.85 FT.
PERMITS	NO
GRADIENT	25
SCENERY	A

US 321 BRIDGE TO SR 1200 (GUYS FORD RD.)

DESCRIPTION: There is a 12-ft. drop about 0.25 mi. below the put-in. This can be seen from the highway. It can be run two-thirds of the way down, but the bottom is packed with boulders. A carry can be made on the right. Other than this, it is primarily a run through gravel bars and small boulder fields.

SHUTTLE: From Boone, take US 321/421 west to the US 321/421 bridge across the river. Continue west on US 321/421 to reach the take-out; turn right onto SR 1200 (Guys Ford Rd.) and stop at the bridge.

GAUGE: USGS minimum for solo is 1.85.

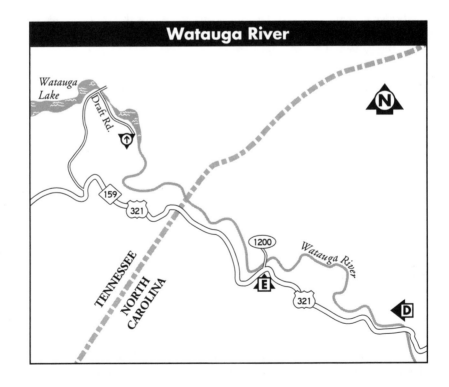

Watauga River

SR 1200 (Guys Ford Rd.) bridge to Watauga Lake

CLASS	III–V
LENGTH	5.7
TIME	4
GAUGE	Visual
LEVEL	See below
PERMITS	No
GRADIENT	90 (3.2 @ 200)
SCENERY	A+

DESCRIPTION: The Watauga River Gorge has been a classic East Coast hardwater run since the East Tennessee Whitewater Club pioneered trips here in the early 1970s. Though it has dropped several rungs on the hair-boating ladder due to comparison with today's banzai runs, it remains a preeminent steep creek for advanced to expert boaters. Note that while the overall gradient is 90 fpm, three sections drop at the rate of 200 fpm for approximately 0.2 mile each.

From Guys Ford bridge there is 0.7 mi. of Class II–III warm-up water before the first boulder clog, which can be eddy hopped. Below here are three major drops within 0.5 mi. The third, and most dangerous rapid on the river, Hydro, should definitely be scouted (on the left). Hydro, a hard Class V at medium and high water, is quite demanding technically, as well as dangerous due to a boulder strainer at the top and a strong keeper at the bottom. Rescue is questionable because it's hard to place ropes.

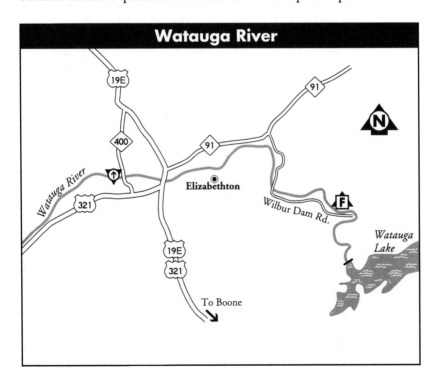

Watauga River

From here the river alternates between reasonably open water and frequent blind drops squeezed between huge boulders. Downstream vision is generally very limited. Vernon's Folly, Edge of the World, and Blowjob are a few of the more significant drops. Heavy Water, another Class V, is noted by a steep, complex entry, as the river narrows and disappears to the right around a macro boulder with the current tending to shove boats into one or two nasty holes below the turn. Scouting is advised here.

Approximately 1 mi. below Heavy Water is the Class V Watauga Falls. The Falls is a 16-ft. vertical drop with 60 percent of the water going over the right center. It is seriously aerated because there is a boulder that is slightly above the surface at the bottom. A distinct horizon line will tell you to take out on the left to carry or scout, about 75 yds. above the drop. If planning to run, it's a good idea to catch the eddy directly above the drop. Cut a hard right angle to boof the drop and hopefully avoid collision with said boulder at the bottom.

From here a house-sized boulder can be seen 200 yds. downstream. Run the 9-ft. drop just to the right of the boulder. Things start to ease up from here down to Watson Island where there is a possible take-out on the left of the island. Don't count on taking out here because the landowners generally have the road shut down to boaters. Instead, run down the right side at Watson Island and continue on easy Class II water to the lake. A 0.5 mi. paddle across the lake will bring you to Phillips Campground, where boaters can leave shuttle cars for two bucks per vehicle.

SHUTTLE: Take US 321 north out of Boone to SR 1200. Take a right on SR 1200 and go 0.25 mi. to the river. Take US 321 north out of Boone to the first paved road on the right (Gregg Branch Rd.) beyond the NC/TN state line. Keep bearing right on this road until the dead-end at Phillips Campground.

GAUGE: Minimum level is 12" below the top of the river left (downstream) piling of the Guys Ford bridge.

CLASS	II–III
LENGTH	I I.5
TIME	5.5
GAUGE	VISUAL
LEVEL	2.68 FT.
PERMITS	No
GRADIENT	I 4
SCENERY	A–B

WILBUR DAM TO 0.5 MI. WEST OF SYCAMORE SHOALS ON US 321

DESCRIPTION: After its emergence from a deep gorge below Wilbur Dam, this section moves on through more pastoral country. Sycamore Shoals, just above the take-out, is where the Over Mountain Men began their historic march to Kings Mountain.

At lower water levels, when the dam isn't operating, there are no dangerous areas, but Sycamore Shoals should be approached with caution. At higher levels the picture changes. About 300 yds. downstream from the overhead foot bridge in the gorge, a series of ledges build up 3–4 ft. standing waves in a bend to the left. If not prepared to handle this, stay close to the left bank.

Downstream from the US 19 E. bridge, the Beaunit Plant on the left and the Elizabethton sewage plant on the right of the river dump waste into the river, which gives one added motivation to stay upright through Sycamore Shoals. It can be recognized by a long flat stretch and the fort on the left side. The shoals can best be scouted from the left. It consists of a series of ledges on the right, running diagonally downstream from right to left. The safest passage is to the right of the main channel.

SHUTTLE: Take TN 91 north from Elizabethton to the community of Hunter (alongside river) and take the first main road to the right after TN 91 leaves the river. Proceed approximately 4 mi. to the dam. For take-out, go west on US 321 from Elizabethton approximately 0.5 mi. beyond Sycamore Shoals Historical Area.

GAUGE: The USGS Gauge is on the left bank at the US 19 E. (Bristol Highway) bridge. Minimum reading for solo is 2.68. There is no regular schedule for water releases from Wilbur Dam, as power is furnished on demand. The only apparent pattern of release occurs on Saturdays shortly after noon during the summer.

ELK RIVER

The Elk originates in Avery County in the valley between Beech and Sugar Mountains, both popular ski resorts. The river flows generally west and north into Tennessee, eventually reaching the impoundment at Watauga Lake. The Elk Gorge is very remote, beautiful, and difficult. Other sections are appropriate for skill levels running the gamut from novice to expert. The river can generally only be run during or shortly after heavy rains, with Section D being the possible exception.

MAPS: Elk Park (NC); Elk Mills (TN) (USGS); Avery (NC); Carter (TN) (County)

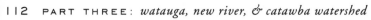

CLASS	III–V
LENGTH	3.4
TIME	3.5
GAUGE	VISUAL
LEVEL	-5 IN.
PERMITS	No
GRADIENT	135
	(1 @ 240)
SCENERY	B

A

SR 1326 BRIDGE TO SR 1305 BRIDGE

DESCRIPTION: This run has two distinct, steep sections. After a 0.75 mi. warmup, one enters a 1 mi. section that drops 240 ft. This piece ends above the NC 194 bridge and the other begins just downstream of the bridge. The highway parallels most of the hard water, so aborting trips is simple. You'll find yourself scout-

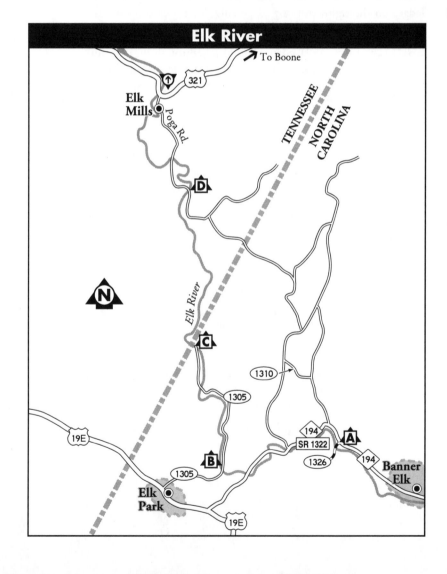

ing Class V rapids in someone's backyard. There is one mandatory portage that comes toward the end of the run. It's a 10-ft. drop choked down with boulders. Carry on the left. The rest of the run is complex, steep, and doable. The larger drops include a couple of 10-footers and an 18-ft. cascading slide. Bow pins have occurred in the middle slot of the lead-in rapid to the first 10-ft. waterfall. High-volume creek boats are essential on this run. This section is more difficult than the gorge downstream and is only appropriate for groups of experts.

SHUTTLE: Take NC 194 west of Banner Elk to SR 1326. Take a left and drive 200 yds. to the river. For the take-out, return to NC 194, turn left, and go into Elk Park. Turn right on SR 1305 (Elk River Rd.) and go to the first bridge over the river.

GAUGE: It's located on the river left piling of the SR 1326 bridge. Minimum level is 5" below "0."

B

SR 1305 BRIDGE TO DEAD END OF SR 1305

CLASS	II
LENGTH	3.6
TIME	2
GAUGE	VISUAL
LEVEL	-6 IN.
PERMITS	No
GRADIENT	28
SCENERY	A–B

DESCRIPTION: There are no difficulties. Just be sure to take out at the park because Big Falls (55 ft.) is 100 yds. downstream.

SHUTTLE: In Elk Park, go west on US 19 E. and take a right on SR 1305 (Elk River Rd.); go to the first bridge over the river. For take-out, continue past this bridge to where the road dead-ends.

GAUGE: It's located on the river left piling of the SR 1326 bridge. Minimum level is 6" below "0."

C

DEAD END OF SR 1305 TO BRIDGE BELOW STONE MOUNTAIN CHURCH

CLASS	III–V
LENGTH	5
TIME	4.5
GAUGE	VISUAL
LEVEL	-5 IN.
PERMITS	No
GRADIENT	112
SCENERY	A+

DESCRIPTION: The Elk River Gorge, from Big Falls to Twisting Falls, is truly a classic piece of water. It is seldom run due to a small watershed, mandatory (hard) portages, and general remoteness. This is experts-only country that even the most jaded of hard boaters will enjoy. The gorge alternates between complex boulder gardens and steep, gnarly ledge drops. Few of the larger drops have crystal clear routes, but all can be run cleanly at medium or higher flows. Large-volume creek boats are recommended.

From the put-in, you can paddle 100 yds. before reaching Big Falls. Carry on the left around this 55-footer. For the next 1.5 mi. enjoy the scenery and easy gradient. A 12-ft. drop denotes the beginning of the "interesting water" and the end of paying attention to anything other than the confrontation of boat and water.

The 2.5 mi. of serious water ends with Twisting Falls, where the river cascades 160 ft. in 0.3 mi. The entrance to Twisting Falls is noted by the vertical rock walls that pinch the river down to a width of 20 ft. Prudent boaters will take out 100 yds. upstream to avoid a nasty entrance rapid that leads to a 15-ft. waterfall and an unrunnable 35-footer. Carry on the left, either up and over the mountain or along the rocks beside these first two falls.

Below here are other rapids and two more vertical drops of 16 and 45 ft. in succession. These drops have been run, but are not recommended unless you've been in some serious car wrecks and enjoyed the sensation. Below Twisting Falls there is fun Class II–III water for a mile down to the take-out.

SHUTTLE: For take-out, drive east from Elk park on US 19 E. Turn left on NC 194 and drive to US 321/421 just west of Boone. Turn left (west) and drive across state line toward Elk Mills. Turn left on Poga Rd. to second bridge across the Elk.

GAUGE: See Section A. Gauge reading should be 5" below for a minimum level.

CLASS	II–III
LENGTH	5.5
TIME	3
GAUGE	VISUAL
LEVEL	-6 IN.
PERMITS	No
GRADIENT	39
SCENERY	A

DESCRIPTION: There are several ledges that may require scouting through the area of the greatest drop. This stretch is located downstream from the second bridge and can be recognized by the bluffs which rise some 300 ft. above the river.

SHUTTLE: From US 321 just west of Boone, go south on the first paved road east of the US 321 bridge over the Elk. Go through the community of Elk Mills to the second bridge. Take out below the US 321 bridge at Elk Mills.

GAUGE: It's located on the northeast side of the US 321 bridge. Minimum for solo run is 6" below "0." This section is runnable most of the year, except during long dry spells. It's best in spring and early summer.

BUCK CREEK

Buck Creek has its headwaters in the Mt. Mitchell Wildlife Management Area below the Blue Ridge Parkway. It flows along NC 80 into Lake Tahoma. Above the lake it is a small, fast dropping stream while below it flattens out somewhat, flowing over small ledges and rocks. Property above the lake is posted as well as patrolled. Don't be tempted.

MAPS: Marion (USGS); McDowell (County)

A

LAKE TAHOMA DAM TO US 70 BRIDGE

CLASS	I–II
LENGTH	3.2
TIME	1.5
GAUGE	VISUAL
LEVEL	-6 IN.
PERMITS	NO
GRADIENT	23
SCENERY	A–B

DESCRIPTION: There are no difficulties, but fast maneuvering will be required in several tight passages.

SHUTTLE: From Marion, drive north on US 221 to US 70. Turn left (west) onto US 70. The take-out is on the east side of the US 70 bridge just east of the community of Pleasant Gardens. Continue past the take-out and turn right on NC 80. Turn off NC 80 on the first road below the dam. There is little space for turning around at the end of this road.

GAUGE: It's located on US 70 on the northeast side of the bridge. Minimum for solo run is reading of 6" below "0." Buck Creek drains a small area and can be run in later winter, spring, and following rain.

NORTH FORK CATAWBA RIVER

The North Fork has its headwaters on Humpback Mountain below the Blue Ridge Parkway. It is a small shallow stream which US 221 follows down the mountain, until Armstrong Creek comes in and it picks up considerably. Also, in the Sevier area, it receives some degree of industrial pollution. Below Sevier it enters a small gorge and continues on its way to Lake James. The river runs parallel to and below the western ridge of the Linville Gorge Wilderness Area. With the exception of the Clinchfield Railroad running along the east bank for about half way down, this is an uninhabited area. It remains fairly narrow as it courses over ledges and through small boulder gardens.

MAPS: Little Switzerland, Marion East (USGS); McDowell (County)

A

CLASS	II–III
LENGTH	5.6
TIME	3.5
GAUGE	VISUAL
LEVEL	-2 IN.
PERMITS	No
GRADIENT	29
SCENERY	A

ON MCDOWELL CR 1559 TO RT. 1552 BRIDGE

DESCRIPTION: Six hundred yds. below the put-in a boulder garden runs about 100 yds. This will require a great deal of maneuvering. It would be best to scout on the right bank.

There are several interesting rapids before arriving at the railroad bridge; below it an 8-ft. slanting falls should be approached

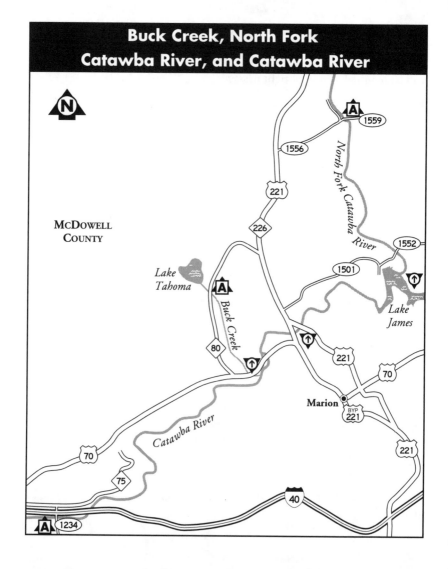

Buck Creek, North Fork
Catawba River, and Catawba River

with caution. Three 2- to 3-ft. ledges follow it closely. Run on the right. The river drops about 16 ft. within 150 yds. through this area. Scout on the right bank again.

With a reading of approximately 4" above the bottom of "0" on the gauge, several of the rapids will require scouting.

SHUTTLE: From Marion, drive north on US 221 to Woodlawn, east on Rt. 1556 to Rt. 1559, then 100 yds. to the put-in on the river's edge, between the creek bridge and railroad bridge. For take-out, return to US 221 and go east on Rt. 1501 (Hankins Rd.) to Burnett's Landing. Turn left on Rt. 1552 to the bridge. A slightly easier take-out can be made at the Wildlife Access Area 0.5 mi. downstream from the Rt. 1552 bridge. Look for the sign on the right, after passing Burnett's Landing.

GAUGE: It's located on the northwest side of the railroad bridge at the put-in. Minimum level for solo is 2" below "0." The river generally can be run during wet seasons or immediately after a rain. Run off will be fast.

CATAWBA RIVER

The Catawba heads up above Catawba Falls in the extreme western portion of McDowell County and flows into Lake James north of Marion. Below Linville Dam on Lake James, it continues until it reaches the backwaters of Lake Rhodhiss. After Lake Rhodhiss the river is impounded several times with little fast free-flowing water, therefore the reason for no further description.

The river is small and fast in Section A but carries industrial pollution east of Old Fort. Except for this it could be a very pretty run. However, there are several areas where gravel operations are evident.

Below Lake James the river flows primarily through woodlands until it reaches Morganton.

MAPS: Marion, Glen Alpine, Morganton South, Morganton North (USGS); McDowell, Burke (County)

McDowell CR 1234 BRIDGE TO US 221 BRIDGE

DESCRIPTION: There are several series of ledges, the first of which is below the confluence of Crooked Creek on the right. This one in particular should be scouted. An earlier take-out can be made along McDowell CR 1214 for those who desire a shorter run.

CLASS	I–II
LENGTH	12
TIME	6
GAUGE	VISUAL
LEVEL	-6 IN.
PERMITS	No
GRADIENT	7
SCENERY	B–C

SHUTTLE: From Marion, drive south on US 221, then go west on I-40, just past Old Fort, and go south on McDowell CR 1234 at the Parker Padgett Rd. Exit. Take-out is at the old US 221 bridge in Marion.

GAUGE: It's located on the south side of the CR 1234 bridge. Minimum level for solo paddling is 6" below "0." This section can be run year round except during extreme dry seasons.

B

BURKE CR 1223 BRIDGE TO RT. 1147 BRIDGE

CLASS	I–II
LENGTH	8
TIME	3
GAUGE	VISUAL
LEVEL	N/A
PERMITS	No
GRADIENT	5
SCENERY	B

DESCRIPTION: The volume of water coming from the Bridgewater Plant of Duke Power Company is completely unpredictable. This presents a situation where the water level increases approximately two feet within a matter of seconds and can be rather dangerous in the first 200 yds. below the put-in, particularly so 50 yds. downstream, where a large tree blocks most of the channel on the right. Put in on the left of the bridge to be safe.

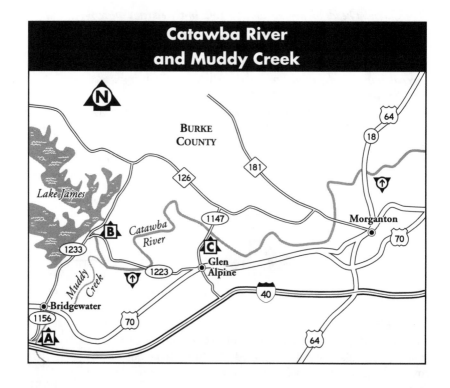

The stretch above the second bridge has several islands that should be approached carefully when the water is up.

SHUTTLE: Drive east on US 70 to the exit at Glen Alpine. Get on Burke CR 1233 and go east to old road bed about 100 yds. upstream from the bridge on river left of the Catawba. The old bridge abutment is evident here. The put-in is located further east on CR 1223 400 yds. east of Bridgewater Power Plant at Lake James.

GAUGE: None. The power plant is operating if there are no significant mud flats along the banks. This will provide plenty of water. When it is not in operation, the first two gravel bars in Section B probably will need to be walked. After these two the remainder can be negotiated.

BURKE CR 1147 BRIDGE (WATERMILL RD.) TO NC 18 BRIDGE

CLASS	I
LENGTH	7.5
TIME	3
GAUGE	VISUAL
LEVEL	N/A
PERMITS	No
GRADIENT	2
SCENERY	A–B

DESCRIPTION: Watch out for a low head dam located just around the bend above Independence Blvd. in Morganton. It is well marked. Carry on the posted trail on the left. For those wishing to shorten the trip, an access area has been constructed as part of Morganton's greenway at Judges Riverside Restaurant off Airpark Road.

SHUTTLE: The take-out is located at the NC 18 bridge north of Morganton on the south bank at a gravel pit. Return to Glen Alpine for put-in, driving north on CR 1147 to the bridge.

GAUGE: See Section B.

MUDDY CREEK

North Muddy Creek heads up in the hills south of Marion and wanders east and north before meeting the South Muddy downstream of I-40 and the put-in. It then flows northerly entering the Catawba River about 1 mi. down from the Bridgewater Power Plant at Lake James.

MAPS: Glen Alpine (USGS); Burke, McDowell (County)

CLASS	I
LENGTH	5.1
TIME	2.5
GAUGE	VISUAL
LEVEL	-6 IN.
PERMITS	NO
GRADIENT	9
SCENERY	A–B

McDOWELL CR 1763 TO BURKE CR 1223
ON THE CATAWBA RIVER

DESCRIPTION: There are no difficulties.

SHUTTLE: To reach the take-out, drive east on US 70 to exit at Glen Alpine. Get on Burke CR 1233 and go east to the old road bed about 100 yds. upstream from the bridge on river left of the Catawba. The put-in is located off US 70 in Bridgewater. Take Burke CR 1156 south, which becomes McDowell CR 1763, to the creek.

GAUGE: It's located on the I-40 bridge piling. Minimum for solo is 6" below "0."

LINVILLE RIVER

The Linville River originates approximately 1 mi. east and down slope of Sugar Mountain, just across the valley from Grandfather Mountain. From its origin, the river flows quietly for several miles before reaching Linville Falls, a drop of some 85 ft. Below this point the Linville Gorge proper begins, and the river and its immediate environs are protected by the Linville Gorge Wilderness Area, an 11,000-acre tract that is part of Pisgah National Forest. This remote, rugged, beautiful country lends itself to hiking, rock climbing, and fishing, pursuits much saner than attempting to paddle this river.

Due to its length, inaccessibility, and gradient, Linville River Gorge is arguably the most difficult stretch of whitewater in the eastern United States. The gorge is 17 mi. long and drops 1,880 ft. The first 14 mi. are Class IV, V, and VI water, and the lower 3 mi. slow down to Class II and III. The entire Gorge is seldom run due to the following:

1. The river runs infrequently, generally only after extended rainfall, and has a small window of runnability.

2. The remoteness makes for difficult put-ins and take-outs. Evacuations would be extremely strenuous and time-consuming.

3. Scouting and portaging are hard and sometimes dangerous.

4. The rapids are long, complex, unforgiving, and often undercut.

In short, unless you're quite comfortable on every other high-caliber hair run in the East, you're about to get in over your head if considering a run down the Gorge. This is full contact boating at its finest.

Linville River

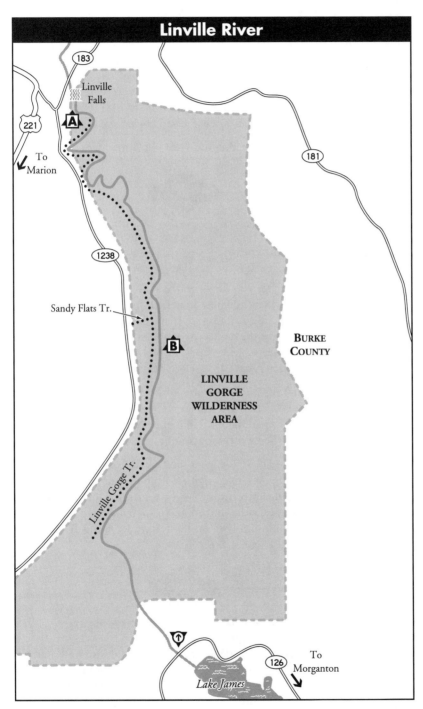

183

Linville
Falls

221

A

To
Marion

181

1238

Sandy Flats Tr.

B

BURKE
COUNTY

LINVILLE
GORGE
WILDERNESS
AREA

Linville Gorge Tr.

126

To
Morganton

Lake James

Although the Gorge has been run in a single, bone-jarring, glycogen-depleting day by at least one group, it should be considered a two-day trip. The break point between Linville Falls and NC 126, Sandy Flats Trail, is the most logical place to split the trip due to similar time requirements for the section above and below. This also divides the hardest section of the river (the middle 10 mi.). The most popular section for a single day of paddling is from Conley Cove Trail to NC 126, which has about 3.5 mi. of hard water and 3.5 mi. of easy rapids.

MAPS: Linville Falls, Ashford (USGS); Burke (County)

CLASS	IV–VI
LENGTH	7
TIME	8
GAUGE	VISUAL
LEVEL	I FT.
PERMITS	No
GRADIENT	I 25
SCENERY	A+

LINVILLE FALLS TO SANDY FLATS TRAIL

DESCRIPTION: The first 2.5–3 mi. below Linville Falls are a natural slalom course of primarily Class III rapids. The first big drop of 14 ft. lets you know you're about to enter more serious water. The next several miles do not let up. It gets generally harder and harder. The scouting is strenuous and the portages even more so. Some of the rapids encountered are First Falls, Harvey's Folly, Group Grope, and Map Falls. It is advisable to know something of the trail system in case of evacuations or aborted trips.

SHUTTLE: Take NC 181 north of Morganton to a left on NC 183. Follow NC 183 to a left on NC 1238 (Old Hwy. 105). Go to Linville Falls parking lot. Hike in below Linville Falls on river right side. See Section B for take-out.

GAUGE: The USGS Gauge is located 100 yds. upstream of the NC 126 bridge on river right. The minimum level has been changed significantly from the first printing of this edition, probably due to the streambed being altered during the flood of 1994. The minimum level on both Sections A and B should be approximately 1 foot.

CLASS	IV–V+
LENGTH	I 0
TIME	8
GAUGE	VISUAL
LEVEL	I FT.
PERMITS	No
GRADIENT	I 00
SCENERY	A+

SANDY FLATS TRAIL TO NC 126 BRIDGE

DESCRIPTION: The rapids and their complexities are numerous. There will be about 6.5–7 mi. of hard water before the gradient starts to slow down. This section has been done in two portages, both mandatory. One is a 10-yd. walk and the other is a 40-yd. walk (longest portage on the river) ending above

Cathedral Falls. Cathedral Falls will come about 2 mi. into this section. The rapid is composed of a 6-ft. horseshoe-shaped ledge feeding a fast runout to a 16-ft. vertical drop where one must be on line. Other significant drops include The Narrows, Kidney Reducer, The Slot, Slam Dance, Twist and Shout, and The Wall.

SHUTTLE: See Section A for put-in. Take NC 126 west of Morganton to the bridge over the Linville River. Take-out 100 yds. upstream of the bridge.

GAUGE: See Section B. Minimum level should be 1 foot.

STEEL CREEK

Steel Creek is born in northeastern Burke County just east of Linville Gorge. The first several miles are a beautiful wilderness run, then the creek begins to parallel NC 181. The entire drainage lies within Pisgah National Forest ensuring excellent water quality. Below the put-in, this section is continuous Class III for 2 mi. after which the gradient subsides somewhat down to the confluence with Upper Creek. The natural slalom course is provided by the boulder garden nature of the river bed. This is strictly a high-water run with a window of one to two days at best.

MAPS: Chestnut Mtn., Oak Hill (USGS); Burke (County)

FR 228 TO SR 1405 (ADAKO RD.) BRIDGE

CLASS	III
LENGTH	6
TIME	2.5
GAUGE	VISUAL
LEVEL	3 IN.
PERMITS	No
GRADIENT	66
SCENERY	A+−B

DESCRIPTION: There are no major drops and everything can be boat-scouted. Eddy hopping and ferrying abilities will be strongly tested because the upper part of this run is very fast and tight. Below the first 2 mi. the gradient gradually decreases to the take-out. Beware of one low-water bridge approximately 3.5 mi. into the run. Carry on the right.

SHUTTLE: Take NC 181 north of Morganton. Go 4.5 mi. beyond SR 1405 and take a left onto FR 228. Follow this road until it literally runs into the creek. Take out at the SR 1405 bridge.

GAUGE: The Upper Creek Gauge on FR 982 (see Section A on Upper Creek) should read 3" above "0" for a minimum level.

UPPER CREEK

Upper Creek originates in the Jonas Ridge area of northern Burke County. The upper stretches are within Pisgah National Forest, which ensures excellent water quality. The creek flows through one unrunnable gorge in the Jonas Hole area before entering the long abandoned Greentown community where the remains of an old railroad track are still visible. Downstream of Greentown is the Raven Cliff Gorge section. Below Section A the creek progressively slows down and runs through rural areas before its confluence with the Catawba River, just above Lake Rhodhiss. Upper Creek is reportedly one of the best smallmouth bass fishing streams in the Southeast.

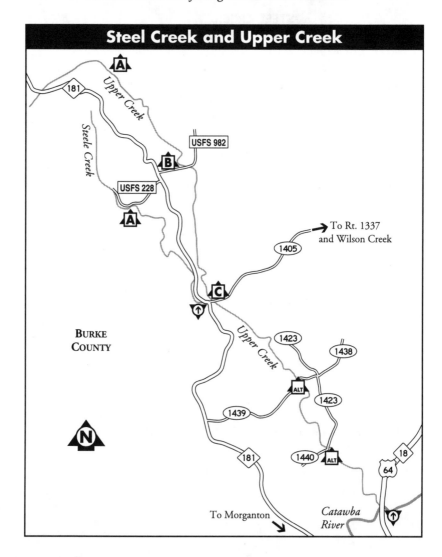

MAPS: Chestnut Mtn., Oak Hill, Morganton North (USGS); Burke (County)

GREENTOWN TRAILHEAD TO FR 982

CLASS	III–V
LENGTH	4.3
TIME	4.5
GAUGE	VISUAL
LEVEL	3 IN.
PERMITS	No
GRADIENT	177
SCENERY	A+–A

DESCRIPTION: Due to the difficulty of the water, the hike to the put-in, and the mandatory 45-minute portage, this section is only for dedicated experts in good condition. The gradient is somewhat skewed on this stretch due to the 0.4 mi. gorge, known as Raven Cliffs, where the river tumbles 280 ft. (essentially unrunnable even by today's gnarly standards). At high water this is serious Class IV with an occasional Class V drop thrown in to keep everyone honest. This section was first run at 2 ft. above the suggested minimum and things were somewhat out of control at times. Less than 1 mi. into the run, the beautiful Burnthouse Branch Falls tumbles in on river left.

Approximately 0.5 mi. downstream, Raven Cliffs starts. Take out on the left well above to carry over the mountain. Entry into the Raven Cliffs section at high water is cheap thrills suicide. The water below Raven Cliffs is steeper than above. Pay particular attention to one long Class IV rapid that feeds a drop with a major-league strainer, which one boater luckily survived on the first descent. Things don't ease up until you're about 1 mi. above the take-out.

SHUTTLE: Take NC 181 north of Morganton. Go 8.8 mi. beyond SR 1405 (Adako Rd.); look for a small sign on the right for the Greentown/Upper Creek trailhead. Hike 1.1 mi. to the creek. The take-out is located 4.5 mi. beyond SR 1405 (Adako Rd.) at FR 982 on the right. Go to the first bridge over the creek.

GAUGE: It's located on the river left piling of the FR 982 bridge. Minimum level is 3" above "0."

B

FR 982 BRIDGE TO SR 1405 (ADAKO RD.) BRIDGE

CLASS	II–III
LENGTH	5.4
TIME	2.5
GAUGE	VISUAL
LEVEL	1 IN.
PERMITS	No
GRADIENT	44
SCENERY	A–B

DESCRIPTION: Though there are no major drops on this section, there is plenty of maneuvering necessary at high water. A log dam, a few low-water bridges, and an 8-ft. dam at Optimist Park are mandatory portages. This stretch meanders through pasture

land for the last 2 mi. above Optimist Park and its subsequent confluence with Steel Creek.

SHUTTLE: Take NC 181 north of Morganton. Go 4.5 mi. beyond SR 1405 (Adako Rd.) to FR 982 on the right. Go to the first bridge over the creek. Take out at the SR 1405 bridge, 100 yds. from NC 181.

GAUGE: Minimum level 1" above "0."

CLASS	I (II)
LENGTH	11.2
TIME	7.5
GAUGE	VISUAL
LEVEL	-6 IN.
PERMITS	No
GRADIENT	6
SCENERY	B–C

Rt. 1405 BRIDGE (ADAKO RD.) TO NC 18 BRIDGE ON THE CATAWBA RIVER

DESCRIPTION: Look out for one ledge about 0.5 mi. below the put-in. There's also a fast narrow chute about 2 mi. below the Rt. 1439 bridge at Worry. Watch for downed trees throughout the entire section. The river is basically flat below Rt. 1440 (Bost Rd.).

SHUTTLE: Take NC 181 north of Morganton to SR 1405 (Adako Rd.). Turn right and go 100 yds. to the bridge. The take-out is reached by driving north of Morganton on NC 18 to the bridge over the Catawba River. The bridge is immediately below the confluence of Upper Creek with the Catawba.

This section can be shortened by taking out/putting in at the Rt. 1439 bridge at Worry (Henderson Mill Rd.) or at the Rt. 1440 bridge (Bost Rd.).

GAUGE: It's located on the southwest piling of the Rt. 1405 bridge. Minimum for solo is 6" below "0." An alternate gauge is located on a concrete slab under the Rt. 1439 bridge on the east side.

NORTH HARPER CREEK

North Harper Creek is born high in the Pisgah National Forest between Headquarters Mountain and Big Lost Cove Ridge. It is a beautifully scenic run alternating between fast current through steep gorges and quiet water through the valley floor. A large portion of the gradient is comprised of unrunnable falls and very congested (read unrunnable) boulder chokedowns. Indeed, the creek has been run/walked by walking in the Little Lost Cove trail. This tacks an additional 1.6 mi. of distance and 480 ft. of drop to the run, most of which is unrunnable.

MAPS: Grandfather Mtn., Chestnut Mtn. (USGS); Avery, Caldwell (County)

North Harper Creek, Lost Cove Creek, Wilson Creek, and Johns River

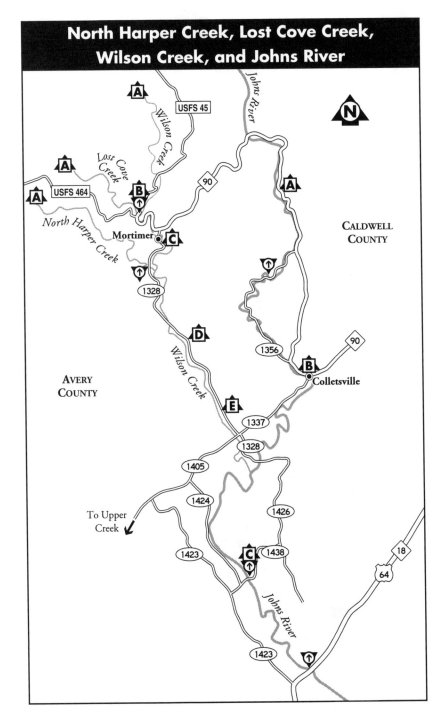

CLASS	III–IV
LENGTH	5.4
TIME	5
GAUGE	VISUAL
LEVEL	0 IN.
PERMITS	No
GRADIENT	141
SCENERY	A+

FR 464 TO SR 1328 BRIDGE OVER HARPER CREEK

DESCRIPTION: From the 266A trailhead put-in, there is 0.5 mi. of easy water and then the gradient increases for 0.3 mi. and culminates in a 50-ft. waterfall. Carry on the right. From here everything is runnable down to Harper Falls, a triple stage drop of 100 ft. Carry on the left. Approximately 1.5 mi. above Harper Falls, the creek joins with Hull Branch Creek, doubling the volume and forming Harper Creek. The run is primarily easy Class III water, though quite technical. This is a true wilderness run; you're guaranteed to see none but the occasional, hard-core fisherman. North Harper Creek is only runnable after heavy, extended rainfall and has a window of one to two days at best.

SHUTTLE: The take-out is located just south of Mortimer on SR 1328 at the bridge over Harper Creek, just above the confluence with Wilson Creek. For put-in, take NC 90 west out of Mortimer. Go left on FR 464 to the Harper Creek trailhead sign. Walk 1 mi. to the creek.

GAUGE: It's located on the river left piling of the SR 1328 bridge over Harper Creek. Minimum level is bottom of "0."

LOST COVE CREEK

Lost Cove Creek is born deep in the mountains between Lost Cove Cliffs and Sassafras Knob. A beautiful, sparkling stream, its entire drainage is within Pisgah National Forest. It is the major tributary of Wilson Creek. This is strictly a high-water run with a window of two days at best. A good flow is probably 150 cfs. Make sure you're well warmed up before putting in. There is continuous Class III water for 2 mi. after pulling out of the first eddy, with more interesting stuff below. This is a true wilderness run and you must hike 2.2 mi. to get to the put-in. The run is well worth the walk.

MAPS: Grandfather Mtn. (USGS); Avery, Caldwell (County)

FR 464-A to Edgemont Church Rd. at NC 90 bridge

CLASS	III–IV (V)
LENGTH	5
TIME	4
GAUGE	Visual
LEVEL	2 ft.
PERMITS	No
GRADIENT	104
SCENERY	A+

DESCRIPTION: The creek forks in several spots making for very tight maneuvering. After 2.5 mi. of continuous boulder gardens, the stream enters a 0.75-mi. gorge and changes character with several ledge drops. The first and most difficult, Hunt Fish Falls, is a low Class V rapid consisting of two drops of 7 and 10 ft. in close succession. Scout or carry on the right. The rapid has been run by staying far right on both drops. Note the beautiful waterfall tumbling down the mountain on the right. Below Hunt Fish Falls is a 12-ft. slide best run right center. The next rapid should be entered far right with a cut to the left down the runout trough. A tight boulder garden is below here. This is followed by Air Baker, the last large drop on the run, which should be entered far left and finished with a traverse to the right. Below Air Baker the gradient subsides somewhat but continues with entertaining Class II and III rapids for the next 2 mi. to the take-out.

SHUTTLE: Take NC 90 west out of Mortimer. Take a left onto FR 464 and go 4.75 mi. to FR 464-A. Walk 464-A the 2.2 mi. to the creek because the road is not in good shape. For take-out, take NC 90 west from Mortimer to Edgemont Church Rd. and park. This is right above the confluence with Wilson Creek.

GAUGE: Wilson Creek Gauge should read a minimum of 2 ft.

WILSON CREEK

Wilson Creek has its headwaters on the eastern slopes of Grandfather Mountain. With its watershed primarily within the Pisgah National Forest, it has exceptional water quality. This quality quite often fools even the experienced paddler into underestimating water depth.

Section A, which is quite technically challenging, can only be run after heavy rains, and has a small window during which it can be paddled. Sections B and C drop over the occasional ledge and stubblefield and are suitable for low intermediate skill levels. Section D drops through a ruggedly beautiful gorge with several memorable rapids. It is one of the more popular advanced runs in the Southeast. After leaving the gorge at Brown Mountain Beach, the creek slows down considerably upon its confluence with the Johns River. The gorge, as well as most of the creek, can be enjoyed by everyone, not only those with the skill to paddle it. Wilson Gorge is highly recommended to all—whether boating, mountain biking, or just driving. Be aware that the creek, especially through the gorge, has become a very popular area. The traffic on the narrow road is quite heavy on weekends from late spring through the summer.

MAPS: Grandfather Mtn., Chestnut Mtn., Collettsville (USGS); Avery, Caldwell (County)

FR 45 TO INTERSECTION OF SR 90 AND FR 981

CLASS	III (IV)
LENGTH	4.9
TIME	3
GAUGE	VISUAL
LEVEL	1.5 FT.
PERMITS	No
GRADIENT	106
SCENERY	A–B

DESCRIPTION: This is a bang-up section of almost continuous Class III water. Though not as impressive as the popular gorge downstream, this stretch requires excellent boat control, as there are many tight moves. With the exception of one rapid, everything can be boat scouted. Approximately 0.75 mi. into the run is a steep Class IV rapid which is best scouted and entered on the right. There is a potentially nasty undercut at the bottom of the drop. There is a trail on the left paralleling most of the run. The scenery, while not outstanding, is pristine, down to the first bridge. Be aware of the private property (owned by a hunting club) that is posted throughout the lower portion of the run, and precludes taking out at the first bridge you come to.

SHUTTLE: Take SR 90 north from Mortimer. SR 90 turns into FR 45. Stay on FR 45 to 0.5 mi. south of the intersection at Gragg, where the trailhead is on the left. Hike in approximately 1.5 mi. to the creek. For take-out, take NC 90 west from Mortimer to the intersection of NC 90 and FR 981. The bridge is on the right 50 yds. up from the intersection.

GAUGE: It's located on the river left piling of the SR 1405 (Adako Rd.) bridge. A minimum level is 1.5 ft.

INTERSECTION OF SR 90 AND FR 981 TO SR 1328 BRIDGE

CLASS	II
LENGTH	2.5
TIME	1
GAUGE	VISUAL
LEVEL	9 IN.
PERMITS	No
GRADIENT	40
SCENERY	A–B

DESCRIPTION: There are no difficulties.

SHUTTLE: The take-out is on the Rt. 1326 bridge just south of Mortimer. For put-in, take NC 90 west from Mortimer to the intersection of NC 90 and FR 981. The bridge is on the right 50 yds. up from the intersection.

GAUGE: The Gauge at the Adako Rd. bridge should be a minimum of 9" above "0."

RT. 1328 BRIDGE TO NFS BOUNDARY SIGN

CLASS	I–II (III)
LENGTH	5
TIME	2.5
GAUGE	VISUAL
LEVEL	-5 IN.
PERMITS	No
GRADIENT	24
SCENERY	A–B

DESCRIPTION: Most of Sections C and D can be scouted from the road. About 0.5 mi. below the put-in, as the creek bends to the right, there is a low foot bridge that can be missed by a quick move to the left.

Lunch Stop Rapid, a Class III, narrows down, piling the water against it and forcing it to the left of a rock wall. This should be scouted on the left and run on the inside. The rock makes for an excellent stopping place for lunch.

There are several ledges and stubblefields below the steel bridge that may require scouting depending on the water levels. Be sure that the take-out is checked out and that it can be easily recognized, or the gorge may see you before you see the gorge.

SHUTTLE: The put-in is on the SR 1326 bridge just south of Mortimer. Take out at the NFS boundary marker on Rt. 1328.

GAUGE: It's located on river left of Rt. 1337 (Adako Rd. bridge). Minimum for solo is 5" below "0." Call the store at Brown Mountain Beach (704) 758-4257 for a rough estimate of the water level.

NFS BOUNDARY SIGN TO BROWN MOUNTAIN BEACH

CLASS	III–IV+
LENGTH	2.4
TIME	3
GAUGE	VISUAL
LEVEL	-3 IN.
PERMITS	No
GRADIENT	92
SCENERY	A

DESCRIPTION: Wilson Gorge is primarily a drop/pool run, although there are several boulder gardens that provide natural slalom courses. There are five major drops on this section and plenty of good action between them. They are (in order): Ten Foot Falls, Boatbuster/Thunderhole, Triple Drop, Razorback, and Huntley's Retreat. These rapids are all Class IV at levels of "0" and below. As levels rise from "0" to 1 ft., they progress to Class V. Above 1 ft. they are quite intimidating with sketchy lines and big keeper hydraulics that invite unwilling boaters back in for an extended chat.

With a road following the river closely for most of the run, scouting or aborting trips is a simple matter. As car break-ins are not uncommon, valuables should be left at the take-out because

that area is less secluded. If you would like to park across from the Brown Mountain Beach store and carry boats through the property to reach your car, be aware their is a small fee to either park on or walk across their property. If this is unappetizing to you, take out 0.75 mi. upstream at the first pull-off past the old take-out.

SHUTTLE: Put in at the NFS boundary marker on Rt. 1328. Take out at Brown Mountain Beach on Rt. 1328.

GAUGE: Minimum level is 3" below "0."

CLASS	I–II
LENGTH	8
TIME	3.5
GAUGE	Visual
LEVEL	-6 in.
PERMITS	No
GRADIENT	5
SCENERY	B–C

200 YDS. ABOVE RT. 1337 BRIDGE ON RT. 1328 TO BURKE CR 1438 BRIDGE OVER THE JOHNS RIVER

DESCRIPTION: There is one rapid, Eddie's Icebox, approaching Class III in difficulty at higher water levels, about 0.5 mi. below Adako bridge, which requires a hard right turn. It will carry the unwary paddler directly onto the rock ledge straight in front. Step out on the small island to the left to scout.

One other rapid between Perkins Park and Playmore Beach can be trouble at lower water levels. Most of the water runs off a ledge on the far right, which is where it should be run.

SHUTTLE: Put-in at Rt. 1328 north of Rt. 1337 1 mi. northeast of the Burke-Caldwell County line. A low-water bridge is 0.6 mi. south of Mortimer. For take-out, drive west on Rt. 1337 (Burke CR 1405) 2.2 mi. from the Wilson Creek bridge, to Burke CR 1424 (Grade Rd.). Go south on it to Rt. 1438, then east to Corpening.

GAUGE: Minimum for solo is 6" below "0."

JOHNS RIVER

The Johns heads up in the Globe area of the Pisgah National Forest. It wanders through farm land and wooded areas until it reaches the backwaters of Duke Power Company's Lake Rhodhiss, north of Morganton. A gap, between Sections A and B, has been left due to the many low-water bridges located through that stretch.

MAPS: Globe, Collettsville, Morganton North (USGS); Burke, Caldwell (County)

CLASS	I–II
LENGTH	4.5
TIME	2.5
GAUGE	VISUAL
LEVEL	-4 IN.
PERMITS	No
GRADIENT	26
SCENERY	B

JOHNS RIVER CAMP BRIDGE TO
SECOND LOW-WATER BRIDGE AFTER LEAVING NC 90

DESCRIPTION: None, other than a couple of very tight passages that might be blocked by downed trees. Do not trespass on private property through here, which can prove rather difficult with some seven low-water bridges.

SHUTTLE: Take NC 90 north of Collettsville to Johns River United Church of Christ Camp bridge. Ask permission if the campground is open. For take-out, go to the second low-water bridge on SR 1356 southwest off NC 90.

GAUGE: It's located on the east side of the Caldwell CR 1337 bridge in Collettsville. Minimum for solo is 4" below "0." There is also a corresponding Gauge on the east side of the Burke CR 1438 bridge. With a level of 2" above the bottom of "0" the trip can be extended 3.5 mi. by putting in at the Caldwell CR 1367 low-water bridge.

CLASS	I–II
LENGTH	12.5
TIME	5
GAUGE	VISUAL
LEVEL	-6 IN.
PERMITS	No
GRADIENT	7
SCENERY	B–D

CALDWELL CR 1337 BRIDGE IN COLLETTSVILLE
TO BURKE CR 1438

DESCRIPTION: Watch out for one area below the old sand and gravel pit, which may be clogged with debris after high water.

SHUTTLE: Put-in at the Caldwell CR 1337 bridge at NC 90 in Collettsville. Take SR 1405 (Adako Rd.) into Burke County to Rt. 1424. Turn left onto Burke CR 1438 to the bridge. You can cut this trip in half by putting in/taking out at the Rt. 1328 bridge.

GAUGE: Minimum for solo: 6" below "0."

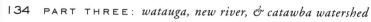

CLASS	I
LENGTH	5.5
TIME	2.5
GAUGE	VISUAL
LEVEL	-6 IN.
PERMITS	No
GRADIENT	2
SCENERY	B

BURKE CR 1438 BRIDGE (30 YDS. UPSTREAM ON EAST BANK) TO NC WILDLIFE ACCESS AREA AT NC 18 BRIDGE

DESCRIPTION: There are no difficulties.

SHUTTLE: Take SR 1405 (Adako Rd.) into Burke County to Rt. 1424. Turn left onto Burke CR 1438 to the bridge. Take out at the NC 18 bridge northwest of Morganton.

GAUGE: Minimum level for solo is 6" below "0."

JACOB FORK RIVER

The Jacob Fork flows out of the South Mountains through an area of rolling hills, until it joins with the Henry Fork. It has been designated as Outstanding Resource Waters by the state. Most of this stretch of river is closed in, with little signs of habitation except in the immediate areas around the bridges. The banks generally abound in laurel and rhododendron.

MAPS: Casar, Banoak, Longview, Hickory (USGS); Burke, Catawba (County)

CLASS	I–II
LENGTH	28.8
TIME	10
GAUGE	VISUAL
LEVEL	2.75 FT.
PERMITS	No
GRADIENT	13
SCENERY	A–B

BURKE CR 1901 BRIDGE TO TO RT. 1139 BRIDGE

DESCRIPTION: In the horseshoe bend between the Burke CR 1907 bridge and the Rt. 1910 bridge there are remains of a 10-ft. dam. Approach very cautiously in higher water levels. Portage on the left.

SHUTTLE: For put-in, take Burke CR 1924 (old NC 18) south of Morganton approximately 12 mi., then go west on Burke CR 1901 to the bridge. To reach the take-out, drive south out of Hickory on the US 321 bypass, turning west at NC 10 and diving to the intersection with Catawba CR 1139. Turn right (north) and drive 3.1 mi. to the CR 1139 bridge. There several other places to set shuttle, including the NC 18 bridge south of Morganton and the Catawba CR 1116 bridge.

GAUGE: The USGS Gauge is at the Burke CR 1924 bridge (old NC 18). Minimum for solo is 2.75. The river can be run

most of the year except during dry spells. There's also a gauge on the NC 127 bridge on the northwest side. Minimum for solo is 4" below "0."

HENRY FORK RIVER

The Henry Fork heads up in the South Mountains and flows east out of Burke County into Catawba County, where it meets the Jacob Fork and forms the South Fork of the Catawba River. The upper sections have been designated as Outstanding Resource Waters by the state. The first 15 mi. flow through an area abounding in laurel and

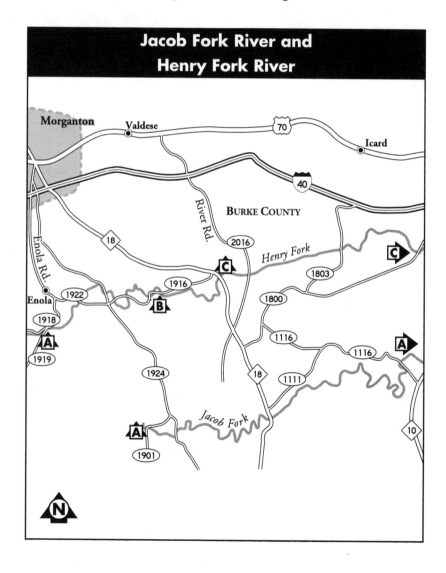

rhododendron, making a very scenic run. The stretches below are generally flat and include two dams. Also, sewage is pumped into the river below the dam at Brookford.

MAPS: Morganton South, Valdese, Longview, Hickory (USGS); Burke, Catawba (County)

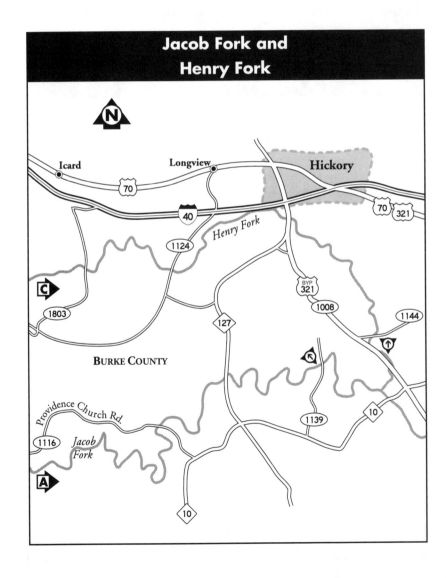

BURKE CR 1919 BRIDGE SOUTH OF ENOLA TO CR 1916 BRIDGE

CLASS	II–III
LENGTH	4.4
TIME	2
GAUGE	VISUAL
LEVEL	1 FT.
PERMITS	No
GRADIENT	36
SCENERY	A–B

DESCRIPTION: There are no difficulties that are dangerous, but a constant gradient of 48 fpm through the first 2.5 mi. will demand great caution. This section consists of many small ledges which are generally followed by pools.

SHUTTLE: Take Enola Rd. south off I-40 at the Western Carolina Exit in Morganton. Proceed to Rt. 1918, the first paved road to the right beyond the community of Enola, and continue to the end of the pavement. To reach the take-out, continue past the first paved road until you reach CR 1924 (old CR 18). Cross the road and continue to the CR 1916 bridge.

GAUGE: It's located on the south side of the NC 18 bridge. The reading should be at the bottom of "1" for a solo run through the first 2.3 mi. to the Rt. 1922 bridge; 4" below "0" from Rt. 1922 to Rt. 1916 is a minimum. Run only after rain.

BURKE CR 1916 BRIDGE, JUST OFF RT. 1924 (OLD NC 18),
TO NC 18 BRIDGE

CLASS	I–III
LENGTH	10.2
TIME	5
GAUGE	VISUAL
LEVEL	-4 IN.
PERMITS	No
GRADIENT	16
SCENERY	A–B

DESCRIPTION: There are no difficulties. You'll find primarily shallows and small shoals in the first half. The second half has several shoals that drop quickly.

SHUTTLE: To reach the put-in, take CR 1924 (old CR 18) out of Morganton and turn left at CR 1916 and continue to the bridge. The take-out is on the CR 18 bridge, though you could shorten the trip by setting shuttle at the second bridge on CR 1916.

GAUGE: Minimum for solo is 4" below "0." This section can be run most of the year except dry seasons.

NC 18 BRIDGE TO CATAWBA CR 1143 BRIDGE

CLASS	I–II
LENGTH	18.5
TIME	7.5
GAUGE	VISUAL
LEVEL	-6 IN.
PERMITS	NO
GRADIENT	151
SCENERY	A–C

DESCRIPTION: Watch for one small rock garden below the NC 18 bridge. A 20-ft. dam at the Henry River Mills is located just below the Catawba CR 1002 bridge, and requires a portage of 150 yds. on the left side around the mill. A 30-ft. dam in the town of Brookford can be portaged on the right bank. Approach with caution.

SHUTTLE: The put-in is south of Morgantown at the CR 18 bridge. The take-out can be reached by taking the US 321 bypass and taking the River Rd. (CR 1144) Exit to the bridge.

GAUGE: Minimum for solo is 6" below "0." The section between the NC 18 bridge and the CR 1803 bridge can be run year round except during extremely dry spells.

SOUTH FORK NEW RIVER

The South Fork begins at the confluence of several small streams southeast of Boone and meanders across the three most northwesterly counties in North Carolina. Then it joins the North Fork and forms the New just south of the Virginia line. It is primarily an easy flowing stream over rocky beds, with occasional riffles as it threads its way between mountains on one side and fields on the other. The South Fork is an excellent stream for canoe camping, even though there are low-water bridges on practically every section that will generally require carrying.

The South Fork is by far the more popular canoe stream of the two forks of the New River. Its popularity is due primarily to its greater length of canoeable water and its easier accessibility. Trips ranging in length from an hour or so up to several days are possible on the South Fork, all in water with only Class I rapids suitable for novice canoeists and canoe camping. There are many open areas and pastures along the South Fork that make beautiful spots to stop for lunch or to camp. There are also four public campgrounds along the South Fork with facilities for camping; all charge a small fee.

The Forks, as well as the New itself, were known as the Teays River on maps showing ancient rivers, and at one time was the master water system of North America. The New cuts north and west across Virginia into West Virginia, where it is joined by the Gauley and becomes the Kanawha.

The river, perhaps the oldest in the country, appeared to be short lived when plans for a giant hydroelectric plant were firming up in the early 1970s. Two dams were planned which would have flooded some 42,000 acres, mostly in North Carolina. After a long hard battle which gathered national support, the river was saved when President Ford signed a bill on September 11, 1976, establishing a 26.5 mile section as a National Wild and Scenic River. This section consists of 22 mi. of the South Fork, plus the first 4.5 mi. of the main stem (most of Sections G and H).

Naturally this has brought an influx of paddlers to the river—especially on the Wild and Scenic section, which quite often has resulted in property damage and hard feelings by residents. Perhaps we can keep this in mind when floating here.

MAPS: Deep Gap, Todd, Glendale Springs, Jefferson, Laurel Springs, Mouth of Wilson (VA) (USGS); Watauga, Ashe, Alleghany, Grayson (VA) (County)

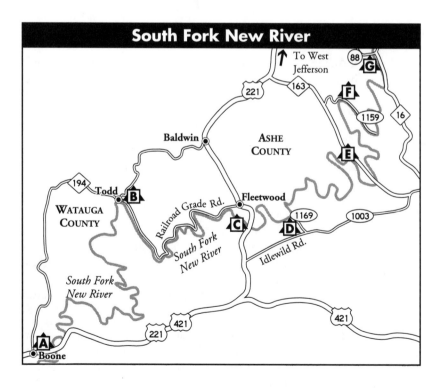

US 421 BRIDGE TO WATAUGA CR 1347

CLASS	I
LENGTH	18
TIME	6
GAUGE	VISUAL
LEVEL	2.5 FT.
PERMITS	No
GRADIENT	6
SCENERY	A–B

DESCRIPTION: There are no difficulties other than low-water bridges and shallow gravel bars at lower water levels. There are, however, many low, overhanging branches.

SHUTTLE: For take-out, go north from Boone on NC 194. River access is in Todd. Return to Boone for put-in, taking US 221/421 east until it crosses river.

GAUGE: The USGS Gauge is on the right bank, 200 yds. upstream of NC 16/88. Minimum for solo is 2.50. There's another gauge on US 221/441 on the southwest side. Minimum for solo is 5" below "0." The river below Todd can be run year round. It would be wise to check the Gauge during spells of extreme dryness to determine the advisability of running the upper section in particular.

TODD TO FLEETWOOD

CLASS	I–II
LENGTH	12
TIME	4.5
GAUGE	VISUAL
LEVEL	2.4 FT.
PERMITS	No
GRADIENT	7
SCENERY	A–B

GAUGE: The river below Todd can be run year round. It would be wise to check the Gauge during spells of extreme dryness to determine the advisability of running the upper section in particular.

DESCRIPTION: Although the section of the river upstream between Boone and Todd is passable in the spring, for most of the year Todd is as far upstream as paddling is practical. SR 1347 runs along the South Fork in the small town of Todd, NC. Railroad Grade Rd. (SR 1100), the pathway of the old railroad bed to Todd, runs alongside the river for this whole section, making it somewhat more populated and less scenic than other sections of the river. There are also many low-water bridges that require portaging. For this reason, this section is not as popular as those further downstream.

There are no difficulties, other than low-water bridges. Watch for one set of shoals about 2 mi. above the take-out.

SHUTTLE: Put in at Todd. The take-out for this section is a low-water bridge just off Railroad Grade Rd. upstream from Fleetwood. This is private property, so permission should be sought before using it or leaving a car there.

FLEETWOOD TO WINDY HILL RD. (SR 1169)

CLASS	I
LENGTH	4.5
TIME	1.5
GAUGE	VISUAL
LEVEL	N/A
PERMITS	No
GRADIENT	5
SCENERY	A–B

DESCRIPTION: The short section of the South Fork between Fleetwood and Windy Hill Rd. is a pretty section that flows under the US 221 bridge along the way. Because of its short length, this section of the river is seldom paddled except as part of a longer trip.

SHUTTLE: The put-in is at the first low-water bridge along Railroad Grade Rd. above Fleetwood. The US 221 bridge is not a practical put-in point because the bridge is very high off the water, necessitating a long carry from the road to the river. There is one low-water bridge downstream from US 221. The take-out is at the low-water bridge on Windy Hill Rd. (SR 1169).

GAUGE: See Section B.

WINDY HILL ROAD (SR 1169) TO DANIEL'S DAUGHTER (NC 163)

CLASS	I
LENGTH	10
TIME	4.5
GAUGE	VISUAL
LEVEL	N/A
PERMITS	No
GRADIENT	5
SCENERY	A

DESCRIPTION: This section of the river is one of the prettiest and most popular for day trips, although there are three low-water bridges to portage along the way. The scenery is spectacular, and the fishing is often quite good in this part of the river. The shuttle to the take-out point is also easy by following Idlewild Rd. to Highway 163 and then toward West Jefferson to Daniel's Daughter.

SHUTTLE: The put-in is at the low-water bridge where Windy Hill Rd. (SR 1169) crosses the river. Windy Hill Rd. runs between US 221 just south of Fleetwood and Idlewild Rd. (SR 1003).

The take-out is at a low-water bridge alongside Highway 163 where it runs next to the river. There is a sign on Highway 163 for Daniel's Daughter, a small development on the opposite side of the river. Please be careful not to block the road or bridge at this take-out point. The low-water bridge just upstream would be a more convenient take-out, but the land is privately owned, and canoeists are not allowed. The Highway 163 bridge just downstream is not practical, since it is high above the river with only a barely passable road going down to the water.

GAUGE: See Section B.

CLASS	I
LENGTH	7
TIME	2.5
GAUGE	VISUAL
LEVEL	N/A
PERMITS	No
GRADIENT	5
SCENERY	A–B

DANIEL'S DAUGHTER (NC 163) TO ELK SHOALS (SR 1159)

DESCRIPTION: This is probably the most popular short (half-day) trip on the South Fork. It is a very scenic section of the river, there are no low-water bridges, and the shuttle is very convenient.

SHUTTLE: The put-in is at the low-water bridge at Daniel's Daughter as described above.

The take-out is at the beach at the Elk Shoals Methodist Campground along Bogg's Rd. (SR 1159). Take Bogg's Rd. off Highway 163 and cross the river on a low-water bridge at the sign to the Elk Shoals Campground. Elk Shoals is open to the public, but since it is a church camp, no drinking is allowed and canoeists should respect the rights of others using the beach.

GAUGE: See Section B.

CLASS	I
LENGTH	I O
TIME	3.5
GAUGE	VISUAL
LEVEL	N/A
PERMITS	No
GRADIENT	5
SCENERY	A–B

ELK SHOALS TO NC 16/88 BRIDGE

DESCRIPTION: The section between Elk Shoals and the Bogg's Rd. bridge is seldom paddled except on longer trips that pass through this section. The 6-mi. section below the Bogg's Rd. bridge is very pretty until the last mile where it runs along NC 16.

SHUTTLE: Put-in is possible at the low-water bridge going into the Elk Shoals Campground, but this necessitates portaging two low-water bridges just downstream. A better put-in is at the bridge where Bogg's Rd. crosses the river about two miles further downstream.

The take-out is at the bridge where NC 16/88 crosses the river. This is shown as Index on USGS maps and is known as Sheet's Store locally. Please do not leave cars along the small road next to the river. There is plenty of room for parking along NC 16.

GAUGE: See Section B.

CLASS	I
LENGTH	10
TIME	3.5
GAUGE	VISUAL
LEVEL	N/A
PERMITS	NO
GRADIENT	5
SCENERY	A–B

NC 16/88 BRIDGE TO GENTRY ROAD BRIDGE (SR 1595)

DESCRIPTION: This is the most heavily used section of the South Fork due to its accessibility and a livery located just upstream. If you want solitude, this is not a part of the river to paddle! About 4 mi. downstream is the old Cockerham Mill, a grist mill used from the late 1800s until the early 1950s. The land is privately owned, and canoeists should not stop. Just downstream on the right bank, opposite a large island, is the Wagoner Rd. Access Area of the New River State Park. Trips can be started or ended here, and the park makes a nice stop-over point for lunch or camping. Canoe-in camping only is allowed, and a small fee is charged.

SHUTTLE: The put-in is at the bridge where NC 16/88 crosses the river. The take-out is at the bridge on Gentry Rd. (SR 1595). Take SR 1593 off US 221 at Nathan's Creek north of Jefferson. Both the put-in and take-out for this run are heavily used, and canoeists should take care in parking to avoid blocking access by other canoeists and the two liveries that service the river in this area.

GAUGE: See Section B.

CLASS	I
LENGTH	15
TIME	6
GAUGE	VISUAL
LEVEL	N/A
PERMITS	NO
GRADIENT	5
SCENERY	A–B

GENTRY RD. TO PINEY CREEK BRIDGE

DESCRIPTION: About 3 mi. downstream of the put-in is a low-water bridge at Fulton Reeves Rd. (SR 1602). This can be used as an alternative take-out to lengthen the trip above or as a put-in to shorten this trip. Another 4 mi. downstream, US 221 crosses the river. This is not a practical put-in or take-out because the bridge is very high over the river, and all the land is privately owned.

SHUTTLE: Put in at the bridge on SR 1595 as described above. The take-out is at the low-water bridge where the old Sparta Rd. (SR 1560) crosses the river. Just downstream from here is the Twin Rivers Campground, a popular camping spot for canoeists. Don't, however, use the campground as a take-out unless you are camping there.

GAUGE: See Section B.

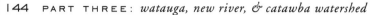

CLASS	I (II)
LENGTH	8
TIME	3
GAUGE	VISUAL
LEVEL	N/A
PERMITS	No
GRADIENT	5
SCENERY	A–B

PINEY CREEK BRIDGE TO MOUTH OF WILSON CREEK

DESCRIPTION: Just downstream is the Twin Rivers Campground, just below which is the only rapid approaching Class II on the whole South Fork. Around the bend from the campground the North Fork joins the South Fork to form the New River itself. From this point on the river is much larger, and offers some beautiful scenic vistas. About 3 mi. below the confluence is the Alleghany County Access Area of the New River State Park. This can be used as a camping or picnic area but does not currently have road access to use as a take-out point.

SHUTTLE: The put-in is at the bridge on SR 1560. The take-out is at a river access site built by the state of Virginia just off Highway 58 under the bridge where NC 93 crosses the river just east of Mouth of Wilson, VA. Shortly downstream from here is a dam that backs up almost to the bridge, so there is little reason to go further.

GAUGE: See Section B.

NORTH FORK NEW RIVER

The North Fork heads up in the extreme western end of Ashe County just over the Tennessee line. It flows northeast in the shadows of The Peak, Three Top Mountain, and Phoenix Mountain on the south before confluencing with the South Fork and forming the New River.

It is primarily a stream of shallow ledges with an occasional gravel bar through its upper reaches. Then it flattens out to where it presents a few riffles and a ledge now and then. River access is quite easy with roads following alongside most of the entire distance. This also gives it a pastoral setting through most of the sections.

MAPS: Baldwin Gap, Warrensville, Jefferson, Grassy Creek, Mouth of Wilson (VA) (USGS); Ashe (County)

South Fork New River and North Fork New River

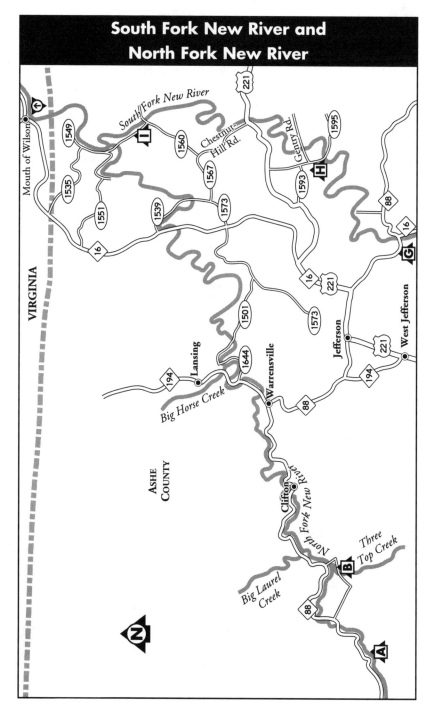

South Fork New River

221

Mouth of Wilson

Chestnut Hill Rd.

Genry Rd.

VIRGINIA

1549

1535

1551

1560

1567

1573

1539

1593

1595

H

88

16

G

16

1501

16

221

1573

194

221

Jefferson

West Jefferson

1644

194

Lansing

Warrensville

88

221

Big Horse Creek

ASHE COUNTY

Clifton

North Fork New River

Three Top Creek

B

Big Laurel Creek

88

A

N

CLASS	I—II
LENGTH	6.6
TIME	3
GAUGE	VISUAL
LEVEL	-4 IN.
PERMITS	No
GRADIENT	11
SCENERY	B

ASHE CR 1119 BRIDGE AT COMMUNITY OF MAXWELL TO RT. 1100 BRIDGE

DESCRIPTION: Watch for a series of gravel bars in the first 1.5 mi. which drop at a rate of about 25 fpm.

SHUTTLE: From Warrensville, go west on NC 88 to Ashe CR 1119, and south to the bridge. The take-out is located on the NC 88 bridge at Creston.

GAUGE: It's located on the northeast piling of the Rt. 1644 bridge at Sprague Electric (Rowie McNeil Rd.). Minimum for solo is 4" below "0." The river can be run from Clifton down most of the year except during extremely dry seasons.

CLASS	I
LENGTH	36.2
TIME	15
GAUGE	VISUAL
LEVEL	-6 IN.
PERMITS	No
GRADIENT	11
SCENERY	A–B

RT. 1100 BRIDGE AT CRESTON TO ASHE CR 1549 BELOW THE CONFLUENCE WITH THE SOUTH FORK

DESCRIPTION: Watch for low-water bridges throughout this section. Below Clifton where the river bends sharply away from NC 88 and then back, there is a 12-ft. dam which can be seen from the highway. Carry on the left. There is a 4-ft. slanting ledge immediately below the dam which can be run with a couple of inches above the minimum.

After passing the NC 16 bridge (north of Jefferson) and just below the next bridge are the remains of a washed out low-water bridge that will require portaging at normal water levels. Carry or scout on the left. One low-water bridge farther downstream should be approached with caution at higher levels.

SHUTTLE: Drive west of Warrensville along NC 88 to the bridge at Creston. To reach the take-out, drive north on NC 16 to Ashe CR 1535 (just south of the Virginia state line). Turn right (east) and go to Ashe CR 1549 along the New River.

There are a number of access points along this stretch to modify the length of your trip. Points along the river include the NC 88 bridge west of Clifton, Ashe CR 1644 low-water bridge (Bernard Miller Rd.) south of Lansing, and the NC 16 bridge.

GAUGE: It's located on the northeast piling of the Rt. 1644 bridge at Sprague Electric (Rowie McNeil Rd.). Minimum for solo is 6" below "0." The river can be run from Clifton down most of the year except during extremely dry seasons.

NEW RIVER

The New begins with the confluence of the North and South Forks. At this point it has already become a fairly wide river although still primarily shallow (see Section F, South Fork, New River). From Mouth of Wilson to Stuart Dam, the New is mostly flat, therefore the reason for omitting these 2.5 mi.

The river flows through forested rolling hills and pastoral lands and in general is a very scenic stream.

MAPS: Mouth of Wilson (VA), Sparta West, Sparta East (NC/VA), Briarpatch Mtn., Galax (VA) (USGS); Grayson (VA), Alleghany (NC) (County)

STUART DAM TO STATE ACCESS AREA ON RIVER LEFT
BELOW US 221/21 BRIDGE (LOCATED ON SR 700)

CLASS	I–III
LENGTH	11.3
TIME	4
GAUGE	VISUAL
LEVEL	N/A
PERMITS	No
GRADIENT	6
SCENERY	B

DESCRIPTION: Downstream 1 mi. from the Grayson CR 601 bridge in the community of Cox Chapel as the river bends to the right there are two rapids. The first, a long Class II, should be scouted from the left in higher water. The second, a couple of hundred yards beyond the first, is a Class III where most of the water flows hard left by a large boulder on the bank. Watch for the drop just beyond the boulder. Attempt to scout on the right. At higher water levels this can be run in the center.

This area of the rapids is where Appalachian Power Company proposed to construct their dam (see South Fork, New River).

SHUTTLE: At Stuart Dam alongside US 58, east of Mouth of Wilson.

GAUGE: None, however the river can be run all year. The river has widened considerably and care should be taken if conditions are such that there might be high water.

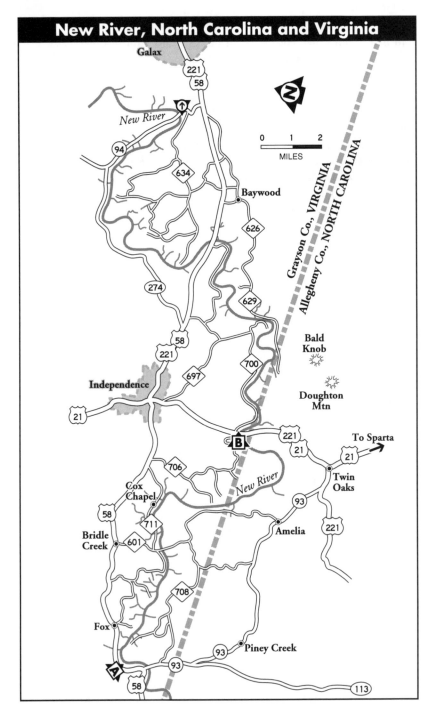

New River, North Carolina and Virginia

Galax

Grayson Co., VIRGINIA
Allegheny Co., NORTH CAROLINA

New River

0   1   2
MILES

Baywood

Bald Knob

Doughton Mtn

Independence

To Sparta

Twin Oaks

Cox Chapel

New River

Bridle Creek

Amelia

Fox

Piney Creek

State Access area below US 221/21 bridge to Access area on Grayson CR 641

CLASS	I–II
LENGTH	26.2
TIME	10
GAUGE	Visual
LEVEL	N/A
PERMITS	No
GRADIENT	5
SCENERY	A–B

DESCRIPTION: There are no difficulties. This is primarily flat with occasional riffles and a few shoals. This is a favorite float trip for canoe camping.

SHUTTLE: Go north on Rt. 634 from US 58/221, then left on Grayson CR 641.

GAUGE: None. The river can be run year round.

LITTLE RIVER

The Little heads up on the slopes of Peach Bottom Mountain and winds its way through the foothills of the Blue Ridge to join the New River in Grayson County, VA. The entire run of the river is quite remote and very scenic.

MAPS: Sparta East (USGS); Alleghany (NC), Grayson (VA) (County)

Alleghany CR 1424 bridge to CR 1433 bridge

CLASS	I–III
LENGTH	7.8
TIME	3.5
GAUGE	Visual
LEVEL	-5 IN.
PERMITS	No
GRADIENT	19
SCENERY	A

DESCRIPTION: Watch for cables and barbed wire below the second bridge (Rt. 1426). About 2 mi. below this bridge, at a point just upstream from where Rt. 1428 comes down to the river on the south side, the river narrows down. About 50 ft. below is a 3.5-ft. ledge, forming a natural dam, followed immediately by a 2-ft. ledge. Carry on the right. At higher levels move right immediately below the narrow chute, since a strong hydraulic is formed below.

Approximately 1 mi. below the confluence of Glade Creek there is a 3-ft. ledge that should be scouted on the far left. Approach it cautiously.

SHUTTLE: Go northeast on NC 18 from Sparta for 1.1 mi., to CR 1424, then east for 1.1. mi. to the bridge. For take-out, continue north on NC 18 to CR 1433, then turn right and continue to the bridge.

GAUGE: It's located on the northwest side of the CR. 1424 bridge. Minimum level for solo is 5" below the bottom of "0." Runnable primarily during wet seasons.

CLASS	I–II
LENGTH	3.4
TIME	1.5
GAUGE	-6 IN.
LEVEL	N/A
PERMITS	No
GRADIENT	16
SCENERY	A

ALLEGHANY CR 1433 BRIDGE TO NC 18

DESCRIPTION: At slightly higher levels the stretch from below the confluence of Brush Creek down to NC 18 can become rather heavy.

SHUTTLE: To reach the put-in, drive north on NC 18 to CR 1433, then turn right and continue to the bridge. Take out where NC 18 crosses the river.

GAUGE: Minimum level for solo is 6" below "0."

CLASS	I–II
LENGTH	7.7
TIME	3
GAUGE	VISUAL
LEVEL	-7 IN.
PERMITS	No
GRADIENT	16
SCENERY	A

NC 18 TO GRAYSON CR 632 BRIDGE

DESCRIPTION: At one point about halfway down this stretch, there is a natural weir which funnels most of the water through a rock garden on the inside of a hard bend to the right. It should be approached cautiously.

SHUTTLE: To reach the put-in from Sparta, go north on NC 18 and put in where it crosses the river. The take-out turn-off is just south of the put-in point. Go north on Alleghany CR 1414, turn right on CR 1412, cross the state line, and turn right again on Grayson CR 632 to the bridge. For those who might like to extend the trip into the New River, there is a run of 3 mi. to the US 58/221 bridge west of Galax, VA.

GAUGE: Minimum level for solo on the Gauge at CR 1424 is 7" below "0." There is also a roughly painted Gauge on the NC 18 bridge. Minimum for solo can be judged as the same distance below the bottom of the "0" as the distance between numbers 1 and 2. Measurement between the numbers varies considerably.

part**Four**

YADKIN RIVER BASIN

NORTH FORK MAYO RIVER

The North Fork of the Mayo flows through heavily wooded hills after leaving the pasture lands at the beginning of the section. It has more gradient than the upper reaches of the South Fork, thus providing a more interesting trip. Once it joins the South Fork, the Mayo is formed and it drops over a series of ledges that give the effect of a natural staircase. The latter part of the trip contains some of the best whitewater available to paddlers in the northern Piedmont and eastern North Carolina. It makes for an excellent training course. You can take out above the last ledges at the CR 1358 bridge, run on down through the good stuff, and take your chances at the old takeout or continue on down to the NC 770 bridge.

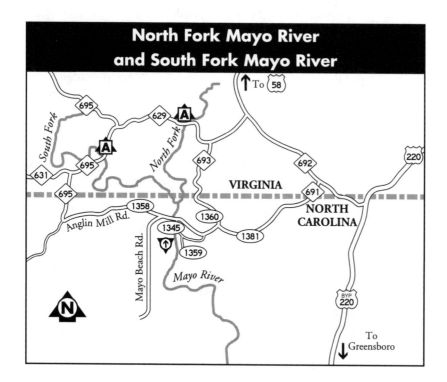

MAPS: Price (VA) (USGS); Henry (VA), Rockingham (County)

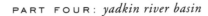

CLASS	II–III
LENGTH	4.2
TIME	2.5
GAUGE	VISUAL
LEVEL	1.55 FT.
PERMITS	NO
GRADIENT	13
SCENERY	B

HENRY CR 629 BRIDGE TO ANGLIN MILL RD. (CR 1358)

DESCRIPTION: Two ledges on the upper section might require scouting. Both are recognizable before getting too close. Both can generally be run on the far left.

Below the confluence, the staircase will require a great deal of maneuvering to locate the best passage in low water, and a great deal of care in high water. Below the CR 1358 bridge, a 3-ft. ledge has a wide open chute on the left. Thirty yds. below it, a series of ledges drop some 8 ft. within 15 yds. This is best entered at left center and by angling diagonally right across the current, before dropping through a slot not much wider than a canoe. A hard left turn must be made immediately, in order to miss the rock in the center of the bottom of the passage. The gradient averages 20 fpm through this last mile.

SHUTTLE: From Rockingham CR 1358 (the extension of Rt. 1381), go north on Rt. 1360 and Henry CR 693 (1.1 mi. east of the CR 1358 bridge) to Henry CR 629, west to the bridge. An old homestead northeast of the bridge has a road down it, which leads to the riverside. This is private property. If in doubt, check at the house across the river before entering. The take out is on Anglin Mill Rd. (CR 1358). For an extended trip, one may wish to paddle on down the Mayo to the NC 770 bridge (distance is 6 mi.; time is 2–2.5 hrs.; Class I, easy take-out directly under the bridge on the east side). Take NC 770 west of US 220 at Stoneville, NC.

GAUGE: The USGS Gauge is 400 ft. south of the CR 629 bridge, on the east bank. Minimum level for solo run is 1.55. Maximum for the lower part of the section is 2.6. Another USGS Gauge is located 300 ft. downstream from the Rockingham CR 1358 bridge, on the west bank. Minimum for solo is 1.38, maximum 2.3. The river can be run year round, except during long dry spells.

SOUTH FORK MAYO RIVER

The South Fork of the Mayo meanders through woodlands, presenting the paddler with easy riffles, until it confluences with the North Fork. From there down to the take-out, the river drops faster over a series of ledges and gives a more challenging course.

MAPS: Spencer, Price (VA) (USGS); Henry (VA), Rockingham (NC) (County)

A

HENRY CR 695 BRIDGE TO ANGLIN MILL RD. (CR 1358)

CLASS	II–III
LENGTH	5
TIME	3
GAUGE	VISUAL
LEVEL	1.38 FT.
PERMITS	NO
GRADIENT	11
SCENERY	A–B

DESCRIPTION: This is primarily a run of easy riffles. For more information on the area below the confluence, refer to the Mayo River, North Fork.

SHUTTLE: Go west on the Rockingham CR 1358 bridge (Stokes CR 1625) to Stokes CR 1630, north to Henry CR 695, then northeast to the bridge. Rt. 695 can also be reached from Rt. 629 west of the North Fork bridge, and then southwest on Rt. 695. The take-out is on Anglin Mill Rd. (CR 1358). For an extended trip, one may wish to paddle on down the Mayo to the NC 770 bridge (distance is 6 mi.; time is 2–2.5 hrs.; Class I, easy take-out directly under the bridge on the east side). Take NC 770 west of US 220 at Stoneville, NC.

GAUGE: The USGS Gauge is 300 ft. downstream from the Rockingham CR 1358 bridge, on the west bank. Minimum level for solo run is 1.38. The river can be run year round except during long dry spells.

DAN RIVER

The Dan River flows off the crest of the Blue Ridge beneath the Pinnacles of Dan. It is piped down the mountains through the turbines of the City of Danville Power Plant above the community of Kibler. From the power plant, it wanders southeast through hills of laurel and rhododendron before turning northeast and entering Virginia just east of Eden. It then flows generally east until it confluences with the Roanoke River.

The Dan was named after Danaho, a Saura Indian chief. The Saura Indians lived along the river, with Saura Town situated near the junction of the Smith and Dan and lower Saura Town located near the former town of Draper.

On the upper section in North Carolina, paddlers will catch glimpses of the Sauratown Mountains to the south. This range is one of the most easterly mountainous areas in the state and is home to Hanging Rock State Park. The park consists of rugged mountain terrain and has excellent camping facilities. The Dan is a North Carolina State Water Trail.

MAPS: Claudville, Stuart S.E. (VA); Hanging Rock, Danbury, Ayersville, Belews Lake, Walnut Cove, Mayodan, South West Eden, South East Eden; Draper, Brosville (NC/VA) (USGS); Patrick (VA); Stokes, Rockingham (NC) (County)

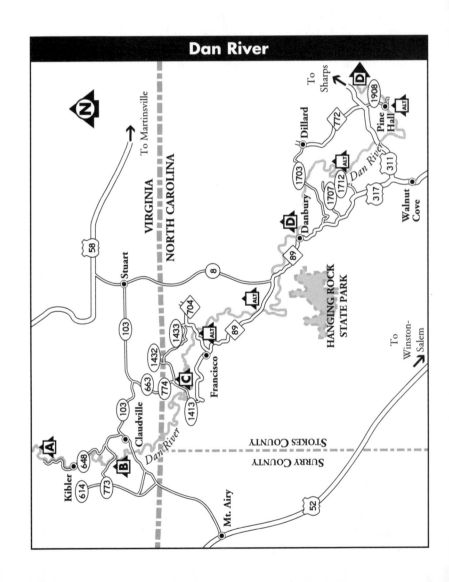

PINNACLES POWER PLANT AT KIBLER TO PATRICK CR 773 BRIDGE

CLASS	I–II
LENGTH	8
TIME	3.5
GAUGE	PHONE
LEVEL	5 600–
	9,600 KW
PERMITS	No
GRADIENT	32 (1 @ 65)
SCENERY	B

DESCRIPTION: The first 0.5 mile below the put-in drops very fast. About 200 yds. below the first bridge, a 3-ft. drop pushes much of the water into a large boulder on the right. If entered too far to the right, much of the boat is also pushed against the boulder. This rock is undercut, so be very cautious in trying to dislodge a broached canoe.

SHUTTLE: From Mt. Airy, NC, drive northeast on VA 103 to Patrick CR 773, northeast to Rt. 648, then north to the end of the road at the city of Danville Power Plant. Ask permission at the plant to launch below. There is not much parking space in the immediate area, so be very careful not to block driveways in any way. For take-out, return to CR 773 and go west to the bridge.

GAUGE: None. To check on the water flow, call Pinnacles Hydroelectric Station, (276) 251-1255 and ask for the water flow. A minimum would be 5,600 kw. Maximum possible flow is 9,600 kw, at which open canoes can run safely. The plant will run 7,500 kw on Saturdays July through October from 9 a.m. to 3 p.m. unless unusual conditions exist.

PATRICK CR 773 BRIDGE TO STOKES CR 1432

CLASS	I–II
LENGTH	12.5
TIME	5.5
GAUGE	VISUAL
LEVEL	1.7 IN.
PERMITS	No
GRADIENT	18
SCENERY	A

DESCRIPTION: Primarily fast water approaches through small rock gardens and over small ledges.

Following the second bridge (Stokes CR 1416) below the VA 103 bridge there are a series of ledges ending in a tight S turn presenting a high Class II. Scout on the left. Old Rt. 1417 (Joyce Mill Rd., which is now closed) is immediately downstream.

SHUTTLE: From Mt. Airy, NC, drive northeast on VA 103. Take Patrick CR 773, and drive past CR 648 to the CR 773 bridge. The take-out is accessed by VA 103, continuing east past the CR 773 turn-off, to CR 663. Go south to CR 774, then continue to CR 1432 (Collinsville Rd.). Turn right and go to the bridge.

GAUGE: The USGS Gauge is located 75 ft. above the NC 704 bridge on the north bank. A reading of 1.7 is minimum for solo, or phone Pinnacles for a reading (5,600 kw minimum).

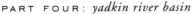

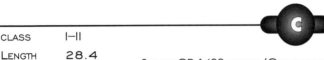

CLASS	I–II
LENGTH	28.4
TIME	13.5
GAUGE	VISUAL
LEVEL	1.7 FT.
PERMITS	No
GRADIENT	10
SCENERY	A–B

STOKES CR 1432 BRIDGE (COLLINSTOWN RD.) AT JESSUPS MILL TO
MORATOCK PARK ACCESS AT DANBURY OFF STOKES CR 1695

DESCRIPTION: Above the NC 704 bridge, there is one rapid where the river drops abruptly over a bed of rocks and narrows down between two large boulders. It is easily recognizable and an excellent lunch stop. There is one sharply undercut bank in a sharp bend to the left, just below the NC 89 bridge access point. Otherwise, paddlers will see small gravel bars at lower water levels.

One more item of note. Past the second bridge after Hanging Rock State Park, be on the lookout for some caves on river right. The more ambitious paddler may be tempted to climb up to them. The problem is the great clusters of poison ivy growing at the entrance.

SHUTTLE: For put-in, drive north from Danbury on NC 8/89. Continue on NC 89 when it veers left, drive through Francisco, and turn right (north) on Asbury Rd., then right again on CR 1432 (Collinstown Rd.) to the bridge. For take-out, take NC 8 south out of Danbury and turn left at Delta Church Rd. to reach the Moratock Park access.

Other possible access points include the NC 704 bridge (Hart's Access), Whitts Highway 89 Access at NC 89, and the Hanging Rock State Park Access off Stokes CR 1487.

GAUGE: A reading of 1.7 is minimum for solo.

CLASS	I–II
LENGTH	57.7
TIME	22.5
GAUGE	VISUAL
LEVEL	N/A
PERMITS	No
GRADIENT	4
SCENERY	A–B

MORATOCK PARK TO RT. 1761 BRIDGE (VA 880)
AT VA STATE LINE

DESCRIPTION: Just above the CR 1712 access points are the remains of a dam that was blown up with dynamite and could prove dangerous. Scouting is easy from river right. A 6-ft. dam located just above CR 1138 and opposite the brick yard can best be carried on river right (a 40-yd. carry).

Paddlers should also be wary of a series of small, washed-out dams downstream from the US 220 bridge. They extend for some 100 yds., with steel rods exposed; however, the center is clear. Finally, another 6-ft.-high dam located 1.2 mi. downstream from the NC 14 bridge has a fairly strong hydraulic. A short carry on the right will be necessary.

Dan River

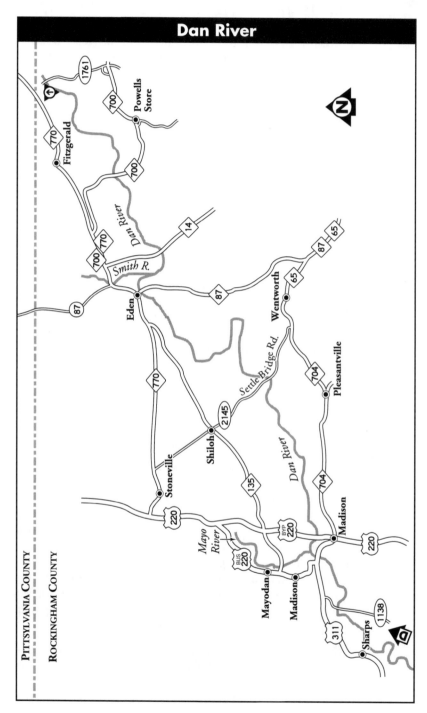

PITTSYLVANIA COUNTY

ROCKINGHAM COUNTY

1761

700 Powells Store

770 Fitzgerald

700

Dan River

14

87 65

65 Wentworth

87

700 770

Smith R.

700

87

Eden

770

Settle Bridge Rd.

704 Pleasantville

2145

Shiloh

Stoneville

Dan River

704

135

220

Mayo River

BYP 220

Madison

220

BIS 220

Mayodan Madison

311

1138

Sharps

SHUTTLE: For put-in, take NC 8 south out of Danbury and turn left at Delta Church Rd. to reach the Moratock Park access. To reach the take-out from Eden, drive east on NC 770 to the Virginia state line. Turn right at Berry Hill Bridge Rd. (VA 880) and drive south to the bridge.

Since this is a long section, there are many places to shorten the trip. Some of these include the Hemlock Golf Course Access of Power Dam Rd. (CR 1712) on CR 1732, the NC 772 bridge access in Pine Hall, Rockingham CR 1138 (Lindsay Bridge Rd. access), CR 2145 bridge access, and the Wildlife Access area off CR 2309 south of Leaksville.

GAUGE: This section is runnable year round except during dry seasons.

BUFFALO CREEK

The Buffalo flows from the junction of several small streams in Buffalo Cove. It courses through a small valley until it cuts through a deep remote gorge. After leaving the gorge it comes back along the highway before leveling out slightly as it confluences with the Yadkin. The Buffalo throughout its course is a small, low-water stream flowing over gravel bars with a few small ledges.

MAPS: Buffalo Cove (USGS); Caldwell (County)

CLASS	IV
LENGTH	5.2
TIME	2.5
GAUGE	VISUAL
LEVEL	3FT
PERMITS	YES
GRADIENT	888
SCENERY	B

RT. 1503 BRIDGE TO NC 268 BRIDGE

DIFFICULTIES: There are two broken dams on this section, the first of which is located in the first gorge the stream enters below the put-in. The chute appears open but a large rock and an iron bar which are barely under the surface can easily damage a boat attempting to pass through.

The second dam, about 10-ft. high, can be seen from the Rt. 1505 bridge where the Gauge is located. It should be approached very carefully when the water is high enough to be flowing over the top. It can be portaged on the left bank.

SHUTTLE: From the US 321 and NC 268 intersection at Patterson, drive northeast to CR 1504 and turn left. Drive north to the Rt. 1503 bridge. Take out at the junction of Buffalo Creek with the Yadkin River, about 50 yds. from the NC 168 bridge over the Yadkin.

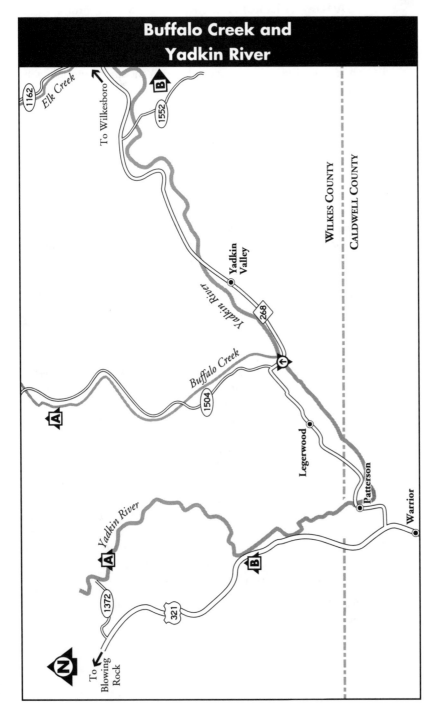

Buffalo Creek and Yadkin River

GAUGE: It's located on the Rt. 1505 low-water bridge on the northwest side. Go to water level on the northeast side to read. A minimum level of 6" below "0" is required for solo. Rt. 1505 is the first road on the right off Rt. 1504 after leaving NC 268. The best water level will be obtained during the spring and following runoffs from rain.

YADKIN RIVER

The Yadkin heads up in the mountain resort town of Blowing Rock and flows through a remote mountainous area of Caldwell County before coming alongside US 321 about 3 mi. north of Patterson. It moves generally northeasterly through Happy Valley into Kerr Scott Lake, and then meanders through five counties before entering the impoundment at High Rock Lake in Davidson County. Two additional impoundments, Badin and Tillery, follow immediately after which the Yadkin becomes the Pee Dee and flows into South Carolina.

The river is primarily pastoral down from Patterson, moving over occasional low ledges and through shallow rock gardens. Below Kerr Scott Dam it continues on much the same, although considerably wider and with fewer rapids, until it makes the big bend to the south below Siloam. Here, it drops fairly fast for a couple of miles over a series of shoals, which can become formidable in medium high waters.

The one other point of difficulty on the river is Idols Dam, which is downstream from the I-40 bridge and just below Tanglewood Park. Water flows over the dam and it should be approached with great caution.

Naturally, a water way crossing as much of a state as the Yadkin does carries with it much history—in fact, too much to delve into here in any detail. However, it is of interest to note that in the 1760s, the Daniel Boone family had two home sites in the vicinity of Section B, between the NC 268 bridge and NC 26 bridge. The first was near Beaver Creek, about 0.75 mi. south of the river, where the hearth still stands; the second was on the north side of the river just below the mouth of Beaver Creek. It was from here that Boone left on his trek to Kentucky in April, 1775.

MAPS: Buffalo Cove, Lenoir, Grandin, Boomer (USGS); Caldwell, Wilkes (County)

CR 1372 (Richland Rd.) bridge to US 321

CLASS	III–IV+
LENGTH	7
TIME	3
GAUGE	VISUAL
LEVEL	-4 IN.
PERMITS	No
GRADIENT	63
SCENERY	A

DESCRIPTION: The upper Yadkin is strictly a high-water run. As with any tiny watershed, it must be caught during or after major rainfall. The river, like most headwater tributaries, picks up volume quickly. The scenery is quite pleasant, though not as spectacular as many gorges in the area. The stream flows through pasture land for the first half mile, making the bulls on shore the largest danger. The first 1.5 mi. are Class I and II and then there is a 6-ft. drop that is best run in the center. The meat of the run begins in 1.5 mi.

Once into the gorge, the river drops 200 ft. in 1.8 mi., and is somewhat reminiscent of the Chauga Gorge. The entrance to the steep section is noted by a very constricted run through large boulders. This is followed by an 8-ft. drop into a boulder choke that is best run on the left. Below this drop are several long, steep boulder gardens that will test any boater. The steepest drop on the river, Main Squeeze, is quite undercut and should only be attempted at higher levels due to bow pin possibilities. Beware of downed trees, some in very critical places. About 0.75 mi. above the take-out, the gradient slows down to Class II. This stretch is well worth your time if you can catch it with water.

SHUTTLE: Take US 321 north of Lenoir to SR 1372 (Richland Rd.). Take a right on SR 1372 and go 1.7 mi. to the bridge over the river. The take-out is located on US 321 north of Lenoir. Take out 100 yds. upstream of the store on the old roadbed.

GAUGE: Check the first wooden plank bridge 0.5 mi. downstream of take-out. The gauge is on the river right piling and water should be 4" below the bottom of "0" for a minimum level.

US 321 to the end of Wilkes CR 1137 on Kerr Scott Lake

CLASS	I–II
LENGTH	23
TIME	10.5
GAUGE	VISUAL
LEVEL	SEE BELOW
PERMITS	No
GRADIENT	21
SCENERY	B

DESCRIPTION: There is one portage around a 12-ft. dam about 1.75 mi. into the run. Below the NC 268 bridge near Patterson, the river narrows considerably just below the put-in, so the possibility of blocked passages always exists.

SHUTTLE: Take US 321 north of Lenoir to Annes Country Cubbard. Put in 100 yds. upstream of the store on the old roadbed. For take-out, drive 3.9 mi. east of the community of Ferguson, on NC 268 to Wilkes CR 1137 and north 1.5 mi. to the lake.

Paddlers have the option to shorten the trips, by accessing the river at these places: the NC 268 bridge at Patterson, the NC 26 bridge at Buffalo Creek, or the Caldwell CR 1552 bridge.

GAUGE: Above the NC 268 bridge, check the first wooden plank bridge 0.5 mi. downstream of the put-in. The gauge is on river right piling and water should be 4" below the bottom of "0" for a minimum level. There is also a USGS Gauge located 50 yds. above the NC 268 bridge in Patterson, on the east bank. Minimum reading for solo is 1.28. Below the NC 268 bridge, the river can be run all year. It would be tight through a couple of shoals in very dry periods.

ELK CREEK

Elk Creek cuts through the deep valley below Elk Ridge on its way to join the Yadkin River just below Elkville. It is a small, fast-moving stream meandering through farmlands before making a last dash, dropping through a beautiful gorge above Elkville.

MAPS: Grandin (USGS); Wilkes (County)

CLASS	I–II
LENGTH	8.4
TIME	4
GAUGE	VISUAL
LEVEL	1.15 FT.
PERMITS	No
GRADIENT	23
SCENERY	A–B

Ⓐ

RT. 1162 ABOVE DARBY TO NC 268 BRIDGE

DESCRIPTION: Watch for the many small pebble fields and rock gardens. The last 600 yds. through the gorge drop rather fast over ledges that will require a lot of maneuvering. Much of the gorge can be scouted from CR 1162 when the foliage isn't too thick. With higher water levels (above 1.55), scouting closely will become a necessity.

SHUTTLE: Go to Wilkes CR 1162 off NC 268 at Elkville, to where the road touches the river just above the community of Darby. At low-water levels, put-in can be made 4.3 mi. above NC 268 alongside the road. This cuts the trip almost in half. Take out below the last ledge, about 100 yds. above the NC 268 bridge, on the east bank. This is private property; ask permission at the building above.

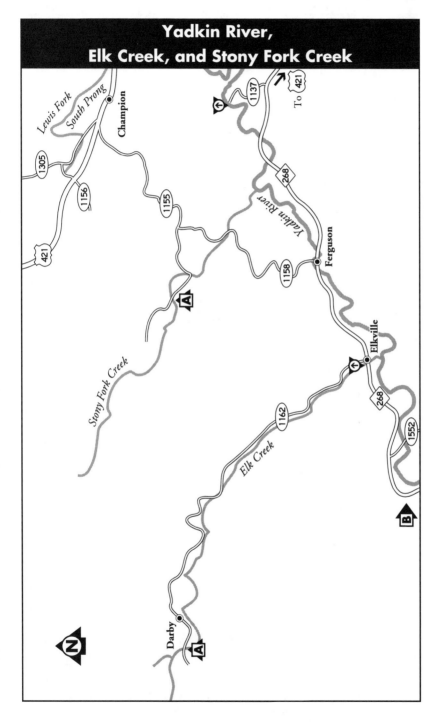

Yadkin River, Elk Creek, and Stony Fork Creek

GAUGE: The USGS Gauge is located 100 ft. above the last ledge on stream, above the NC 268 bridge on the east bank. Minimum reading for solo paddling is 1.15. This is a low-water stream which can be run in the spring and during or following rains.

STONY FORK CREEK

The Stony Fork runs off of the slopes of Tompkins Knob, off the Blue Ridge Parkway, and winds its way between Dividing Ridge and Elk Ridge, before confluencing with the Yadkin River above Kerr Scott Reservoir. It is a small, fast-moving stream, dropping over many small ledges.

It might be worth noting that it was in this area, between the Stony Fork and Elk Creek, that Tom Dooley of "Hang Down Your Head" fame supposedly did his dastardly deed.

MAPS: Grandin, Boomer (USGS); Wilkes (County)

CLASS	I–III
LENGTH	6
TIME	3
GAUGE	VISUAL
LEVEL	-6 IN.
PERMITS	No
GRADIENT	15
SCENERY	A

WILKES CR 1155 (MT. ZION RD.) TO RT. 1137, ON KERR SCOTT LAKE

DESCRIPTION: Watch for primarily ledges of 12- to 18-in. high, until just above the Yadkin, where it drops considerably faster. This can be recognized by a large tree, which blocks most of the river. Directly behind it on the right, most of the stream pours down a 4-ft. drop into a great deal of turbulence and continues on down through a boulder garden. The total drop is some 9–10 ft. within about 50 ft.

SHUTTLE: From US 421 go approximately 9 mi. west of Wilkesboro to CR 1154, then south to CR 1155 and left approximately 2 mi. to the put-in, just above a bridge crossing a small stream coming into the Stony Fork. From Ferguson on NC 268, go northwest on CR 1135 (which becomes 1158 after crossing the Stony Fork) to CR 1155 and left approximately 2 mi.

For take-out, go 3.9 mi. east of Ferguson on NC 268 to Wilkes CR 1137, and north 1.5 mi. to the lake. Approximately 0.75 mi., mostly backwaters, can be eliminated by taking out up a rather steep bank along NC 268, about 2.5 mi. east of Ferguson.

GAUGE: It's located on the northeast side of the Rt. 1135 bridge (Mt. Pleasant Rd.) facing west. Minimum for solo is 6" below the bottom of "0." The creek is generally runnable during wet seasons.

LEWIS FORK NORTH PRONG

The North Prong of the Lewis Fork heads up on the slopes of the Blue Ridge, and winds its way through the valley between Yates Mountain on the south and Judd Mountain on the north, before joining the South Prong and running on into the Kerr Scott impoundment. The stream is primarily one of ledges, presenting a natural slalom course in several stretches. Most of the run is through a secluded area, until the last mile or so, where it becomes more pastoral.

MAPS: Purlear (USGS); Wilkes (County)

WILKES CR 1304 BRIDGE TO RT. 1307,
JUST BELOW THE CONFLUENCE OF THE SOUTH PRONG

CLASS	II–III
LENGTH	4.2
TIME	2.5
GAUGE	VISUAL
LEVEL	-5 IN.
PERMITS	NO
GRADIENT	34
	(0.6 @ 66)
SCENERY	A

DESCRIPTION: About 10 yds. below the first ledge, extending across the entire river bed, are two strands of barbed wire. The first can be raised and the second can be paddled over at a decent water level.

In the second mile, just beyond a bend to the right, there is a drop of some 20 ft. within 80 yds. This stretch can best be scouted from the left.

A few hundred feet above the take-out, a large tree blocks the passage at the Rt. 1311 bridge. This can become a dangerous spot at higher water levels. At lower levels a boat can be worked around on the left slide.

SHUTTLE: Go west on US 421 approximately 8 mi. from Wilkesboro, to CR 1307 (just beyond the 421 bridge over the Lewis Fork), then north to CR 1304 and right for approximately 1 mi. to the 1304 bridge. There is limited parking here, so be careful not to park in yards. The take-out is a couple of hundred yds. north of US 421 on CR 1307.

A run of an additional 4 mi. can be made by extending the trip down the Lewis Fork into Kerr Scott Lake, and taking out at Smithey's Creek Public Use Area. This can be reached by going east 1 mi. from CR 1307 on US 421, to CR 1145 and then south.

GAUGE: It's located on the east side of the Rt. 1304 bridge, at the put-in. Minimum for solo is a reading of 5" below the "0." The river is generally runnable during wet seasons. A reading of 1" or 2" above the bottom of the "0" is probably maximum.

LEWIS FORK SOUTH PRONG

The South Prong of the Lewis Fork runs along US 421 between Dividing Ridge and Yates Mountain, to join the North Prong before entering Kerr Scott Lake. The run here is primarily over small gravel bars interspersed with an occasional ledge, through a fairly remote wooded area.

MAPS: Purlear (USGS); Wilkes (County)

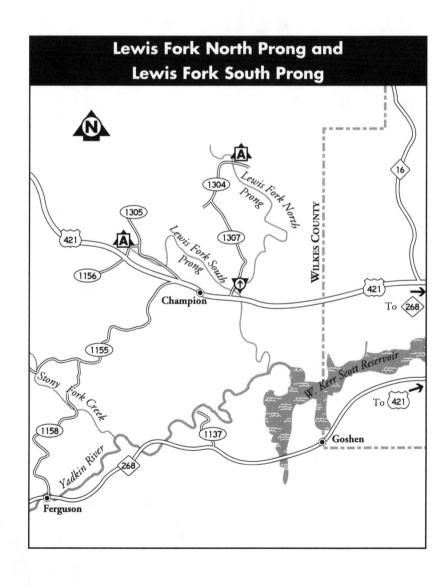

WILKES CR 1156 BRIDGE TO CR 1307,
JUST BELOW THE CONFLUENCE OF THE NORTH PRONG

CLASS	I–II
LENGTH	3.5
TIME	2
GAUGE	VISUAL
LEVEL	-6 IN.
PERMITS	No
GRADIENT	25
	(0.4 @ 50)
SCENERY	A

DESCRIPTION: There is one slanting ledge, easily recognizable, which should be approached rather cautiously at higher water levels. The overall drop throughout the entire run is fairly gradual.

SHUTTLE: Travel west on US 421 approximately 9 mi. from Wilkesboro to Rt. 1154; then go northwest to the bridge, then left beyond the bridge on Rt. 1305 for 0.6 mi. to the put-in. The take-out is a couple of hundred yds. north of US 421 on Rt. 1307.

GAUGE: It's located on the south side of the Rt. 1154 bridge. Minimum for solo is a reading of 6" below the "0." The river is generally runnable during wet seasons.

REDDIES RIVER

The Reddies flows out of the Blue Ridge Mountains between Judd Mountain and Burke Mountain to North Wilkesboro, where it joins the Yadkin River. Mostly it flows through forested land interspersed with farm land. The first 2 mi., with a 20 fpm gradient, is where it's at—the whitewater, that is—but the entire section, except for the last mile, will give the paddler a pleasant float trip.

MAPS: Wilkesboro (USGS); Wilkes (County)

RT. 1546 TO CITY LIMITS OF NORTH WILKESBORO

CLASS	I–II (III)
LENGTH	10
TIME	4.5
GAUGE	VISUAL
LEVEL	1.30 FT.
PERMITS	No
GRADIENT	12
SCENERY	A–B

DESCRIPTION: The Class III rapid is in the first mile, where a series of three ledges drop about 12 ft. within 20 yds. Scout on the left and enter on the left. This stretch of 2 mi. from the put-in to Rt. 1540, which includes the Class III, can be run in less than one hour.

SHUTTLE: Take NC 16 about 8.5 mi. north of US 421 to Rt. 1546, and then east about 0.5 mi. to a gravel pit. This is private property, so observe it as such. For the take-out, drive to the

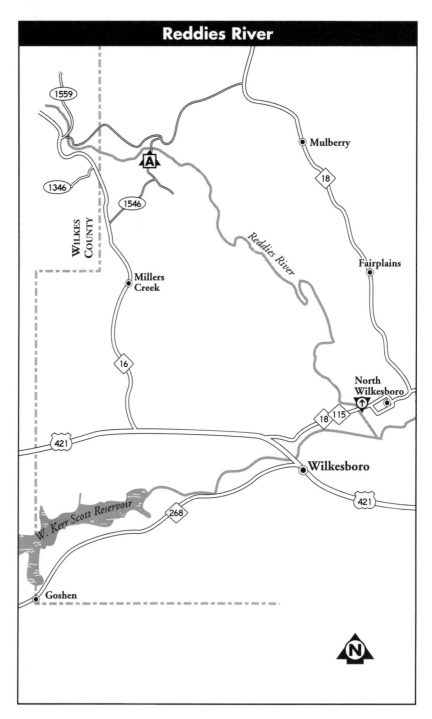

Reddies River

grade road immediately east of the US 421-A bridge, and north to North Wilkesboro city limits, which is beyond the city sewage treatment plant.

GAUGE: The USGS Gauge is on the east bank 400 ft. upstream from the Rt. 1517 bridge. Minimum for solo is 1.30. The river can be run year round, except during prolonged dry spells.

MITCHELL RIVER

The Mitchell flows off the foothills of the Blue Ridge to join the Yadkin. It is a fast, low-water stream flowing over small ledges and through rock gardens. The water quality is generally quite clear, while the heavily wooded banks give the impression of complete wilderness. If the water table remained at a high enough level much of the year, this would surely be one of North Carolina's most popular float streams.

MAPS: Elkin North (USGS); Surry (County)

A

RT. 1315 BRIDGE TO NC 268 BRIDGE

CLASS	I–II
LENGTH	10.5
TIME	5
GAUGE	VISUAL
LEVEL	2.5 FT.
PERMITS	No
GRADIENT	19
SCENERY	A

DESCRIPTION: This river is characterized by fast water running through rock gardens. There is also a 3-ft. ledge located just above the take-out. This can present a hydraulic at higher water levels.

GAUGE: The USGS Gauge is located at the end of CR 1498 just off Rt. 1001 and west of the bridge. A minimum reading of 2.5 is necessary for solo running. The river can be run during the spring and after rain.

SHUTTLE: Put in at the Surry CR 1315 bridge, east off US 21 and 1 mi. east of the town of Mountain Park. Take out at the NC 268 bridge, 4.5 mi. east of the Elkin city limits, and just above its confluence with the Yadkin River. A run of an additional 4.5 mi. can be made by extending the trip into the Yadkin and taking out at the US 601 bridge at Crutchfield. The trip can also be shortened by taking out at the CR 1001 bridge just south of Zephyr.

FISHER RIVER

The author feels the Fisher is the ideal stream for the novice to begin his fast water paddling. It presents no very difficult rapids, primarily

small riffles, but does require one to maneuver the craft and read the water well. The banks are pretty with many hillsides solid with rhododendron and for the most part there is little evidence of habitation. In the spring, the Fisher appears to teem with wildlife. For a nice leisurely paddle, try the Fisher.

MAPS: Dobson, Copeland (USGS); Surry (County)

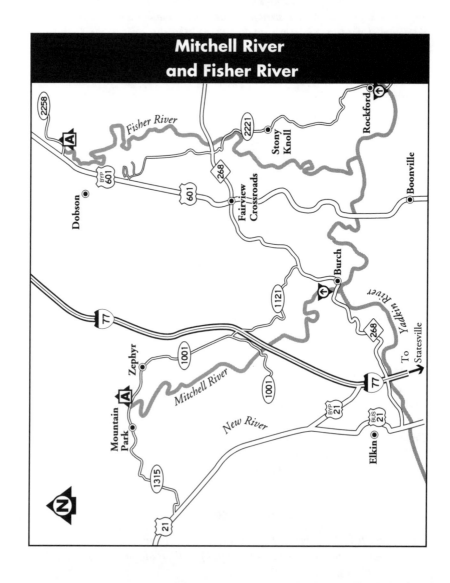

A

SURRY CR 2258 BRIDGE TO ROCKFORD

CLASS	I–II
LENGTH	20
TIME	9
GAUGE	VISUAL
LEVEL	2.20 FT.
PERMITS	No
GRADIENT	8
SCENERY	A–B

DESCRIPTION: Paddlers will find shallows and pebble fields throughout the 20-mile section. A washed-out dam just below the NC 268 bridge should be approached cautiously. A Class II located between the second and third bridges can be recognized by the large flat rock blocking most of the stream. Best passage at lower levels is on the far left. At 2.90 or above, the right side of the left channel can be run. If one looks closely one will find the large rock is pock-marked with garnets.

Watch out for the low-water bridge at higher water levels after entering the Yadkin.

A slightly shorter run can be made by combining the last part of Section A and the major part of Section B. Put in at approximately the 8 mi. point.

SHUTTLE: Put in at the old US 601 bridge northeast of Dobson. For take-out, drive south on Surry CR 2221, off NC 268 (0.3 mi. west of the 268 bridge), to Rockford Community Park, 0.3 mi. south of Rockford. This will be 200 yds. downstream from the Yadkin CR 1510 low-water bridge on the north bank. If Yadkin is high, take out on the north bank just above the low-water bridge.

Other access points include the CR 1100 bridge, the NC 268 bridge, or the Rt. 2233 bridge.

GAUGE: The USGS Gauge is at the NC 268 bridge, 500 ft. upstream on the east bank. Minimum level for solo run is 2.20.

UWHARRIE RIVER

The Uwharrie heads up west of Asheboro and flows generally south through the Uwharrie Mountains and across portions of the Uwharrie National Forest before it flows into Lake Tillery. The river meanders greatly through small floodplains and steep valley walls, which present some very scenic bluffs. The streambed is primarily one of long pools with occasional ripples.

The area is widely known for its gold mining activity. North Carolina's first deep gold mines were found in Montgomery County in the early 1820s. In fact, several mines were worked along the river itself late in the nineteenth century. The largest of these was the Coggins Mine, just up Rt. 1301, west of the river. This was the most important

Uwharrie River

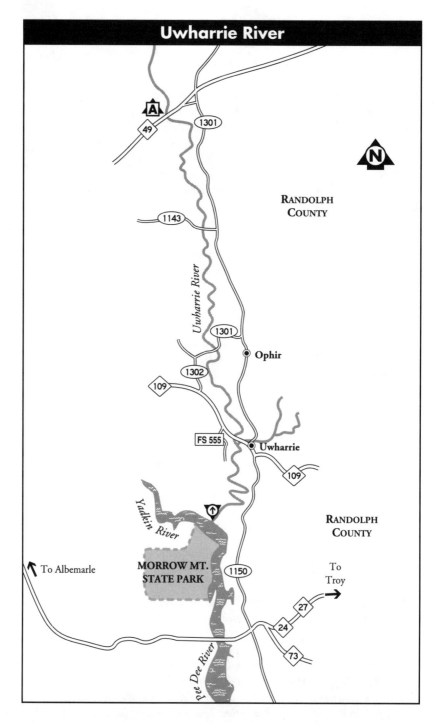

RANDOLPH COUNTY

RANDOLPH COUNTY

Uwharrie River

• Ophir

• Uwharrie

Yadkin River

MORROW MT. STATE PARK

To Albemarle

To Troy

Pee Dee River

mine in the state from 1915 until the late 1920s. The paddler may want to bring along a pan and take a longer than usual lunch break. It may pay for the gas to run the shuttle—one way, that is!

Note to hikers: *The Uwharrie National Recreational Trail runs beside the Uwharrie. This 21-mile trail starts on SR 1306 near Ophir and goes south to NC 24/27.*

MAPS: Asheboro, Albemarle (USGS); Randolph, Montgomery (County)

NC 49 BRIDGE TO RANDOLPH MORROW
MOUNTAIN STATE PARK

CLASS	I–II
LENGTH	36.4
TIME	14
GAUGE	VISUAL
LEVEL	1.6 FT.
PERMITS	No
GRADIENT	3
SCENERY	A–B

DESCRIPTION: Watch for an occasional downed tree. A 5-ft. dam located just above the CR 1143 bridge can be carried fairly easily on the left side. Approach cautiously at higher water levels. Some two miles of back water will be found above here.

SHUTTLE: From Asheboro, drive southwest on NC 49 to where it crosses the Uwharrie River. The take-out is at Morrow Mountain State Park, off of NC 740, northeast of Albemarle. For those who wish to extend the trip some 6 mi. down the lake, a boat launching ramp is located on the east side below the NC 24/27/73 bridge, southeast of Troy. Other access points include the Randolph CR 1143 bridge, the Montgomery CR 1301 bridge, and the bridge to the side of FS 555 (Cotton Place Rd.), 2.9 mi. below the NC 109 bridge.

GAUGE: The USGS Gauge is 100 yds. downstream from NC 109 on the north bank. Minimum for solo is 1.6. The river is runnable year round except during extremely long dry periods.

part**Five**

Nearby Rivers

CHATTOOGA RIVER

The Chattooga rises as a sparkling mountain stream near Cashiers, NC, in the vicinity of Whitesides Mountain. It flows 10 mi. before leaving North Carolina, and continues on for some 40 mi. as the boundary line between South Carolina and Georgia, before entering the impoundment at Lake Tugaloo. In this 50 mi. the river drops 2,469 ft., for an average drop of 49.3 fpm.

The river cuts down the magnificent Chattooga Gorge, providing many rugged whitewater cascades through an area that is almost totally wild and natural. Upon reaching Nicholson Fields above Rt. 28, it becomes a more pastoral area and continues as such to Turn Hole. Beyond there, it slowly begins to revert back to its wild and rugged characteristics and is accessible at only five points within the next 24 mi.

It is one of the longest and largest free-flowing rivers in the Southeast and is the only mountain river in a four state area without substantial development along its banks. Its outstanding scenery and unspoiled wilderness is protected with its status as a National Wild and Scenic River. With this protection the river hopefully will be preserved in a natural state for generations to come, so that they may see what their forefathers saw—a wild and free-flowing river. In order to continue this preservation, certain conditions must be followed:

1. Each float party leader must register.
2. All floaters, including inner-tubers, must wear a life jacket rated "Coast Guard Approved."
3. All persons in decked craft, and ALL floaters below Woodall Shoals, must wear a helmet.
4. Minimum party size: Above Earls Ford—2 persons, 1 craft; Below Earls Ford—2 persons, 2 craft.
5. Inner-tubes are prohibited below Earls Ford.
6. Rafts must have a minimum of two air chambers.
7. All floating is prohibited north of SC 28.

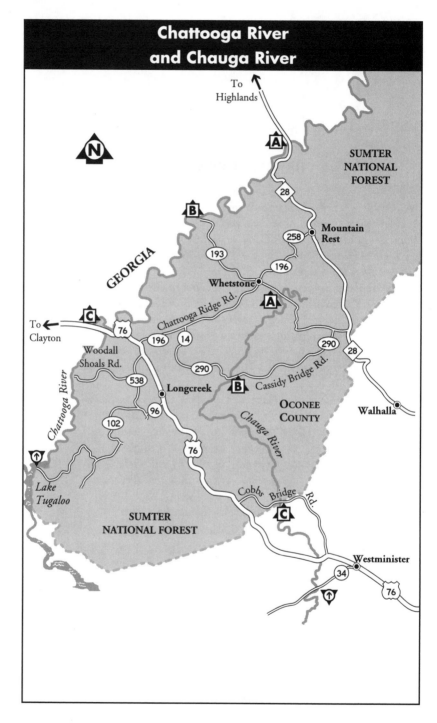

Chattooga River and Chauga River

8. *Air mattresses, motorized craft, or other craft deemed unsuitable by the US Forest Service, are prohibited.*

As of the summer of 2001, the Forest Service has proposed to limit the number of private boaters floating on the Chattooga. This was still unresolved as the book went to press. For current information, contact the Andrew Pickens Ranger District at (864) 638-9568. Also of note: There is a parking fee of $3 at Thrifts Ferry, Highway 76, and Woodall Shoals parking areas.

The stretch from Burrels Ford to the SC 28 bridge, usually referred to as Section A, has not been included because of the extreme gradient of the upper part of the section. Also, floating above Rt. 28 is prohibited at this time by the Forest Service.

The stream that heretofore had been known to a few trout fishermen, backpackers, and canoeists was made famous by the 1972 film, Deliverance. *It brings many canoeists and rafters to the river who know little of what to expect and who quite often are ill equipped to handle what they find. It is for this reason that the author has gone into greater detail in describing certain rapids in the river than has been done on other rivers. Hopefully such knowledge will persuade the unprepared adventure seeker to reconsider and arm himself with the skill that the Chattooga demands of those who seek her unspoiled beauty.*

MAPS: Satolah, Rainy Mtn., Tugaloo Lake (GA); Whetstone (SC) (USGS); Oconee (SC); Rabun (GA) (County)

RT. 28 BRIDGE (RUSSELL BRIDGE) TO EARLS FORD

CLASS	I–III
LENGTH	7
TIME	3.5
GAUGE	VISUAL
LEVEL	0.72 FT.
PERMITS	YES
GRADIENT	11
SCENERY	A

DESCRIPTION: The water is generally shallow and slow to the mouth of the West Fork where the current picks up.

Long Bottom Bridge, about 2.5 mi. downstream, must be carried, so the novice paddler should approach with care.

Turn Hole is the first rapid of any consequence. Here the water pushes the canoe into the left bank and a strong pull to the right is necessary in order to stay out of the branches. Following Turn Hole is a series of rapids which require one to maneuver back and forth across the streambed.

Big Shoals, the Class III, can be recognized by the big rock ledges that appear to block most of the center and left side. The run is to the far right through an open chute which twists slightly to the left at the bottom. The drop is about 5 ft. Scout from the ledge in the center and carry over there if necessary.

Small riffles and shoals continue on down to just above Earls Ford where passage becomes a little more complex. Beginners and novices should not attempt to continue beyond here.

SHUTTLE: Put in along the SC/GA border at the Highway 28 bridge. To reach the take-out, drive south on Highway 28 to Mountain Rest, and turn right on Chattooga Ridge Rd. Drive to the four-way stop (Whetstone). Turn right on Whetstone and drive to the end of the pavement and beyond on the graded road to the river and Earls Ford. There is a 1,400-ft. carry from the river to the parking area.

GAUGE: There's a metal gauge on the Georgia side of the Rt. 28 bridge. A minimum reading of 0.72 and a maximum of 2.23 indicate the optimum levels.

EARLS FORD TO US 76 BRIDGE

CLASS	III–IV (V)
LENGTH	12.5
TIME	6
GAUGE	VISUAL
LEVEL	1.3 FT.
PERMITS	YES
GRADIENT	30
SCENERY	A+

DESCRIPTION: The second rapid below Earls Ford should be entered on the left side of the river, then turn hard left dropping over a 3-ft. ledge, which in lower water levels, puts the bow on a rock just under the surface at the bottom. This rapid gives the paddler a quick idea of whether he should be here or not. If trouble occurs here, it is not too late to head back, for several rapids follow that are much more difficult.

About 400 yds. beyond, the river passes through Rock Gardens, where great slabs of angular rock stick up out of the river. Several scenes in *Deliverance* were filmed here.

The next rapid of any consequence is Dick's Creek Ledge, which is recognized by Five Finger Falls cascading down on the Georgia side. Scout on the right center, which is also the best place to portage. For those wishing to run this, an S turn is required. The first drop should be entered with the bow angled to the right as the canoe slides down the ledge and drops into the small pool above the next ledge. Do not attempt to enter from the left side at the top.

The next two rapids should be run to the right of the respective islands. Below these rapids is Sandy Ford, which is the last place to take out for those who find the river more than they can handle. There is a very rough road negotiable only by four-wheel-drive vehicles, on the Georgia side.

Mild rapids follow, and then a calm pool before the river bears left. Around the bend is the Narrows, where three concentric ledges funnel the river into a constricted canyon. Enter toward

the left. Two more drops follow as the river narrows down even more. Beware of the turbulent cross-currents below these drops. It is very difficult to get through the entrance ledges without swamping if paddling tandem. A beautiful cliff overhangs the river below the last drop. This makes an excellent lunch stop.

Second Ledge is around the next bend. Scout or portage it on the right. This can be run on the left side by sliding down across the face of the falls, not too easy by any means. At higher levels, run down the right center, if possible, with a hard right turn into the pool; eddy turn, then drop through a small slot in the bottom ledge.

Eye of the Needle, about 1.5 mi. beyond Second Ledge, is entered on the extreme left. A rock ledge extends about halfway across the river from the right, forcing most of the water through a twisting chute dropping to the right. Don't lean to the right and you'll arrive upright. *Note to decked boats:* there is a good spot for "pop ups" at the bottom.

There are some 4 mi. of easy rapids before arriving at Fall Creek Falls, entering on the left. Just below the falls is the Roller Coaster, a delightful ride through a series of big waves, and also a very good place for the unwary to fill the craft.

The next rapid is a large ledge called Keyhole. Scout on the left. Enter on the right center and cut to the right. A very large boulder sits on the left center in the bottom. If entering to the left, a mishap can push a boat square into the rock.

There are several interesting ledges and shoals in the next 3 mi., before arriving at a bend to the left. A huge rock formation extending from the right bank is just beyond. This marks the entrance rapid to Bull Sluice, a series of 2 falls totaling 10 ft. in height. The rock formation and large boulders block the "Sluice" from view, so immediately upon spotting the bend and the rocks pull out on the right. Portage on the right also.

The entrance rapid to Bull Sluice is a Class III, which can splash a great deal of water into the canoe before ever arriving at the first falls. The hydraulic below the first falls can easily hold a body or a boat in, so give it all due respect. The second has a rock just under the surface which is generally well hidden. What appears as a fast open chute isn't. The author broke a rib bouncing off this rock, and on another occasion saw a swamped 17 ft. Grumman do an end over end when the bow met with said rock. So if attempting to run Bull Sluice, don't assume that it's been made if one makes it beyond the hydraulic. Keep in mind that several drownings have occurred here.

The US 76 bridge is about 300 yds. downstream around the bend. For those who wish to see the "Sluice" before or without running the river, a trail leads up along the South Carolina side.

SHUTTLE: Take-out is at the South Carolina–Georgia border at the US 76 bridge. For put-in, go east on US 76 approximately 2 mi. to Chattooga Ridge Rd. (SC 196) and turn left. Proceed north approximately 6 mi. to the first 4-way stop intersection. Bear left onto Whetstone Rd., which becomes a graded road, until reaching the parking area, some 1,400 ft. above Earls Ford and the river. You guessed it, neighbor, you get to warm up before you reach the water.

GAUGE: The USGS Gauge is 75 yds. downstream from US 76 bridge on the South Carolina side. Readings of 1.3 to 2.0 are considered a minimum and maximum for open boats.

CLASS	III–V
LENGTH	7.5
TIME	5
GAUGE	VISUAL
LEVEL	1.1 FT.
PERMITS	YES
GRADIENT	90
	(0.5 @ 200)
SCENERY	A–B

US 76 BRIDGE TO TUGALOO LAKE

DESCRIPTION: This section offers the paddler some of the most beautiful and challenging whitewater in the East. There are many rapids throughout the stretch which an intermediate would find difficult, but only the major falls and rapids will be discussed. In other words, only those rapids that will prove difficult to even the advanced canoeist will be mentioned.

The first, Surfing Rapid, is entered from the right after coming around the first bend of the river below the put-in. Some distance downstream, a large sandbar appears on the Georgia side. About 200 yds. below is Rock Jumble, a single drop which is dotted with rock. Scout to determine the best place to run.

About 0.5 mi. downstream, where the river bends left, a large rock ledge extends out from the South Carolina side, forcing the water to the right. Pull out on the ledge before the current does the same to the canoe, and scout. At the end of this ledge is the entrance falls to Woodall Shoals. It forms a strong, dangerous hydraulic at the bottom, which has kept boats, rafts, people, or anything else that floats, for extended periods of time. Due to the power of the hydraulic, this is probably the most dangerous spot on the river. It definitely is not the place to play. A slanting ledge on the far right might be run without the danger the hydraulic presents at levels above 1.4, though this hole can get sticky above 2 ft.

The rest of the Shoals is a twisting turning ride for another 60 yds. before ending in a quiet pool. A forest road enters into Woodall on the South Carolina side.

Below the Shoals the river enters a gorge containing two fairly long rapids with standing waves. Let this be the warning of

Seven-Foot Falls coming up. Scout it on the right, where instead of the abrupt drop of the left, a slanting drop can be run.

Following several rapids, the river widens and Stekoa Creek drops in from the right, indicating the beginning of Stekoa Creek Rapids, a quarter mile of constant whitewater. The creek is the source of the pollution that has prevented the rest of the section from qualifying in the Wild, Scenic, or Recreation River class, but hopefully this will soon be remedied by a new sewage treatment plant. It has been listed in a Conditional Scenic River class.

Long Creek Falls, a beautiful waterfall which was shown in *Deliverance,* enters on the left into the pool at the end of Stekoa Creek Rapids.

Following several ledges the river runs into a house-size boulder. It has become known as "Deliverance Rock" due to several scenes in the movie having been shot here.

A beautiful cliff, Raven Rock, rises on the left high above the river, as one paddles beyond "Deliverance Rock." Just above the cliff is Raven Rock Rapid, which should be scouted on the left and run on the far left across the face of the slanting rock.

For a little over a mile, the river courses over small rapids which appropriately enough have been called "Calm Before the Storm." Below here the river pulls out all stops as it enters The Five Falls, one of the most exciting stretches of water to be found anywhere.

The first, Entrance (or First Fall), is entered down a long stubblefield running diagonally left to far right into a small pool. At this point it is best to scout, perhaps the rest of the falls, before continuing. Entrance should be run on the right and angling to the left. If trouble develops upon attempting Entrance, get to shore immediately, because 100 ft. downstream is Corkscrew, the toughest rapid for an open boat on the river, and a mass of surging cross-currents.

Crack-in-the-Rock, which in reality is three cracks, follows. The 5-ft. crack on the right is the safest of the three, although it can be dangerous as it sometimes becomes partially clogged by logs and debris. Scout on the right. There is a good pool for rescue below the crack. Avoid "left crack" at all costs. Two boaters have drowned there in recent years.

Jawbone comes up next. Scout on the left. It should be entered from right center. Drop left into the eddy on the far left, make an eddy turn, and then cut back into the main chute to be flushed out at the bottom. To the right and two-thirds of the way down the diagonal curler, there is a badly undercut rock to avoid. Below here Hydroelectric Rock bisects the current. Go left or right, but be aware there is water flowing through this boulder.

The final falls, Sock 'Em Dog, is a 7-ft., vertical drop on the far right. Jawbone in itself isn't terribly difficult, but with Sock 'Em Dog awaiting to chew up a swamped craft, one must consider carefully before attempting the run. The eddy on the left is the best spot to get out to scout or to carry. The run is to the far right over a slight rise at the very top of the falls. For those who can't resist the temptation, there is a long pool to reassemble whatever needs to be.

The last rapid of any consequence above the lake, Shoulder Bone, is at the end of the pool. Run it at left center. After that one can relax somewhat before the fun begins—a 2-mi. paddle down Lake Tugaloo.

SHUTTLE: The take-out is on Tugaloo River. From the put-in on US 76 at the SC/GA border, drive east on US 76 approximately 2 mi. to Orchard Rd. Turn right and go until it Ts up on Battle Creek Rd. Turn right and at sharp turn, keep on the paved road (name changes to Damascus Church Rd.). Just past the church on the left, turn right onto Bull Sluice Rd. and follow to where it ends at Lake Tugaloo. Parking can be a problem here, so be considerate. Be wary of outfitters' buses coming up the narrow road.

GAUGE: See Section B. A reading of 1.1 is a minimum level.

CHAUGA RIVER, SC

The Chauga heads up on the eastern slopes of Chattooga Ridge in Sumter National Forest, wherein flow the first two sections. It moves south, then sharply east and south again, until it reaches the backwaters of Lake Hartwell. On its way it cuts through several small gorges that rival the Chattooga River for spectacular beauty.

MAPS: Whetstone, Holly Springs (USGS); Oconee (County)

A

WHETSTONE RD. BRIDGE (BLACKWELL BRIDGE) TO CASSIDY BRIDGE RD.

CLASS	II–III
LENGTH	5.4
TIME	3.5
GAUGE	VISUAL
LEVEL	2 IN.
PERMITS	No
GRADIENT	38 (2 @ 63)
SCENERY	A

DESCRIPTION: Within the first 0.5 mi. there is a 45-ft. waterfall, which can be carried on the right. It is followed by a 10-ft. sliding drop that can be run at slightly higher water levels. One should watch for downed trees throughout the section.

SHUTTLE: From US 76, take Chattooga Ridge Rd. north for 6.1 mi. to Whetstone (four-way stop). Take a right onto Whetstone Rd. and go to the bridge. For take-out, from US 76, take Academy Lane north 2.1 mi., then take a right onto Cassidy Bridge Rd. Turn into the gravel parking lot on the left before you cross the bridge.

GAUGE: It's located on the Oconee CR 290 bridge. Minimum run for solo is 2" above "0." The gauge on the US 76 bridge on the Chattooga will require a reading of 2.3.

CASSIDY BRIDGE RD. TO COBB BRIDGE RD.

CLASS	III–V
LENGTH	9.8
TIME	7
GAUGE	VISUAL
LEVEL	O IN.
PERMITS	No
GRADIENT	43 (1 @ 140)
SCENERY	A+

DESCRIPTION: This section, known as the Chauga Gorge, begins with gentle rapids in the first mile, before dropping quickly through a series of waterfalls and continuous fast water. Access is difficult so the paddler should be skilled enough to handle his boat under very rough water conditions as well as care for any emergencies that might arise.

Watch for downed trees within the first mile. As one enters the gorge, watch for a waterfall which should be carried on the left. Approximately 1 mi. further on is another falls that can possibly be run at a favorable level. The river continues to drop quickly as it turns toward the east. A slanting waterfall, which is best carried, is followed by continuous heavy water for close to 2 mi. Several Class III rapids are interspersed along the way, as the gradient eases up for a couple of miles. Then, some 2 mi. above the take-out, a sheer falls is reached that requires a carry on the right.

SHUTTLE: From US 76, take Academy Lane north 2.1 mi., then take a right onto Cassidy Bridge Rd. For take-out, return to US 76, drive east, then turn left on Cobb Bridge Rd. to reach the bridge.

GAUGE: It's located on the Cassidy Bridge Rd. bridge. Minimum for solo run is "0." Maximum for a safe run is 6".

CLASS	II–IV
LENGTH	7.5
TIME	4.5
GAUGE	VISUAL
LEVEL	1.8 FT.
PERMITS	No
GRADIENT	18
SCENERY	A–B

COBB BRIDGE ROAD TO CR 34 BRIDGE
(HORSESHOE BEND BRIDGE)

DESCRIPTION: Below the US 76 bridge and just above the water pumping facility is Pumphouse, a Class III which can be scouted from the rocks in left center. Just downstream is the Class IV, Canopener—a steep, 5-ft. slide with a sharp rock alongside the chute that can "open" one's boat up if not careful. Scout it before running.

SHUTTLE: From US 76, go north on Cobb Bridge Rd. to reach the bridge. For take-out, return to US 76 and drive east. Turn right onto CR 34 to the bridge.

GAUGE: It's located on the US 76 bridge. Minimum for a solo run is 1.8.

DOE RIVER

The Doe flows off Roan Mountain, through the town of the same name, and cuts through the spectacular Doe River Gorge on its way to join the Watauga in Elizabethton, TN. The Gorge, between Fork Mountain on the south and Cedar Mountain on the north, is 800–1,000 ft. deep. There are several outstanding rock formations, the most prominent being Flagpole Point, jutting out sharply on the right, and Pardee Point, rising high on the left.

A small gauge railroad, where the original "Tweetsie" of the East Tennessee and Western North Carolina ran, makes it fairly easy to scout the gorge on foot. In fact, this is recommended in order for one to fully appreciate the rugged beauty. A hike down the gorge is highly recommended for those who haven't the skill to paddle it.

MAPS: White Rocks Mtn., Iron Mtn. Gap, Elizabethton (TN) (USGS); Carter (TN) (County)

US 19 E. AT BUCK CREEK CONFLUENCE TO US 19 E. BRIDGE

CLASS	I–II
LENGTH	2.6
TIME	1
GAUGE	VISUAL
LEVEL	3.8 FT.
PERMITS	No
GRADIENT	21
SCENERY	B–C

DESCRIPTION: There are no difficulties.

SHUTTLE: To reach the put-in, take US 19 E. in Elizabethton, TN, toward Spruce Pine to where US 19 E. crosses the Doe at Crabtree. The put-in is further east on US 19 E. at the confluence of Buck Creek and the Doe River.

GAUGE: The USGS Gauge is in Section B. Take the road east of Honeycutt Grocery. Minimum reading of 3.80 for solo run. The river can be run all year except after dry spells.

US 19 E. BRIDGE AT CRABTREE TO THE BRIDGE AT BLEVINS

CLASS	II–III
LENGTH	4.6
TIME	3
GAUGE	VISUAL
LEVEL	4.14 FT.
PERMITS	No
GRADIENT	40
SCENERY	A–B

DESCRIPTION: There are two Class III rapids in the second mile. Both should be approached cautiously and scouted to determine if a passage is open. Each is strewn with boulders and has a difficult entrance.

SHUTTLE: To reach the put-in, take US 19 E. in Elizabethton, TN, toward Spruce Pine to where US 19 E. crosses the Doe at Blevins. The put-in is further east on US 19 E. at Crabtree.

GAUGE: Minimum reading for a solo run is 4.14.

BRIDGE AT BLEVINS TO US 19 E. BRIDGE AT HAMPTON

CLASS	III–V
LENGTH	6
TIME	6
GAUGE	VISUAL
LEVEL	4.3 FT.
PERMITS	No
GRADIENT	83 (1 @ 145; 2 @ 115)
SCENERY	A+

DESCRIPTION: The road at the put-in continues along the river for 2.5 mi. to the head of the railroad tracks. The upper section can be scouted from the road. There is one Class IV above the first railroad bridge, where the water piles up on a rock, requiring a hard left turn into a drop of 3–4 ft.

Below the first railroad bridge there are numerous rapids, many of which require scouting. Be on the lookout for a point where the river bends to the right, where the entrance is pretty

well clogged up. This area is quite difficult in an open boat, but the thrill seeker may wish to put back in just above the bottom to try the 7-ft. falls on the right.

Following the falls, the next hairy rapid can be recognized by the rock wall constructed to support the railroad tracks. Here a series of diagonal ledges make for an extremely difficult course.

As the river approaches the next rock wall, the course splits into two channels with a Class V on the left, and on the right a jumble of boulders. This is Flagpole rapid, the crux of the river. One unwary paddler swamped twice here, just portaging.

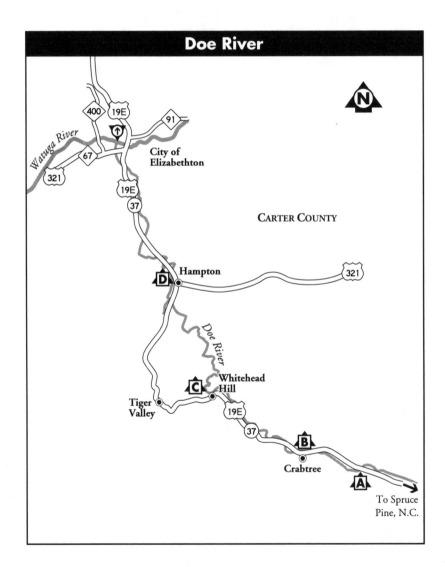

From here to the take-out, there are many exciting rapids remaining, several of which should be scouted. This section is not recommended for the paddler who is not in excellent condition. The stress and strain are sure to take their toll on one who isn't.

SHUTTLE: To reach the put-in, take US 19 E. in Elizabethton, TN, toward Spruce Pine to where US 19 E. crosses the Doe at Hampton. The put-in is further east on US 19 E. at Blevins.

GAUGE: Minimum level for a solo run is 4.3. Due to the gradient and tight passages the river courses through, there is not much leeway between the minimal level and when higher water can cause the run to get out of hand.

US 19 E. BRIDGE IN HAMPTON TO
US 19 E. BRIDGE IN ELIZABETHTON

CLASS	II–III
LENGTH	9.5
TIME	4.5
GAUGE	VISUAL
LEVEL	4.2 FT.
PERMITS	No
GRADIENT	27 (2 @ 50)
SCENERY	A–C

DESCRIPTION: A Class III directly beneath the first 19 E. bridge north of Hampton may require scouting. Beyond the second bridge, a series of ledges form a staircase that will require a good deal of maneuvering to locate the best passage. Other than these, there are a few stubblefields which one should watch for.

SHUTTLE: For take-out, go to the Power Sub Station 100 yds. above the US 19 E. bridge over the Watauga River, on the south bank in Elizabethton. For put-in, drive east on US 19 E. to the bridge in Hampton.

GAUGE: Minimum reading for a solo run is 4.20.

HAW RIVER

The Haw River begins in the northwest corner of Guilford County, and flows east around Greensboro and Burlington before turning generally southeast. It meets the New Hope River in Chatham County, where the Cape Fear River is born. The Haw varies greatly in width—from 50 ft. in some sections to as much as 1,000 ft. at the dam at Bynum.

The river flows through farm lands, forested hills, and some residential areas. As with most rivers in the lower Piedmont, there are long stretches of flatwater, as well as many rapids. There are places where the river branches into two or more channels, each island looking very much like the last one—long, narrow, and heavily covered with trees, shrubs, brambles, and poison ivy.

The creation of Jordan Lake at the end of Section C was controversial due to expected poor water quality, among other things. Over time, the quality of water has improved, although it remains threatened by demands for riverside and watershed development by upstream communities. Citizen watchdog groups maintain a high profile level of activity working to protect and improve the river corridor and its water.

MAPS: Bynum, New Hope Dam (USGS); Chatham (County)

A

CLASS	I–II
LENGTH	6.5
TIME	3
GAUGE	VISUAL
LEVEL	-1.5 FT.
PERMITS	NO
GRADIENT	16
SCENERY	A–B

CHATHAM CR 1545 BRIDGE ("CHICKEN BRIDGE") TO THE DAM, JUST UPSTREAM OF US 15/501 BRIDGE

DESCRIPTION: There are three places of any consequence on this section—Sawtooth Ledge, Lunch Stop, and Final Solution. After about 1.5 mi. of flatwater, a small boulder garden appears and the river bends from river right towards center around a small island. Enter on the right of and as close to the island as the overhanging branches will permit and run straight through, eddying on either right or left at the bottom of the chute.

Sawtooth Ledge is just around the corner, about a mile downstream. This is a rock garden, runnable on the left at normal levels. As the river splits into two channels, stay right in the one with more water. (The left side is unrunnable at low water.) Follow the bend to the left; and on the backside of the island, stay left to avoid rocks in the center of the channel. Then move back to center to avoid rocks at the bottom.

The next rapid, Lunch Stop, is about 4 mi. into the trip. It is a long rock garden spanning the width of the river. At lower water, run it left of center; and once past the island, traverse to river right. At higher water, run center to avoid large holes and swamping waves on the left. (Also at higher water, look for great surfing waves in the heavy flow or else you'll be swept by them before you realize they are available to you.)

After Lunch Stop, the river splits into four channels. Either of the two center channels are runnable; the preferred route is just left of center. After the entrance rapid at the head of the channel, find a slot and paddle over to the next channel on the right for a cleaner route to rejoin the main flow.

Final Solution, the last rapid, is below the wave field just downstream of the gas pipeline right of way. It can be entered left or right of a large boulder that marks the entrance just left of center. Eddy behind this boulder for a look at how to run the chute below. The lake created by the dam at the take-out starts just

downstream from Final Solution. When the river channelizes, stay left for a take-out on river left above the dam.

SHUTTLE: From the US 15/501 bridge, take US 15/501 north to the first intersection and turn left onto Hamlet Chapel Rd. (SR 1525). Go about 2 mi. and turn left onto River Rd. (continuation of SR 1525). Cross the bridge and park on the pavement to the left of the road. Take out at the US 15/501 bridge across the Haw River.

GAUGE: A Gauge has been painted on the bridge piling closest to river right. Minimum for solo open canoe is about -1.5, but at

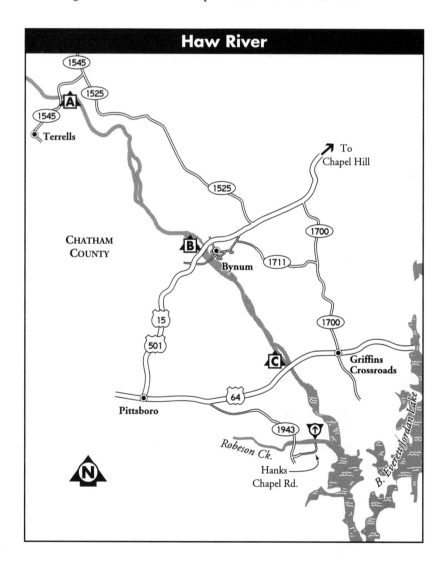

this level the river is low and the trip will be long—4 hrs. not including a lunch stop. If no rocks are visible downstream from the bridge, this section will be pushy, with many holes and waves and few eddies—not good for novices. This section can generally be run all year, except during periods following an unusually long, dry season.

US 15/501 BRIDGE, ON THE SOUTH SIDE OF THE RIVER,
TO US 64 BRIDGE

CLASS	I–II
LENGTH	4.1
TIME	3.5
GAUGE	VISUAL
LEVEL	1.5 FT.
PERMITS	NO
GRADIENT	18
SCENERY	A–B

DESCRIPTION: This section is excellent for skills practice of water-reading, eddy-hopping, peel-outs, surfing, and ferrying (depending on water levels). Ferry from river left just below the dam (and well clear of the backwash) and start your descent right of the island. Paddle this side to enjoy the delightful rock garden until you pass under the Bynum bridge.

Once past Bynum bridge, traverse the river back to the left side of the island. About 1 mi. downstream, the river channelizes further, separated by several islands. Stay with the most flow and widest sections. If you take the far left channel, you'll run Crystal Falls, a shallow ledge S turn entered left of center and run left to right with a subsequent and immediate hard left turn. If you choose to enter the channels in the center, look out for strainers. You'll be rewarded with the channels' intimacy, a channel-wide surfing wave at reasonable water levels, and Thunder Falls, a tight Class II S turn chute. Enter it right of center and turn back left in the chute to avoid being swept into the right bank.

The river becomes wide and flat again where all the channels converge. When it again is separated by islands, stay right for the most interesting run through rock gardens, tiny islands, and finally, a quick S turn chute. If you take the middle channel, you will have to portage the long islands on either side to access river right or river left under the US 64 bridge.

SHUTTLE: Put-in at the US 15/501 bridge across the Haw River. For take-out, from the US 15/501 bridge, take US 15/501 north to the first intersection and turn right onto Durham-Eubanks Rd. (SR 1524). At the stop sign, turn left onto Bynum Rd. and go about 0.5 mi. and turn right onto Bynum Bridge Rd. (SR 1711). At the stop sign, turn right onto Mt. Gilead Church Rd. (SR 1700). At the stop sign, turn right onto US 64 West and cross the bridge and turn left onto the dirt road access.

GAUGE: See Section A.

US 64 BRIDGE TO JORDAN LAKE

CLASS	II–III
LENGTH	2. 1
TIME	2
GAUGE	VISUAL
LEVEL	-6 IN.
PERMITS	No
GRADIENT	2 1
SCENERY	A–B

DESCRIPTION: This is the most difficult section. The higher the water, the less margin for error and the greater the chance for a long, bumpy swim. The section packs a lot into a short run—often paddled after work by locals looking for a one- to two-hour workout before dark. And if darkness comes prematurely, you need not worry as long as you clear the last rapid with daylight because the final 30 to 45 minutes is paddled across the lake.

For the best run and the most action, take the right channel from the US 64 bridge. Within 200 yds., you will enter Lunch Stop, a boulder garden with all the flow to the left of large rocks jutting out into the river from river right. Run the first part just right of center and eddy right just below the rocks if you're not interested in playing. From the eddy, stop at the channel-wide wave below and practice ferrying, surfing, and elevator moves. At 2 ft. and above, try for enders behind the large boulder in the middle. There is flat, slow-moving water below for roll practice.

Fifty yds. below the ender boulder, paddle through a break in the island to enter the center channel. This is Ocean Boulevard. Ocean Boulevard ends on far river right in a small rock garden that boasts a great side-surfing wave. The river pools briefly in the approach to the most difficult rapid on the entire river. Gabriel's Bend, a bona fide Class III at most levels, is identified by a high rock wall on the right. You may pull over and shore scout, although you cannot see the entire run from shore. The best scouting is from an eddy (entered from left or right), in the center of the channel at the top of the rapid.

For a down-river run, stay just left of center, avoiding large, potentially nasty holes to the right. The large, channel-wide wave at the bottom is a very forgiving side-surfer at many water levels, which willingly lets its victims go.

Just below Gabriel's Bend, you have three options. At a level of 1 ft. or more, Moose Jaw Falls on the far right is runnable. At all levels, you can run The Maze, a rock garden at the head of the center channel that requires turning immediately to the right and threading your way through a rock garden descent where the channel joins the right below Moose Jaw Falls.

The most open, least technical run after Gabriel's Bend is Harold's Tombstone—on the far left shore. Traverse the entire river, and as you approach the overhanging trees, work your way left to avoid being washed into the rocks on the right and being

slammed into a jagged rock in the channel just left of center. All three channels rejoin about a quarter mile downstream where the current ends and the Jordan Lake begins, burying forever some of the finest rapids on the river. Paddle to the take-out on river left (approximately 1.5 mi.—30 to 45 minutes).

SHUTTLE: For take-out, take NC 64 west from the put-in and go 0.7 mi. to a left onto SR 1943. Go to the stop sign and take a left on Hanks Chapel Rd., then go 1 mi. and turn left onto the gravel road to the take-out. *Note:* if running the left channel below Gabriel's Bend, you will have to paddle back upstream 100 yds. to reach the take-out.

GAUGE: A Gauge is painted on the US 64 bridge pilings and is visible from the access on river right. Minimum for solo open canoe is about -6 in. On this gauge 6 in. to 2 ft. is an excellent level for eddy-hopping and surfing. Above 2 ft., the river gets pushy, especially in Gabriel's Bend. For example, at 3 ft., extremely strong currents, huge waves, and keeper-holes form throughout, thus transforming this section into a run for only properly equipped advanced to expert boaters.

The National Weather Service gives a reading of the USGS gauge (located about 1 mi. below the Bynum bridge in Section B) in the mornings—usually until 11 a.m. It can be obtained by listening to a weather radio or calling the National Weather Service in Raleigh, NC. A USGS reading of 4.0 is minimum.

NORTH TYGER RIVER

The North Tyger heads up in northern Spartanburg County and flows practically the length of the county, to where we pick it up just upstream of the confluence with the South Tyger. It drops through the Fall Line, presenting several miles of interesting whitewater. This area is composed of long pools, with occasional sharp drops and long shoals.

MAPS: Spartanburg, Enoree (USGS); Spartanburg (County)

CLASS	II–III
LENGTH	7.6
TIME	7.6
GAUGE	VISUAL
LEVEL	-8 IN.
PERMITS	NO
GRADIENT	10
SCENERY	A

SPARTANBURG CR 231 BRIDGE TO
SPARTANBURG CR 113 BRIDGE

DESCRIPTION: This stretch is primarily a series of pools interspersed with ledges and long shoals, several of which can be quite formidable at higher water levels (above 1 on the gauge). The

second rapid drops 7 ft. in some 25 yds. and has a rather sneaky hydraulic in the center that one must punch through.

Nesbitt Shoals runs for about 200 yds. above the Rt. 50 bridge. Below the bridge one encounters another 150 yds. of shoals which should be run right of center, due to a number of large rods in the middle and far left immediately below the first ledge. The last shoals run 0.25 mi. down to the take-out. It has many possible passages.

SHUTTLE: To reach the take-out, take I-26 (Exit 35) east on SC 50. You can shorten the trip 3.3 mi. by setting shuttle where SC

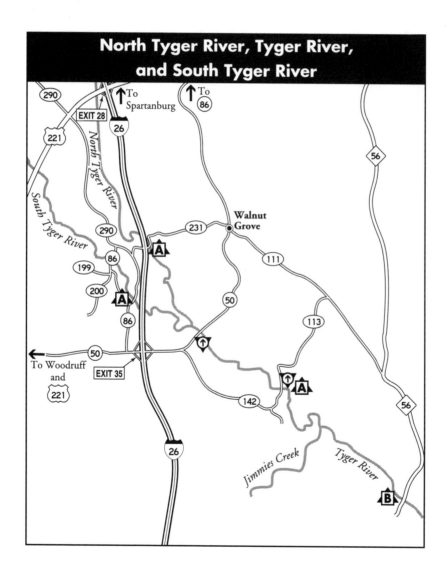

50 crosses the Tyger. Otherwise, turn right on SC 142 just before SC 50 crosses the river, then left onto SC 113 to the bridge. For put-in, return to the interstate, continue underneath it, and take a right at SC 86. Continue over the South Tyger, and take the next right onto SC 231 to the bridge.

GAUGE: It's located at the Spartanburg CR 231 bridge at the northwest corner. Minimum level for a solo run is 8" below "0."

TYGER RIVER

The Tyger is formed in Spartanburg County after the confluence of the North, Middle, and South Forks. It then flows generally south and east to meet the Broad east of Whitmire. As it drops through the Fall Line, it presents a stretch of rather fast and difficult whitewater before it flattens out in the plains and meanders across Sumter National Forest. Other than the occasional bridges spanning the river, one sees little sign of habitation. The entire stretch is fairly wild and scenic.

Rose Hill State Park (at SC 16) is 4.9 mi. down from the 49 bridge.

MAPS: Cross Anchor, Union West, Sedalia, Whitmire North, Blair, Pomaria, Jenkinsville (USGS); Spartanburg, Union, Newberry (County)

CLASS	C-IV
LENGTH	6.2
TIME	9
GAUGE	VISUAL
LEVEL	-8 IN.
PERMITS	NO
GRADIENT	8
SCENERY	A–B

SPARTANBURG CR 113 BRIDGE TO SC 56 BRIDGE

DESCRIPTION: A series of shoals runs for almost a half mile, providing many choices of channels. This stretch ends with a natural 6-ft. vertical dam. Approach with great caution, for at higher levels, one will have a very difficult time scouting this ledge. Beyond this point, one will encounter primarily fast flatwater.

SHUTTLE: To reach the take-out, go south on SC 56 from Spartanburg until it crosses the river. For put-in, return north on SC 56, turn left onto SC 111 toward Walnut Grove, then left again at SC 113 to the bridge.

GAUGE: It's located at the Spartanburg CR 113 bridge on the southwest corner. Minimum level for a solo run is 8" below "0."

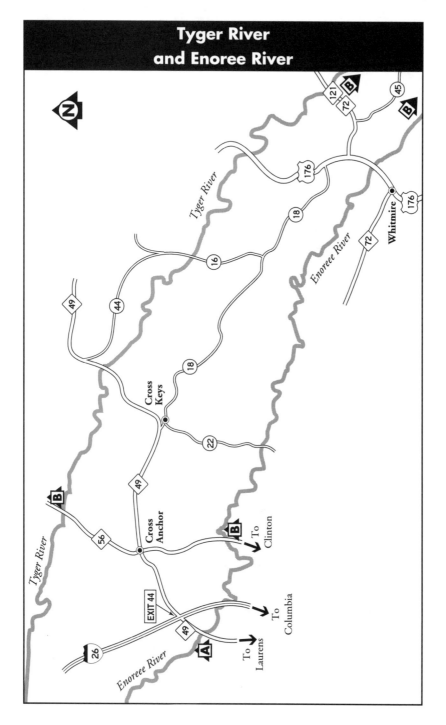

Tyger River
and Enoree River

CLASS	A–I
LENGTH	53.2
TIME	22
GAUGE	VISUAL
LEVEL	N/A
PERMITS	NO
GRADIENT	3
SCENERY	A

SC 56 BRIDGE TO PARR SHOALS DAM

DESCRIPTION: Watch for downed trees, although the channel appears to stay fairly clear. Take care at higher than normal levels.

After entering the Broad, paddlers will hear a rather ominous sound as Henderson Island comes into view. It's only a small shoals extending across the river, but following all the peace and quiet it makes quite a roar. Best passage is probably 20–30 ft. off the right bank. There are a few rock gardens on the way down to the end of the island, where shoals run for 150–200 yds. This area should be approached with caution, especially with canoes loaded with gear and inexperienced paddlers.

From SC 34 down to the dam, winds can provide some difficulty.

SHUTTLE: The take-out can be reached by going south on US 176 from Pomaria, turning left (east) on SC 231, then left again on Broad River Rd. Take the next right to the dam.

There are numerous places along the river where shuttles can be set, including the SC 49 bridge, the US 176 bridge, Union CR 35, the Newberry CR 45 bridge, and The C 34 bridge on the Broad.

GAUGE: None. Runnable all year.

SOUTH TYGER RIVER

The South Tyger heads up in the foothills and cuts across the Pied-mont Plateau before making its final plunge where we pick it up. This section has long pools with occasional sharp drops that make the flatter stretches worth paddling.

MAPS: Spartanburg, Enoree (USGS); Spartanburg (County)

Tyger River
and Enoree River

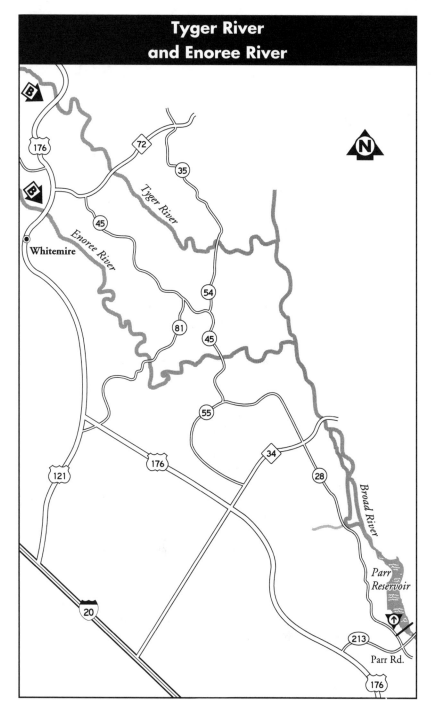

CLASS	II–III
LENGTH	5.2
TIME	1.8
GAUGE	VISUAL
LEVEL	-8 IN.
PERMITS	NO
GRADIENT	7
SCENERY	A

SPARTANBURG CR 86 BRIDGE OVER FERGUSONS CREEK TO
SC 50 BRIDGE OVER THE TYGER

DESCRIPTION: Susan Thomas Shoals drops 5.5 ft. in about 30 yds. It can be scouted at right center. The next shoals, Chesnee, now known as "Sting 'em dog" due to an experience Jack and David Powell had with their canine companion, presents a very technical run. The rapid drops 7 ft. within 50 yds. It can be scouted far left. Nesbitt Shoals runs for some 200 yds. just below the confluence with the North Tyger and continues on to the take-out.

SHUTTLE: To reach the take-out, from I-26 (Exit 35) go east on SC 50 to where the bridge crosses the Tyger. You can lengthen the trip 3.3 mi. by turning right on SC 142 just before SC 50 crosses the river, then left onto SC 113 to the bridge. For put-in, return to the interstate, continue underneath it, and take a right at SC 86 and go to the bridge.

GAUGE: It's located on the Spartanburg CR 231 bridge on the North Tyger at the northwest corner. Minimum level for a solo run is 8" below "0."

ENOREE RIVER

The Enoree heads up on the Piedmont in Greenville County and winds its way southeasterly to confluence with the Broad, northeast of New-berry. On its way, it cuts through the Fall Line, offering a short stretch of interesting whitewater before reaching Sumter National Forest and the coastal plains. From the put-in to the take-out at Parr Shoals on the Broad, one encounters very little evidence of civilization other than highway bridges. It is a most scenic run through rolling hills.

Maps: Ora, Philson, Crossroads, Sedalia, Whit-mire North, Whitmire South, Pomaria, Jenkinsville (USGS); Spartanburg, Union, Newberry(County)

SC 49 BRIDGE TO SPARTANBURG CR 10 (HORSHOE FALLS ROAD)

CLASS	C-III
LENGTH	6.8
TIME	3
GAUGE	VISUAL
LEVEL	YEAR-ROUND.
PERMITS	No
GRADIENT	8
SCENERY	A

DESCRIPTION: The river drops very quickly within the first 0.75 mi., with a series of shoals. This fast stretch ends with a drop of some 8 ft. within 100 yds. At higher levels (above 3.0) pull out well above on the left and scout.

SHUTTLE: For take-out, take I-26 Exit 44 and go north on SC 49 to Cross Anchor, then south on SC 56. Just before SC 56 crosses the river, take the right-hand fork onto Horseshoe Falls Road to where it comes alongside the river (.3 mi. above SC 56 bridge). For put in, take I-26 Exit 44 and go south on SC 49 to where it crosses river.

GAUGE: USGS Gauge is on the east bank 20 yds. above SC 49 bridge. Runnable year round. A reading of 3.0 will require a lot of skill and experience to handle the stretch below Rt. 49.

SC 56 BRIDGE TO PARR SHOALS DAM

CLASS	C-III
LENGTH	54.6
TIME	3
GAUGE	VISUAL
LEVEL	YEAR-ROUND.
PERMITS	No
GRADIENT	3
SCENERY	A

DESCRIPTION: Downed trees in upper sections. With water levels following rains extreme care should be taken, especially with gear-loaded canoes. Winds can become a problem once entering the Broad. If power isn't being generated at Parr Shoals, one will encounter slack water in this area.

SHUTTLE: To reach put-in, take I-26 Exit 44 and go north on SC 49 to Cross Anchor, then south on SC 56. Just before SC 56 crosses the river, take the right-hand fork onto Horseshoe Falls Road to where it comes alongside the river (.3 mi. above SC 56 bridge). Take out just above Parr Dam. There are numerous places along the river where shuttles can be set, including Union CR 22 bridge, US 176 bridge, Newberry Rt. 81 bridge, SC 34 on the Broad.

GAUGE: None. Runnable all year. May be a little scratchy following extremely long dry spells.

part**SIX**

I_NDEX_

Notes

Notes

Notes

Notes

Notes

Notes

Notes